50 *Hikes*

in Vermont
Walks, Hikes, and Overnights in the Green Mountain State

Seventh Edition

The Green Mountain Club

THE COUNTRYMAN PRESS
Woodstock, Vermont

AN INVITATION TO THE READER
Over time trails can be rerouted and signs and landmarks altered. If you find that changes have occurred on the routes described in this book, please let us know so that corrections may be made in future editions. The author and publisher also welcome other comments and suggestions. Address all correspondence to:

Editor, 50 Hikes Series
The Countryman Press
P.O. Box 748
Woodstock, VT 05091

50 Hikes in Vermont: Walks, Hikes, and Overnights in the Green Mountain State
The Green Mountain Club.
ISBN: 978-1-58157-199-8

Series design by Glenn Suokko
Maps by Michael Borop, siteatlas.com

© 2015 by The Green Mountain Club

Seventh Edition

Published by The Countryman Press
P.O. Box 748
Woodstock, VT 05091

Distributed by W.W. Norton & Company Inc.
500 Fifth Avenue
New York, NY 10110

Printed in the United States of America
10 9 8 7 6 5 4 3 2 1

Acknowledgments

Many interested parties made this book possible, including the following individuals who reviewed the hikes in person and in print: Dick Andrews, Pete Antos-Ketcham, Amy Barcomb, John Berry, Cat Eich, Mike Feiner, Marge Fish, Jean Haigh, Dave Hardy, Ruth Hare, Rebecca Harvey, Jocelyn Hebert, Ned Houston, Maisie Howard, David Iverson, Andrea Kane, Alyssa Krebs, Matt Krebs, Wayne Krevetski, Steve Larose, Sheri Larsen, Herb Ogden, Dwight Penfield, Ruth Penfield, Walter Pomroy, Dolores Rebolledo, Mary Lou Recor, Jessica Rossi, Peter Saile, Sue Shea, Kristen Smith, Martha Stitleman, Jim Sullivan, Ted Vogt, Michael Wetherell, Kevin Williamson, and Rich Windish. Since so many people helped out with this book, however, it is entirely possible that I've overlooked some. To them I offer both my heartfelt thanks and my sincere apologies.

– Doug McKain

50 Hikes in Vermont at a Glance

HIKE	LOCATION
1. Mount Olga	East of Wilmington
2. Equinox Mountain	West of Manchester
3. White Rocks/Ice Beds Trail	Near Wallingford
4. Windmill Hill Pinnacle Trails	South of Cambridgeport
5. Haystack Mountain	West of Wilmington
6. Bald Mountain	North of Townshend Village
7. Antone Mountain	West of Rupert
8. Bromley Mountain	East of Manchester
9. Little Rock Pond and Green Mountain	East of Danby
10. Okemo Mountain	West of Ludlow
11. Stratton Pond	Between Arlington and W. Wardsboro
12. Mount Ascutney	West of Ascutney
13. Baker Peak	South of Danby
14. Stratton Mountain	Between Arlington and W. Wardsboro
15. Little Rock Pond and Clarendon Gorge	Between Danby and Clarendon
16. Robert Frost Trail	East of Ripton
17. Thundering Falls	Near Killington
18. Appalachian Trail	North of Woodstock
19. Mount Horrid's Great Cliff	At Brandon Gap
20. Dear Leap Overlook	At Sherburne Pass
21. Mount Independence	West of Orwell
22. Mount Tom	Near Woodstock
23. Rattlesnake Point	Northeast of Brandon
24. Snake Mountain	Northwest of Middlebury
25. Pico Peak	At Sherburne Pass

DISTANCE (miles)	VERTICAL RISE (feet)	DIFFICULTY	VIEWS	GOOD FOR KIDS	CAMPING NEARBY	GOOD FOR WINTER	
2.2	520	E/M	★	★	★	★	X-C skiing; snowshoeing; fire tower
5.4	2,730	S	★				Panoramic views of the Green, White, Adirondack, Berkshire, and Taconic mountains
2.0	460	E	★	★		★	Snowshoeing
3.4	500	E	★	★		★	Snowshoeing
4.2	1,020	M	★			★	Snowshoeing; parking difficult in winter
3.8	1,160	M	★		★	★	Snowshoeing
5.0	890	M		★	★	★	X-C skiing; snowshoeing; limited views
5.0	1,075	M	★				Observation tower
7.0	1,236	M/S	★		★	★	X-C skiing
6.0	1,950	M	★			★	Snowshoeing; fire tower
7.4	201	M			★	★	X-C skiing; snowshoeing
5.8	2,250	S	★		★		Views from rock outcrops
8.1	2,230	S	★		★		Open summit ledges
9.3	1,910	M/S	★		★	★	Strenuous snowshoeing; fire tower
15.0	3,100	E/M	★		★		Overnight hike; need two cars
1.0	120	E	★	★		★	Snowshoeing; x-c skiing
0.5	minor	E		★	★	★	Waterfalls; boardwalk
7.1	1,317	M		★	★		Snowshoeing; parking difficult in winter
1.4	600	M	★		★	★	Snowshoeing; peregrine falcons
2.0	520	E	★	★	★	★	Snowshoeing
4.1	200	E		★			Interpretive center; historical interest
3.6	600	M	★	★			X-C skiing
3.9	1,160	M	★		★	★	Snowshoeing
4.6	1,087	M	★			★	Mountain was once an island
5.8	1,800	M	★		★		Open summit ledges

DIFFICULTY
E Easy
M Moderate
S Strenuous

50 Hikes in Vermont at a Glance

HIKE	LOCATION
26. General Stark Mountain	East of Bristol
27. Mount Roosevelt	West of Granville
28. Bread Loaf Mountain	South of Lincoln
29. Mount Grant	South of Lincoln
30. Monroe Skyline	Between Lincoln and Appalachian Gaps
31. Hires and Sensory Trails	Near Huntington
32. Owl's Head	East of Marshfield
33. Prospect Rock (Johnson)	West of Johnson
34. Mount Philo	North of Ferrisburg
35. Black Creek and Maquam Creek Trails	North of Swanton
36. Little River History Loop	West of Waterbury
37. Stowe Pinnacle	East of Stowe Village
38. Bluff Mountain	Near Island Pond
39. Spruce Mountain	South of Plainfield
40. Elmore Mountain Loop	South of Morrisville
41. Mount Pisgah	South end of Lake Willoughby
42. Jay Peak	East of Montgomery
43. Hubbard Park	In Montpelier
44. Mount Hunger	East of Waterbury Center
45. Mount Monadnock	South of Canaan
46. Sterling Pond and Elephant's Head	At Smuggler's Notch
47. Mount Mansfield	North of Stowe
48. Camel's Hump	West of Waterbury
49. Belvidere Mountain	North of Morrisville
50. Gile Mountain	West of Norwich

Distance (miles)	Vertical Rise (feet)	Difficulty	Views	Good for Kids	Camping Nearby	Good for Winter	
5.8	2,034	M/S	★		★		Snowshoeing
6.8	2,100	M	★		★		Vista just north of summit
8.6	2,235	S	★		★		Highest point in Breadloaf Wilderness
8.0	1,960	S	★		★		Ascend along mountain stream
2.2	2,535	M	★		★		Overnight hike; need two cars
1.2	200	E	★	★		★	Snowshoeing; museum and interpretative center
0.5	160	E	★	★	★	★	X-C skiing; snowshoeing
2.0	540	E	★	★		★	Snowshoeing
2.0	600	M	★	★	★	★	X-C skiing; snowshoeing
2.3	minor	E		★			Wildlife refuge trails
3.5	880	E/M			★		Ghost town; some x-c skiing
2.8	1,520	M	★		★		Snowshoeing
3.6	1,080	M	★		★		Snowshoeing
4.4	1,180	M	★		★		Strenuous snowshoe; fire tower
4.2	1,470	M	★		★	★	Snowshoeing; fire tower
8-4.8	1,590	M	★				Peregrine falcons on cliff over Lake Willoughby
3.4	1,638	M	★		★		Open summit with tramway station
5.8	374	M	★			★	Snowshoeing; x-c skiing
4.4	2,285	M/S	★			★	Strenuous snowshoe to open summit
4.8	2,108	M/S	★				Fire tower
7.7	1,650	S	★		★		High mountain pond
6.7	3,200	S	★		★		Highest peak in Vermont
7.4	2,645	S	★		★	★	Very strenuous snowshoe
7.9	1,980	S	★		★	★	Loop hike; strenuous snowshoe
1.4	413	E	★	★	★		Snowshoeing

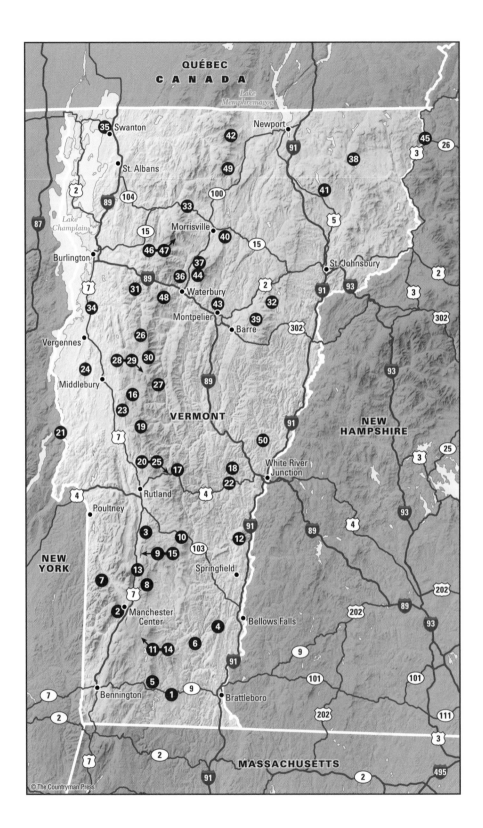

Contents

NORTHERN VERMONT

Foreword to Seventh Edition

Improving on a classic publication is no easy task, but I am pleased to report that editor Doug McKain, the Green Mountain Club's Publications Committee, and the corps of dedicated trail volunteers have done just that with the seventh edition of *50 Hikes in Vermont*. The seventh edition builds on the foundational work of earlier editions and stays true to the creative vision of previous editors Dave Hardy, Bob Lindemann, and Mary Deaett.

The seventh edition contains four new hikes, many updated and enhanced descriptions, more detailed maps, and the GPS coordinates of trailheads. Each hike description has been carefully and thoughtfully crafted by volunteers that know and love the trails. Picking up a copy of the seventh edition, the book feels familiar and comfortable. The passion for the hikes flows naturally from the pages and sets the stage for the reader to get out and enjoy some of the best outdoor experiences that Vermont has to offer.

From alpine classics (Mount Abe and Camel's Hump) to the Champlain Valley (Mount Independence and Snake Mountain) to the Northeast Kingdom (Bald Mountain and Mount Pisgah) *50 Hikes* delivers that perfect blend of hikes to satisfy beginning and seasoned hikers alike.

This book not only serves as a guide to some of the best hiking in the state, it also provides an opportunity to engage the community of hikers and trail stewards who maintain and protect Vermont's trail resources as part of the Green Mountain Club.

Since 1910, the Green Mountain Club has been Vermont's leading organization for trail building and stewardship, hiking trail advocacy, and outdoor education. The 457 miles of the Long Trail system (including 185 miles of side trails), the Appalachian Trail in Vermont, and trails in the Northeast Kingdom represent nearly half of all the miles of public hiking trails in Vermont. This collection has a similar ratio: Roughly half of the hikes are on the Long Trail or Appalachian Trail, and the other half are scattered east and west of the Green Mountain ridgeline in all corners of Vermont.

All of the trails described in this book are loyally maintained by a dedicated group of trail stewards. Every water bar, rock step, cleared blowdown, and freshly painted blaze has been maintained by people whose passion for Vermont and love for hiking makes these trails available for us to enjoy. Vermont is blessed with vast natural beauty and mountains and valleys to explore. Vermont is also blessed with a history and culture of trail stewardship. By reading this book and getting out to hike the trails, you are supporting this culture and helping to pass it on to the next generation.

Wishing you safe and wonderful hiking. Enjoy!

Mike DeBonis
Executive Director
Green Mountain Club

P.S. For more information about the Green Mountain Club and how to join, refer to the "Membership" section in the introduction or check out www.greenmountainclub.org. See you on the trail!

Introduction

For anyone wishing to explore some of Vermont's greatest treasures—the Green Mountains—this book offers hours and days of hiking enjoyment. As a guide through the mountains along a variety of Vermont's hiking trails, this book offers directions for easy walks, ambitious day hikes, and weekend backpacking trips. The editors selected popular and lesser-known trails; some are quite easy, whereas a few are very strenuous. All of these hikes offer crisp mountain air and beautiful wilderness scenery, most with breathtaking views of surrounding pastoral valleys and neighboring mountain ranges. You can hike along sparkling streams, over suspension bridges, across open summits, and through secluded gulches bordered by ferns. Choose the hikes that excite and appeal to you the most.

The editors who selected these trails hiked them and evaluated them thoroughly. Although we encourage enthusiastic exploration of Vermont's hiking trails, we also caution you to consider your health and conditioning, your experience in the woods, the weather, your equipment, and a variety of other factors before exploring Vermont's backcountry wilderness. Please read the advice and information in the following section carefully before beginning your journey. Be prepared and be informed, and then thoroughly enjoy a safe journey into the Green Mountains of Vermont.

HOW TO USE THIS GUIDE

Organized geographically and by difficulty in three regions of the state—south, central, and north—these hikes offer you a variety of terrain and scenery that represents each region. The beginning of each hike lists the general location, approximate distance and hiking time, vertical rise, difficulty rating, and a map of the area. This information allows you to select a hike based on your experience and the time available for your outing.

Before beginning a hike, take time to carefully plan your route, equipment, and supplies. Allow adequate time for unpredictable weather changes, and remember to leave a copy of your itinerary with a friend. Each section in this book contains the following information to help you prepare for your hike:

Total distance means the total number of miles (and kilometers) you can expect to hike on the trails described. Each hike description indicates clearly whether this distance refers to a loop, a return by the same route, or a one-way hike (with cars spotted at both ends of the trail).

Hiking time includes all time spent walking or climbing and some time for resting and enjoying the views. The time listed very likely won't match your own time exactly, but it can serve as a consistent yardstick; your hiking time will likely exceed or be exceeded by the same difference for most any hike in this book, unless hiking conditions change. The "book time" provides a convenient measure of your hiking ability.

Allow extra time for meals and swimming or fishing in the streams and ponds en route (remember that you need a Vermont fishing license). Hiking times assume a steady pace and allow for differences in terrain. If you follow any alternate or side trails not included in the total distance, remember to adjust your hiking time expectations accordingly.

Vertical rise shows the total amount of climb along the route. Although vertical rise may occur all in one climb, it frequently occurs over several climbs. If descents appear between these climbs, the vertical rise for the hike will exceed the difference in elevation between the lowest and highest points on the hike. Remember that substantial vertical rise can turn even a short hike into a real challenge.

Difficulty ratings include easy, moderate, and strenuous classifications—although a few hikes fall in between these categories. Easy hikes are accessible to almost everyone, including first-time hikers, families with children, or someone with limited hiking time and a wish to enjoy Vermont's beautiful scenery. Moderate hikes require a degree of stamina; some previous hiking experience is advisable. Strenuous hikes are challenging outings for experienced hikers in good physical condition.

Maps, listed at the beginning of each hike, show you the area for the hike and provide information to order more detailed maps if you wish. This book contains maps based on United States Geological Survey (USGS) or Green Mountain National Forest (GMNF) topographic sheets. Use the maps in this guidebook only for reference; they are not suitable for map and compass orientation. See the "Route Planning and Ordering Maps" section for more information about where and how to order maps. In Vermont, the compass points about 15 degrees west of true north.

Some of the hikes follow routes on or along the Long Trail (LT), the 272-mile "footpath in the wilderness" through Vermont. See the "Hiking Information Available from the Green Mountain Club" section for relevant guidebooks and maps offered by the Green Mountain Club (GMC).

The maps in this book are intended only as general guides to the trails. Logging, development, and other wilderness disturbances often necessitate changes in trail locations, although the editors took care to ensure the accuracy of trail descriptions and maps at the time of publication.

HIKING GUIDELINES

Guidelines are just that. We can't tell you how to go hiking. We can tell you what we've learned through years of experience and mostly trial and error. It's always best to learn from someone else's mistakes, but we're all going to have learning experiences on the trail—that's part of the adventure!

Hiking season in the Green Mountains begins in late spring and continues through summer and early fall. Most of the trails are not blazed for winter use; snow cover makes trails difficult or impossible to follow. The popularity of snowshoeing in recent years, however, has encouraged more and more winter use, and some trails offer the potential of enjoying the winter experience for appropriately experienced and equipped hikers. The GMC can provide suggestions for winter hikes. The "Winter Use" section contains additional information.

MUD SEASONS

Vermonters joke that spring never comes to Vermont—winter leads directly into "mud season"! When warmth does come to the valleys, trails in higher elevations become wet and muddy. Hiking during "mud season"—from late March through late May—can damage the trails. Please wait until the trails are completely dry before hiking. During mud season:

- Turn back and select another hike if mud forces you to walk on the side of the tread way.
- Plan hikes in the hardwood forest at lower elevations.
- Avoid the spruce-fir (conifer) forests at higher elevations.
- Remember that the state of Vermont closes trails in the Camel's Hump and Mount Mansfield areas from mid-April until Memorial Day weekend. In addition to these areas, avoid Stratton Mountain, the Coolidge Range (Killington to Pico peaks), Lincoln Ridge (Lincoln Gap to Appalachian Gap), and Jay Peak during mud season.

Similar muddy conditions appear in late fall, usually from late October until the snowpack forms. Although early snows leave moisture, the cover cannot protect the ground from damage. The freeze/thaw cycle, combined with overuse during this period, can make trails virtually impassable. Severe winter thaws can create similar conditions. During these times, hikers should find other recreational activities and allow the trails to freeze up or dry out. Such consideration protects the trails from further damage.

If you want to protect and preserve the trails, at all other times of the year walk *through* mud puddles, rather than around them, to minimize damage from "trail spread."

TEMPERATURES

Average monthly Vermont temperature in June, July, and August reaches 60 degrees Fahrenheit (16 degrees Celsius) or higher; in September, 50 degrees (10 degrees C) or higher; in October, around 40 degrees (4 degrees C); and in early November, around 35 degrees (2 degrees C). At any time of the year, however, temperatures can drop below freezing.

WILDLIFE

Insects can make hiking difficult throughout the late spring and summer. Blackfly season usually lasts from mid-May until mid-June, although blackflies can appear throughout the summer in certain locations. Mosquitoes are a summer nuisance at dusk and dawn, especially in wet or swampy areas. Insect repellent, long-sleeve shirts, pants, and mosquito netting help minimize the effects of these pesky critters, so plan accordingly. DEET, an effective ingredient in most insect repellents, may create health problems, particularly in children. If you choose to use a DEET-based product, apply it only to clothing and avoid using it on children. Or, use alternative repellents without DEET.

Hikers in Vermont should be aware of the rise of the deer tick population throughout the state. Deer ticks are carriers of the bacteria that causes Lyme disease. You can take the following precautions when heading outdoors in order to prevent tick bites:

- Wear enclosed shoes and light colored clothing with a tight weave to spot ticks easily. Tuck your shirt into your pants and your pants into your socks or boots.
- Apply repellants that contain 20–30% DEET or 0.5% permethrin to clothes, but avoid contact with skin.
- Check clothes and exposed skin for ticks frequently.
- Stay on the well-traveled trails described in this book and walk in the center of the trail.
- Avoid sitting directly on the ground or on stone walls.

Bathe or shower promptly after your hike (within two hours) and use the opportunity to check for ticks. Remove any ticks found promptly and watch for symptoms, which may resemble the flu and include a stiff neck, chills, fever, swollen lymph nodes, headaches, fatigue, muscle aches, and joint pain. You also may experience a large, expanding "bull's-eye" skin rash around the area of the tick bite. In more advanced states of the disease, nerve problems and arthritis, especially in the knees, may occur. Remember, Lyme disease imitates a variety of illnesses and its severity can vary from person to person. If you have been bitten by a tick or show symptoms of Lyme disease, save the tick and see your doctor right away so that a proper diagnosis can be made and treatment started.

WINTER USE

Hiking takes on a new aura in winter, with clear skies, no bugs, views unimpeded by leaves, and a quiet mountain solitude. Most hiking trails in Vermont are not designed for winter use. Snow usually covers blazes made 4 or 5 feet from the ground; snow-laden branches may block the way. Winter hikers need to anticipate Vermont's unpredictable and ever-changing weather conditions. Deep snow, short days, and the need to carry extra warm clothing and equipment pose practical problems, exacerbated by the winter hiker's need to break trail, a strenuous and exhausting process. Severe wind and weather conditions at higher elevations may make travel difficult or impossible.

Winter conditions extend from November to May in the Green Mountains, and the snowpack lingers until early June at higher elevations below tree line. Maximum snow depth in a typical year occurs in March.

By using snowshoes or skis for backcountry travel, you avoid making knee-deep holes in the snow (post-holing) and keep the trail open and accessible for those coming after you. At higher, windswept elevations, you may need crampons. Sanitation in the winter also poses a challenge. Carry a shovel and dig out the privy whenever possible. Use the privy instead of the snow in front of a shelter. No caretaker likes to arrive after the snowmelt to find piles of human waste left by winter hikers.

The GMC's Education Program offers winter hiking workshops. Today it's possible to walk into a gear store and buy all the equipment you need for a winter trek. You cannot buy experience! We highly recommend you take the time to learn from others the fundamentals of winter travel and safety. Many GMC sections and other outdoor organizations offer trips that help you gain experience with winter equipment and methods of travel. Check out the GMC's *Winter Hiking Guide to Vermont* for more information on winter hiking safety and suggested winter hikes. Additionally, the Catamount Trail, a winter trail that extends the length of Vermont, offers backcountry opportunities with cross-country ski resort facilities. For information and a guidebook, contact the Catamount Trail Association (http://catamounttrail.org/).

SAFETY

The elements of safety include an awareness of weather conditions; packing sufficient clothing, food, and safety gear; carrying or obtaining water; maintaining "situational awareness," including proper route planning and following the blazed trails; and remaining aware of potential hazards along the route. Additionally, always leave a trip itinerary and an estimated return time with a friend.

WEATHER

Expect unpredictable weather in Vermont, including the possibility of high-elevation snowstorms, even in summer! Rain and fog are common, and dangerous storms can appear suddenly. Check a weather report before starting to hike. If stormy weather threatens, either cancel the hike or select a hike at a lower elevation.

CLOTHING AND SAFETY GEAR

Anticipate wet weather by bringing adequate rain gear, a wool or fleece sweater, and a hat. Learn how to use a compass and always carry it—even on short hikes. Keep a first-aid kit and a supply of prepared, high-energy foods, such as nuts and dried fruits, in your pack at all times. The section "Clothing and Equipment" contains more information about what to wear on your hike.

WATER

Water may look pure in the mountains, but it may carry an intestinal parasite called *Giardia lamblia,* even in pristine mountain environments. To prevent giardiasis (an unpleasant infection that often causes cramps, diarrhea, nausea, and vomiting), you should chemically treat, boil, or filter water before drinking it. A 10-minute period of chemical treatment or boiling generally kills all viruses and bacteria. For the majority of hikes in this book, simply carry water with you—and remember to drink water at every rest stop, whether you feel thirsty or not. Everyone requires different amounts of water (usually between two and four quarts per day), depending on the weather conditions and how strenuous the hike.

"SITUATIONAL AWARENESS"

Most trails listed in this book offer parking areas at trailheads. When parking your car, avoid obstructing traffic or blocking access to homes, farms, or woodlots.

Unfortunately, vandalism occurs at trailheads; either remove all valuables from your car or lock them in your trunk. Remove your stereo if possible. Don't leave a note on your car advising friends of your plans. Empty the glove compartment and leave it open (unplug the light first!). Park in the open and parallel to the highway or head-in to the parking space, if possible. If you plan to stay overnight, you might consider leaving the car at a public spot such as a police or service station, or a ski area. Ask permission first; they may ask for a small parking fee. Then you can walk or get a ride to the trailhead.

HUNTING

Hunting, like hiking, is a traditional use of Vermont's woods. Hikers and hunters share the forests of Vermont during the fall, usually from September through December. Deer season mostly occurs in November and wild turkey season in May. Wear bright, visible clothing during hunting season, preferably fluorescent orange. Avoid brown, tan, black, or patches of white that might be mistaken for the white tail of a deer. The Vermont Department of Fish and Wildlife (802-828-1000; www.vtfishandwildlife.com) can provide more information about hunting season and safe practices.

CLOTHING AND EQUIPMENT

The most important rule for clothing, even in summer, is to dress in layers or bring extra clothing with you. The shirt that feels cool with perspiration on a hot summer day may chill you to the bone on a windy and cold mountain summit. Always bring an extra layer of clothing for protection.

No list is perfect, but lists become essential to eliminate the possibility of leaving the camera or other essential item behind.

Boots—Because most of the trails in this book are primitive footpaths, not specially surfaced trails, boots offer the best support and traction. Beginners should wear sturdy and comfortable boots; experienced hikers used to hiking on rough terrain might consider wearing shoes with trail-friendly soles. Some of us hike in sandals. . . .

Socks—Good socks are almost more important than good shoes! Bring an extra pair of socks in case your feet get wet.

Wind jacket/rain gear/breathable shell—Remember, Vermont's unpredictable weather—always be prepared with rain gear!

Sweater or jacket—Warm, dry clothing offers comfort and protection against winds and cooler temperatures at higher elevations. Wool is still the fiber of choice. A wool shirt wears like iron and doesn't melt near campfires or flaring camp stoves.

Hat—You can lose 40 percent of body heat through an uncovered head; headgear keeps you warm.

Day pack—The standard rule of thumb here is whatever size pack you have, you will fill it. It is important to get a pack large enough to carry what you need for a comfortable hike, but bigger is not necessarily better.

Guidebook, maps, and compass—Learn how to use a compass. You may never need it, but when you do, you should know how to use it. The GMC Education Program offers map and compass courses regularly.

Water bottle(s) or canteen(s)—Proper hydration minimizes injuries and fatigue while ensuring your general well-being.

First-aid kit—Include moleskin or similar products for blisters, Band-Aids in assorted sizes, triangular bandage or bandanna, adhesive tape, antiseptic cream, and gauze. Pack everything in a waterproof, sealable plastic bag.

Trail lunch—Food provides the fuel for your hike. Bring a sandwich, fruit, and snacks for the day, and extra high-energy food (energy bars, dried fruit, nuts) for emergencies. Here we recommend carrying food you usually eat. A hike is the wrong time to change your diet. Hikers do march on their stomachs.

Flashlight (or headlamp)—With working batteries, a spare set of batteries, and a spare bulb. Worth checking before each hike—again, when you need it, you really need it.

Matches and/or lighter—Bring waterproof matches or seal everything in a plastic bag.

Toilet paper and trowel

Pocketknife

Whistle—Three short blasts indicate an emergency and help rescuers locate you.

Insect repellent

Sunscreen

Sunglasses (optional)

Camera and binoculars (optional)

Additional Items Required for Backpacking Trips:

Frame pack (internal or external)—Again, get a pack big enough for the gear you need. That 6,000-cubic-inch pack may look great, but you might not want to carry that much gear up the mountain.

Tent or tarp

Sleeping bag and pad—Carry in a waterproof sack. A garbage bag inside that is good insurance. Remember that temperature ratings, like hiking times, vary for individuals. If you sleep cold, get a warmer sleeping bag.

Backpacking stove and spare fuel

Cooking gear and eating utensils

Additional food

Extra clothing—Place in a waterproof sack.

Litter bags—Pack out all trash!

LEAVE NO TRACE

Leave No Trace is a nationwide effort to educate backcountry travelers about the importance of practicing low-impact camping and travel techniques to minimize the potential negative impacts we have on the land, wildlife, and other visitors. "Minimum impact" and "leave no trace" are concepts far more involved than simply giving a hoot and not polluting. Extensive scientific research has revealed widespread damage caused by "loving to death" the favorite places we visit and recreate in. The LEAVE NO TRACE program with its seven principles (listed below) is part of the solution to promoting sustainable use of the backcountry. The GMC offers a variety of education workshops teaching these principles for travelers to understand the ethics and practice the outdoor skills. We encourage you to contact us and find out more about the courses at 802-244-7037, groups@greenmountainclub.org, or www.greenmountainclub.org. The seven principles are as follows:

Plan Ahead and Prepare. Familiarize yourself with local regulations. Visit in small groups; split larger parties into groups of four to eight. Groups should plan to not occupy shelters. Repackage food to minimize waste. Prepare adequately for extreme weather, hazards, and emergencies. Trails can be difficult and travel slower than it appears on a map, *especially in northern Vermont.* Purify *all* drinking water. Carry and know how to use a map and compass. Bring enough tents for everyone.

Travel and Camp on Durable Surfaces. Stay on the trail; avoid shortcuts that erode soil and damage vegetation. Camp in designated sites. Use tent platforms if available to avoid compacting soil. Concentrate activities on existing trails and campsites. Avoid camping where impact is just beginning. Walk single file in the middle of the trail, even when wet or muddy, to avoid widening the tread way. Walk on rocks whenever possible, especially in fragile areas such as shorelines and alpine zones.

Dispose of Waste Properly. If you pack it in, pack it out! Shelters and campsites are equipped with privies. Otherwise, bury human and pet waste in 6- to 8-inch cat holes at least 200 feet away from water sources. Pack out all trash, including hygiene products (opaque bags are helpful). To wash yourself or your dishes, carry water 200 feet away from streams or ponds and use little or no soap. Strain food particles from dishwater and pack out; scatter the dishwater. Keep pets away from water sources to protect water quality.

Leave What You Find. Take only pictures; leave only footprints. Flowers and other naturally occurring objects are best enjoyed in their natural states. Removal of these items is *illegal* on state and federal lands. Altering a campsite is not necessary. Let others enjoy nature and cultural artifacts as you originally found them. Please don't carve into trees or shelters along the trail. After breaking down camp, leave your site cleaner than you found it.

Minimize Campfire Impact. Know local regulations; wood fires may be prohibited. Campfires cause lasting impacts to the backcountry and are discouraged. Use a portable stove for cooking instead of a fire. Where permitted, if you choose to build a fire, use only preexisting fire rings. Keep fires small—using only dead, downed wood. To minimize impacts to the campsite, collect wood on the way in. Burn all wood and coals to ash, extinguish completely, then scatter cool ashes.

Respect Wildlife. Bring binoculars and observe wildlife from a distance. Feeding animals damages their health, alters natural behaviors, and exposes them to predators; *do not feed.* Protect wildlife and your food by storing food securely. If you must bring a pet, keep it leashed and dispose of its waste properly (see above), especially in fragile areas and at campsites. Consider leaving your pet at home.

Be Considerate of Other Visitors. Respect other trail users and protect the quality of their experience. Keep your group size small; no more than 10 on overnighters or trips to fragile areas (alpine summits, pond sites and shorelines, and designated wilderness areas) and no more than 20 on day trips. Be courteous and yield to others on the trail. Take breaks away from the trail and other visitors on durable surfaces. Travel and camp quietly. Let nature's sounds prevail by avoiding loud voices and noises.

For further information about LEAVE NO TRACE, visit www.lnt.org or join a GMC workshop.

SITE AND SUMMIT CARETAKERS

From early May to early November, GMC caretakers are stationed at several sensitive, high-use overnight sites and several alpine areas along the LT. Their informal conversation serves to educate hikers about LEAVE NO TRACE; they also help maintain trails and shelters. At overnight sites, they manage sewage through composting. As summit caretakers, they discuss the fragile alpine ecosystems, enforce camping and fire regulations, and offer first aid and assistance.

As experienced hikers themselves, caretakers can make suggestions and offer basic information about hiking, natural history, and the GMC.

TRAIL COURTESY

Please respect all trail lands. Some trails cross private land, others follow public property. Leave no trace. Carry out all trash. Remember that landowners use the lands adjacent to the trail for farming, grazing, maple sugaring, or logging, all vital to Vermont's economy and way of life.

Private Property—Many of the trails in this guide are located on private property. Please be considerate and appreciative of these landowners, and treat their property with respect to ensure that trails on private property remain open. Do not block traffic or access to private homes when parking at trailheads, and always check with landowners before parking on private property.

Pets—Although your dog may be your best friend, consider leaving it at home. It is often difficult to prevent dogs from contaminating water supplies; they frequently create problems with wildlife, especially porcupines; some hikers or children are afraid of even friendly pets; and dogs may hurt themselves on some of the rougher portions of the trail. If you choose to bring a well-trained dog with you, leash it around tent sites, shelters, water sources, and in the alpine zone. Carry a water bowl so it won't have to drink from water sources, bring extra water for your pet on warm days, and pack biscuits and/or kibble to sustain your pet on longer, more strenuous hikes. Examine your pet's feet for torn pads, bleeding, or sores (pet stores offer "booties" to protect paws from rocks and abrasions). Bury pet waste as you would human waste.

This does seem to be an intimidating list of do's and don'ts; they will quickly become second nature and will ensure an enjoyable hike with your pet and minimize friction with other hikers. We do recommend bringing pliers if you hike with your pet—porcupines are not as common as they used to be, but most every hiking dog will get quilled eventually; being prepared will minimize this trail emergency. And experience has shown that dogs don't learn from this trauma; some of us have had to carry out severely quilled dogs for a veterinarian's attention.

Trash and Waste—The GMC firmly believes in one trail motto: "Pack it in, pack it out." Avoid leaving litter on the trail or in the woods, and pick up litter when someone ignores this rule. Because human waste can damage water quality, use privies when available or bury human (and animal) waste, including toilet paper, 6 to 8 inches deep and at least 200 feet from any trail or water supply.

GROUP USE

Organized groups—such as school groups, camps, and scouts—can use these hikes to plan outings. With experienced leadership, a good leader-to-participant ratio (usually one to four), and a manageable size, each individual in the group can enjoy a successful hike.

GMC promotes a group-use policy that limits group size (including leaders) to 10 individuals for overnights and 20 for day hikes. When possible, the GMC recommends smaller group sizes (4–6 for overnights and 10 for day hikes) so that leaders can provide each participant with maximum attention and security, and the group does not strain existing backcountry resources at shelter and camping sites. At certain shelters, signs encourage groups to use designated tenting areas and avoid shelters entirely. Groups should bring sufficient equipment to tent when shelters are full. Any hiker, and especially those in groups, should accommodate new arrivals and make space for them in shelters or tenting areas.

To minimize impact, some groups break into smaller units and leave at half-hour intervals, and resist the temptation to reconvene until they've returned to the trailhead. Others use different trails to reach a summit or scenic view. Still others hike in opposite directions on the same trail and trade car keys at a middle point. When possible, consider breaking up the group with several experienced leaders and hike in different areas.

GMC staff members can provide planning help and recommendations for group use and suitable hiking areas.

TRAIL WORK

Many trails in Vermont's beautiful mountains include some modifications, which help preserve the tread way and make for drier hiking boots. The Civilian Conservation Corps (CCC), a government work program developed during the Great Depression of the 1930s, completed some of this work. The Long Trail Patrol, the Youth Conservation Corps, and GMC volunteers continue the task of trail construction and maintenance today. This book refers to the following trail construction terms:

Puncheon—Small wooden bridges on one or more log or board planks held off the ground on sills.

Turnpiking—A raised trail bed formed by placing logs on either side of the trail and filling between them with dirt and gravel.

Water Bars—A drainage system of log or rock construction that provides the best defense against trail erosion. Water bars include three parts: the bar, built of log or rock; the apron, a shallow slope to funnel water to the bar; and the ditch, which carries water from the bar and off the trail.

CAMPING AND FIRES

Camping and fires are restricted on most Vermont lands, depending on whether the land is private, state, or federal. Contact the Green Mountain National Forest; Vermont Department of Forests, Parks, and Recreation; or the GMC for more information. Most backpackers carry a portable gas- or alcohol-fueled stove for cooking.

PEREGRINE FALCONS

The following trails in this book pass by the nesting sites of peregrine falcons: White Rocks/Ice Beds (hike 3), Mount Horrid's Great Cliff (hike 19), Rattlesnake Point (hike 23), Mount Pisgah (hike 41), and Sterling Pond and Elephant's Head (hike 46).

The use of the pesticide DDT after World War II almost eliminated these beautiful birds. After the government banned the use of DDT in 1972, the Peregrine Fund at Cornell University and the United States Fish and Wildlife Service started a reintroduction program that released captive-born young falcons on many cliff sites. The Vermont Institute of Natural Science, the Vermont Department of Fish and Wildlife, and the U.S. Forest Service sponsored the peregrine release—or "hacking"—program in Vermont. The first wild nesting pair returned to Vermont at Mount Pisgah in 1985.

Although delisted from the federal Endangered Species List in 1999, the U.S. Fish and Wildlife Service continues to monitor peregrine falcon populations. The Vermont Endangered Species Law still lists the peregrine falcon as endangered, which ensures protection at the state level.

Governmental agencies monitor most peregrine nesting sites in Vermont every year. In Smugglers' Notch, for example, monitoring begins early in the season (around April) to determine nesting sites; the birds historically use several different nesting sites on both sides of the notch. Nesting season usually runs from February through July.

Humans can disturb nesting peregrine falcons and force them to abandon their nests if approached. To protect these birds, the state temporarily closes trails that come close to the nest site or bring hikers onto exposed areas above the nest. Because nesting sites vary year to year, the Vermont Department of Forests, Parks, and Recreation works with the Vermont Department of Fish and Wildlife to minimize both disturbance to the birds and the loss of recreational opportunities.

Watch these majestic raptors only from a distance, using either powerful binoculars or a telescope. Please obey any posted signs, and do not disturb the birds. For more information, contact the GMC or the Vermont Department of Fish and Wildlife at 802-828-1000; www.vtfishandwildlife.com.

ARCTIC-ALPINE VEGETATION

Several of the higher summits in this guidebook feature unique ecosystems with fragile arctic-alpine plant communities. This rare and beautiful plant life remains from an era when ice sheets covered northern New England.

When the most recent glaciers from the Laurentide Ice Sheet retreated between 8,000 and 12,000 years ago, arctic plants grew in exposed areas. As the climate warmed, most of these plants retreated north—except for those on a few mountaintops where the climate resembles the Arctic regions 1,000 miles to the north of Vermont. Shallow soils, high winds, low temperatures, a short growing season, high precipitation (100 or more inches a year), and heavy fog (the alpine plants absorb 5 to 30 inches of fog moisture each year in addition to precipitation) allow only a few species to survive. Those that remain grow very slowly. For example, it takes approximately 80 years for a tree near the timberline to grow 2 inches in diameter.

The survival of this rare vegetation, much of which looks like ordinary grass, is precarious. The same shallow soil and vigorous climatic conditions that allow it to grow make the environment especially vulnerable to hiker disturbances. When a small portion of alpine tundra is destroyed, the wind rapidly scours large holes in the damaged turf, and the soil quickly erodes. Removal of rocks from the grassy tundra is especially harmful in this respect. Fires destroy not only the ground cover plants, but also the thin underlying layer of humus. Because excessive trampling of plants and soil leads to further loss of rare vegetation, please stay on the marked trails and rock outcrops.

THE GREEN MOUNTAIN CLUB

Since its founding, the GMC's primary purpose has been to build, maintain, and protect hiking trails and shelters for the enjoyment of Vermont's residents and visitors.

In 1910, the GMC founded the LT, the nation's oldest long-distance hiking trail. Completed in 1930, the 272-mile LT follows the ridgeline of the Green Mountains from Massachusetts to Canada and encompasses more than 175 miles of side trails and nearly 70 rustic cabins and lean-to shelters. The entire 445-mile LT System is managed and maintained by GMC field staff and hundreds of dedicated volunteers in cooperation with private landowners and state and federal agencies. The LT provided the inspiration for the founders of the Appalachian Trail. Today, the two trails share 105 miles of the same route in southern Vermont.

In 1985, the GMC learned that 34 of the 65 miles of the LT on private land in northern Vermont were for sale. Rising real estate values, the unsettled economics of the forest products industry, and rapid development in Vermont created a volatile land market. The GMC also faced serious problems with landowners who wanted the LT removed from their property or who wanted to use the land for purposes incompatible with the trail.

Convinced of the need to save the scenic quality, environment, wildlife habitat, and continuity of the LT, the GMC started the Long Trail Protection Campaign. The campaign has permanently protected over 60 miles of the LT in Vermont, 18 miles of side trails, and over 25,000 acres of backcountry lands.

The effort to save the LT continues. Vermont is experiencing a construction and population boom as well as tremendous pressures on land use. Nearly 10 miles of the LT system are still in need of protection. The GMC continues the effort to preserve these high mountain lands that are so important to Vermonters and the thousands of people who visit the state each year.

Membership

Anyone interested in hiking and in Vermont's mountains can join the GMC. Membership in the GMC helps protect and preserve the Long Trail System; annual dues support trail maintenance, education, publications, and trail protection activities.

Anyone who wishes to participate in local outdoor and trail activities may join the GMC as a *section* or *at-large* member. Each section (chapter) schedules activities throughout the year, including hikes, potluck dinners, bike trips, cross-country skiing/snowshoeing, and canoeing/kayaking. Section members maintain portions of the LT and its shelters and receive a section-oriented newsletter listing upcoming events. At-large membership lets you support the GMC without joining a section.

Both section and at-large members receive a subscription to the GMC's quarterly periodical, the *Long Trail News,* which provides up-to-date information on trail and shelter conditions, hiking, statewide trails, club history, and a club activity calendar. All members receive discounts on club publications (such as maps and guidebooks), items carried in the GMC bookstore, and opportunities to participate in wide-ranging club activities.

Today's 14 sections include Bennington, Brattleboro, Bread Loaf (Middlebury), Burlington, Connecticut, Killington (Rutland), Laraway (St. Albans), Manchester, Montpelier, Northeast Kingdom, Northern Frontier (Montgomery), Ottauquechee (Woodstock), Sterling (Stowe-Morrisville-Johnson), and Worcester (Massachusetts).

The GMC welcomes volunteers and provides many opportunities for involvement with the club's activities. No experience is necessary, and newcomers are always welcome. The club sponsors education workshops year-round for folks looking for additional information, new perspectives, or just a great day in the woods.

If you would like more information about the GMC, the trails in this book, other hiking opportunities in Vermont, volunteer activities, or membership, please contact us. We will happily help you plan your next hiking adventure.

The Green Mountain Club
4711 Waterbury-Stowe Road
Waterbury Center, VT 05677
802-244-7037
www.greenmountainclub.org

You can visit the GMC in Waterbury Center, Vermont. From I-89 in Waterbury (exit 10), follow VT 100 north 4 miles. The headquarters are located on the left (west) side of VT 100. Alternatively, from the intersection of VT 108 and VT 100 in Stowe, follow VT 100 south 6 miles to the headquarters buildings.

The Marvin B. Gameroff Hiker Center houses the club's information services, educational displays, bookstore, and field programs. The center provides information about backcountry recreational opportunities throughout Vermont. During the winter, the club hosts the James P. Taylor winter slide show and lecture series, which highlights outdoor recreation adventures. Business hours are Monday through Friday from 9:00 AM to 5:00 PM year-round. From Memorial Day to Columbus Day, the hiker center remains open seven days a week from 9:00 AM to 5:00 PM.

HIKING INFORMATION AVAILABLE FROM THE GREEN MOUNTAIN CLUB

The GMC issues a variety of publications about hiking and backpacking in Vermont and welcomes inquiries about trail conditions and planning. To order GMC publications, see the order form in the back of this book.

Guidebooks and Maps

Long Trail Guide (27th Edition 2011)—The latest edition contains 17 color topographical maps, with complete descriptions of the LT, its side trails and shelters, and the Appalachian Trail in Vermont; suggested hikes, helpful hints, and winter-use suggestions.

Day Hiker's Guide to Vermont (6th Edition 2011)—Companion volume to the *Long Trail Guide*. Comprehensive coverage of more than 200 hikes throughout the state with detailed driving directions to trailheads; detailed trail maps and descriptions; summaries of distance, time, and elevation gain; listings of Vermont's trail organizations; and helpful hiking and equipment tips.

The Long Trail End-to-Ender's Guide (19th Edition 2013)—A must-have guide for long-distance LT hikers. Annually updated, this supplement to the *Long Trail Guide* provides detailed information about trail conditions, overnight accommodations, trail towns, mail drops, and transportation.

Mount Mansfield Booklet

The Tundra Walk—An Interpretive Guide to the Mount Mansfield Alpine Region (2002)—This illustrated brochure describes a 0.5-mile natural-history hike along the LT on the summit ridgeline of Mount Mansfield.

Green Mountain Club History

Green Mountain Adventure, Vermont's Long Trail (1st Edition 1985, Second Printing 1989)—An illustrated history of the GMC by Jane Curtis, Will Curtis, and Frank Lieberman. Ninety-six pages of rare black-and-white photographs and anecdotes of the GMC's first 75 years.

A Century in the Mountains: Celebrating Vermont's Long Trail (1st Edition 2009)—A history of the first one hundred years of the LT and Green Mountain Club, illustrated with more than 185 historic and contemporary photographs.

Pamphlets

The Long Trail: A Footpath in the Wilderness—Brochure with information and suggestions on hiking the LT. Free with legal-sized self-addressed stamped envelope.

ROUTE PLANNING AND ORDERING MAPS

The USGS provides mapping services for the United States. Most hikers use the 1:24,000-scale (or 7.5-minute) topographic (or *topo*) maps, although smaller-scale maps are available. Many Vermont topo maps date from the late 1980s, so they may not include all details, such as home or business construction sites. These maps provide topographic details, such as elevations, drainages, and other natural landmarks.

The USGS provides downloadable maps on its website; for hard copies you can obtain maps from both the USGS (http://store.usgs.gov) and a variety of online retailers. Most sources of USGS maps can send you free grids for 7.5-minute topo map quadrants for any state. Order maps from the grid by quadrant. Before ordering, make sure you know the quadrangle (or quad) where you plan to hike (for example, USGS 7.5' Bolton). The USGS defines each quadrangle map by a nearby town or natural feature.

The USGS lists retail vendors across the country who stock government maps. Most offer USGS quads for all states. Many vendors operate on a prepaid basis only. They accept phone orders and forward the maps after receiving your payment.

Your local sporting goods shop or bookstore may also carry USGS maps. Check the phone directory under "Maps—Dealers." The USGS website lists Vermont area map vendors (after clicking on the appropriate link) at http://store.usgs.gov.

In addition, you may order GMNF maps from:

Green Mountain and Finger Lakes National Forests Supervisor's Office
231 North Main Street
Rutland, VT 05701
802-747-6700 or 802-747-6765
www.fs.usda.gov/greenmountain

GMNF maps only include those quadrangles in which the forest is located. Send a prepaid order to receive these maps.

OTHER RESOURCES

For additional information on hiking in Vermont, you may wish to contact one or more of the following organizations.

On Federal Lands

Green Mountain and Finger Lakes National Forests Supervisor's Office
231 North Main Street

Rutland, VT 05701
802-747-6700
www.fs.usda.gov/greenmountain

On State Lands
Vermont Department of Forest, Parks,
and Recreation
1 National Life Drive, Davis 2
Montpelier, VT 05620-3801
www.vtfpr.org

On the Appalachian Trail
(New Hampshire/Vermont Guide)
Appalachian Trail Conservancy
799 Washington Street
P.O. Box 807
Harpers Ferry, WV 25425
304-535-6331
www.appalachiantrail.org

WINTER HIKING AND SNOWSHOEING
The following books contain information
about winter hiking and snowshoeing in
Vermont:

Winter Hiking Guide to Vermont (1st Edition
2013)—This publication contains color
topographical maps and descriptions for
74 winter hikes/snowshoes throughout
the state, winter hiking tips and suggestions, and full color photographs of winter
scenes along the hikes.
The Catamount Trail Guidebook (9th Edition 2009)—A guide to the 300-mile
backcountry ski trail that runs the length
of Vermont. Published by the Catamount
Trail Association and available from
GMC.

Winter Trails Vermont & New Hampshire:
The Best Cross-Country Ski and Snow-
shoe Trails, by Marty Basch (Globe Pe-
quot Press, 2001).

RECOMMENDED REFERENCES
A highly subjective list of references
includes:

The Complete Walker IV, by Colin Fletcher
and Chip Rawlins (Alfred A. Knopf,
2002). An exhaustive and thorough look
at hiking gear with time-tested opinions
and philosophies.
Winterwise, by John Dunn (Adirondack
Mountain Club, 1996). A great guide to
enjoying the great white north safely.
Be Expert with Map and Compass, by
Bjorn Kjellstrom (IDG Books Worldwide,
1994). The guide for understanding map
and compass, not only for staying found
but for getting to where you want to go.
Backwoods Ethics, by Laura and Guy Wa-
terman (Countryman Press, 1993). A
provocative discussion of the balance between management and freedom in the
backcountry, well worth seeking out to
better understand some of the issues and
controversies associated with protecting
and enjoying our recreational resources.
The Nature of Vermont, by Charles W.
Johnson (University Press of New England, 1998). A great guide to Vermont's
environment.
Leave No Trace, by Annette McGivney (The
Mountaineers, 1998). A more detailed
look at walking softly through the woods.

Clarendon Gorge (hike 15)

1

Mount Olga

Total distance: 2.2-mile loop (3.5 km)

Hiking time: 1½ hours

Vertical rise: 520 feet (158 meters)

Rating: Easy to moderate

Map: USGS 7.5' Jacksonville

Trailhead GPS Coordinates: N42° 51.16', W72° 48.88'

The loop trail up Mount Olga is located in Molly Stark State Park, which is named for the wife of General John Stark. During the Revolutionary War in 1777, the general sent Molly a message asking her to "Send every man from the farm that will come and let the haying go." Molly organized the farmers and, along with two hundred other men, went to the general's aid. After the Battle of Bennington, General Stark returned home with one of the six brass cannons captured from the British as a token of gratitude to Molly.

This park, one of the smaller ones in the state park system, is a beautiful place to picnic or camp. A day-use fee is charged during the summer months. Dogs must be leashed.

HOW TO GET THERE
Molly Stark State Park is 3.4 miles east of Wilmington and 15 miles west of Brattleboro, on the south side of VT 9. Ample parking is available.

THE TRAIL
You may want to pick up the free park brochure *Molly Stark State Park Recreational Trails Guide* before beginning your hike. The Mount Olga Trail begins on the east side of the park road opposite the caretaker's home. A sign indicates a distance of 0.8 mile to the fire tower. Follow the blue-blazed trail 30 yards down a short embankment on steps, cross a small wooden bridge over Beaver Brook, and climb a slight to moderate grade on a footpath covered with conifer needles. Cross over an old stone wall, turn sharply left, and continue your ascent through a

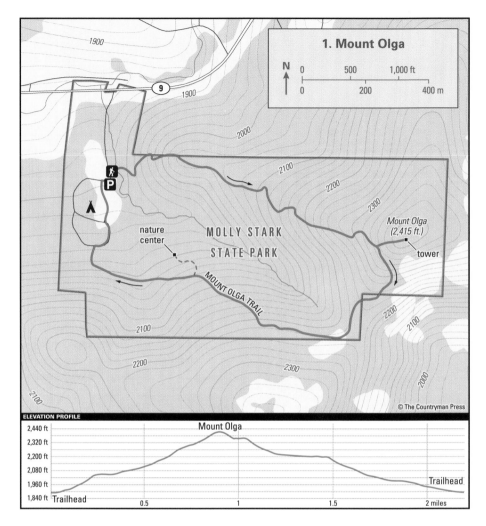

1. Mount Olga

N

| 0 | 500 | 1,000 ft |
| 0 | 200 | 400 m |

MOLLY STARK
STATE PARK

nature
center

MOUNT OLGA TRAIL

Mount Olga
(2,415 ft.)

tower

© The Countryman Press

ELEVATION PROFILE

Mount Olga

| 2,440 ft |
| 2,320 ft |
| 2,200 ft |
| 2,080 ft |
| 1,960 ft |
| 1,840 ft | Trailhead |

Trailhead

0.5   1   1.5   2 miles

forest of stately spruce. At 0.4 mile cross the remains of another low stone wall.

Climb again on moderate grades until, on the left side of the trail, you reach a remarkable rough-barked red maple tree with five stems that sprouted from a cut-over stump, 0.6 mile from the start. In another 100 yards the power and data line for the summit radio relay tower becomes evident on your left.

The trail narrows, becomes steeper, climbs up a few stone steps, and at 0.7 mile reaches a junction. Bear left from the junction, and steeply ascend to the wooded summit (elevation 2,415 feet, 736 meters) at 0.8 mile. Here you will find the fire tower, two old buildings, a shed housing electronics, and a radio relay tower. The white-painted, cement-block building on your right just before the fire tower housed broadcast equipment for a state police communications radio installed in the 1950s.

The summit was established as a fire lookout, with a wooden tower surmounted by a hexagonal cab, in the early 1930s.

Between 1949 and 1950 the wooden tower was removed, and the steel tower from Bald Mountain in Townshend was transferred to Mount Olga. This tower was last used for a fire lookout in 1974. Climb the tower for a beautiful 360-degree panoramic view of southern Vermont and northwestern Massachusetts.

Directly opposite the relay tower is Haystack Mountain (see hike 5), the only mountain with a significant peak apparent. Mount Snow is to the right of Haystack, at the end of the Deerfield Ridge. Stratton Mountain is the large mountain farther to the right. Looking to the left of Haystack, VT 9 leads to the village of Wilmington. The Searsburg Wind Power Facility turbines and Haystack Mountain stand out on the horizon, and a portion of Harriman Reservoir is visible. Mount Greylock, the highest point in Massachusetts, can also be seen to the west.

Return to the trail junction, turn left onto the blue-blazed return leg of the loop, and descend on easy grades through numerous rock outcrops. Pass between giant boulders and ledges, and cross a small bridge at 1.1 miles. The area beyond the boulders, in contrast to the evergreen forest through which you passed on your ascent of Mount Olga, is composed of maple, beech, birch, and ash; no conifer are in sight. Continue your gentle descent to a long, straight section of trail, which follows a skid trail last used to haul timber during horse logging days.

At 1.4 miles turn left. Here the trail parallels an old stone wall, reaching a junction in 50 yards with a trail on the left leading to Shearer Hill Road. The Mount Olga Trail continues to follow the wall through overgrown, sometimes wet pastureland. The old stone wall and trail turn right at 1.7 miles, and at 1.8 miles the trail reaches a junction with a spur trail to the right that leads just over 0.1 mile to the state park nature center.

If you take the walk to the nature center and back, you will be rewarded by displays and information on the natural history of the park. Of particular interest is a photograph of more than one hundred young men of 1179 Company of the Civilian Conservation Corps (CCC), which occupied Camp P-63 on what is now Molly Stark State Park from June 1935, through September 1937. The nature center building itself is a renovated CCC building, and the spur trail to it passes several moss-covered fireplaces built by the CCC three-quarters of a century ago, as sound today as the day they were built despite a total lack of maintenance. The CCC display includes many fascinating details of life in Camp P-63.

From the spur trail junction with the Mount Olga Trail, it is 20 yards to the campground road, across from campsite 9. Turn right, and follow the road 0.2 mile back to your car at 2.2 miles (2.4 miles if you walked to the nature center).

2

Equinox Mountain

Total distance: 5.4 miles (8.7 km)

Hiking time: 4½ hours

Vertical rise: 2,730 feet (832 meters)

Rating: Strenuous

Maps: USGS 7.5' Manchester; 7.5' West Rupert

Trailhead GPS Coordinates: N43° 9.75', W73° 4.94'

Equinox Mountain is the highest peak in the Taconic Mountains and also the highest peak in Vermont not in the Green Mountains. At 3,848 feet (1,173 meters) above sea level, the summit offers panoramic views of the Green, White, Adirondack, Berkshire, and Taconic Mountains. The Valley of Vermont and the Green and the White Mountains are to the east, the Taconic Mountains to the north, the Green Mountains to the northeast and southeast, the Adirondack Mountains to the west, and the Taconic and Berkshire Mountains to the south.

Common theory holds that the origin of the mountain's name is a corruption of Native American words meaning either "place of fog" or "place where the very top is."

Access to the summit is by foot along the Blue Summit Trail, formerly known as the Burr and Burton Trail, as well as by car along the paved Equinox Mountain Skyline Drive (toll charged). There are several trails to the summit from parking areas on the upper third of the Skyline Drive as well. From the parking area at the summit, trails from the Saint Bruno Scenic Viewing Center, built by the Carthusian Foundation, lead to several points of interest. Additionally, the Equinox Preservation Trust (EPT), established in 1993 to protect and maintain some of the lands of Equinox Mountain, maintains several lower-elevation multiuse trails in the vicinity of Equinox Pond. For a brochure and trail map, stop by the Equinox Resort or contact the EPT at P.O. Box 986, Manchester, Vermont 05254; 802-366-1400; www.equinoxpreservationtrust.org.

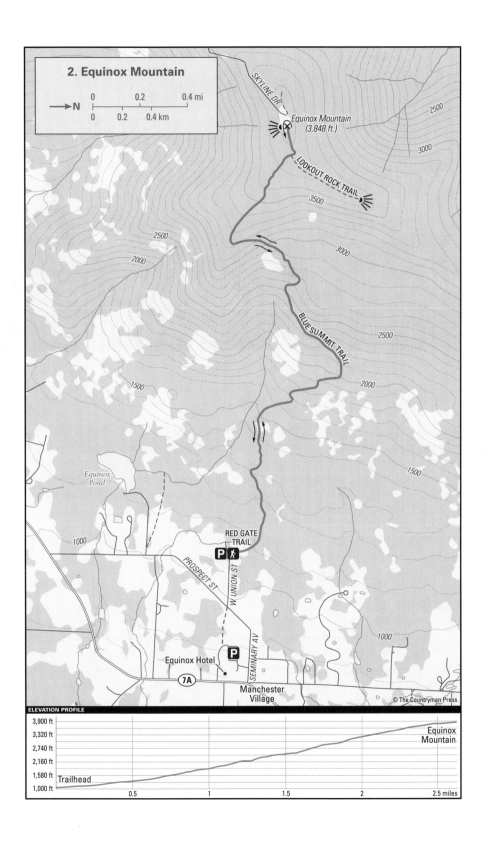

2. Equinox Mountain

0	0.2	0.4 mi
0	0.2	0.4 km

→N

SKYLINE DR

Equinox Mountain
(3,848 ft.)

LOOKOUT ROCK TRAIL

2500

3000

3500

3000

2500

BLUE SUMMIT TRAIL

2500

2000

2000

1500

1500

Equinox
Pond

1000

1000

RED GATE
TRAIL

🅿 🚶

PROSPECT ST

W UNION ST

SEMINARY AV

1000

Equinox Hotel   🅿

7A

Manchester
Village

© The Countryman Press

ELEVATION PROFILE

| | Equinox Mountain |

3,900 ft
3,320 ft
2,740 ft
2,160 ft
1,580 ft   Trailhead
1,000 ft

0.5   1   1.5   2   2.5 miles

View from Equinox Mountain

The Blue Summit Trail was first established and later maintained for many years by students from the Burr and Burton Seminary, now a semipublic high school renamed the Burr and Burton Academy, in the village of Manchester. The trail is maintained by the Friends of Equinox Preservation Trust, a dedicated group of volunteers who maintain all the trails on the Mount Equinox Preserve. The trail is rated strenuous by the EPT because it is steep for most of the way.

HOW TO GET THERE
Parking for the Blue Summit Trail, as well as all the lower mountain trails maintained by the EPT, is on West Union Street. Just north of the Equinox Resort and Spa, turn left on Seminary Avenue, go to the end and bear left on Prospect Street, and turn right on West Union Street. Go about 0.1 mile and there will be a parking lot on the right.

Additional parking for the Blue Summit Trail is available at the Equinox Resort and Spa on VT 7A in Manchester Village. Hikers should leave their cars at the upper (west) end of the large parking lot at the hotel. Park behind the hotel and follow the West Union Trail (blazed in green) to the top of West Union Street. Turn right onto a gravel road and follow the Red Gate Trail to the Blue Summit Trail.

THE TRAIL
From the parking lot, go up the trail past the kiosk with maps to the top of the hill, where there is a T-junction with the Blue Summit Trail. The right turn goes down to the Burr and Burton Academy playing fields. Turn left and begin following the blue-blazed Summit Trail. At about 0.2 mile the Flatlanders Pass Trail leaves on the left and almost immediately the Snicket Trail leaves on the left.

Continue uphill and at 0.3 mile reach a fork. The Red Gate Trail bears left and the Blue Summit Trail bears right.

Continue ascending on the woods road to an overgrown clearing and an unmarked trail crossing (0.5 mile). There is a sign on a tree on the right that says THOMPSON FLATS and a small building on the left. At this junction the Trillium Trail departs left and descends southerly for about 0.6 mile to Equinox Pond. To the right, the Trillium Trail leads to the Southern Vermont Arts Center Loop, which accesses the lower slopes of the Southern Vermont Arts Center and connections with its local trails.

Continue straight through the junction on the Blue Summit Trail and, after some steady climbing, cross the Maidenhair Trail (0.6 mile). Still following the woods road, begin a steep and winding climb northwest. Eventually swinging southwest, the trail continues its steady ascent to the end of the road (1.4 miles). Bear right and continue a steady southwesterly ascent on the Blue Summit Trail, now a rough and narrow footpath, and pass several overgrown but increasingly revealing views of the Manchester area and the Green Mountains. Reach the south shoulder of the mountain (2.0 miles) and ascend westerly on easier grades through spruce woods. After another steep pitch, make an easy ascent to the ridge and reach a junction with a cross trail. From the junction, continue straight in the woods on the Blue Summit Trail and soon cross the terminus of a narrow gravel road at a television repeater station. Skirt the left side of the fenced-in facility and continue 100 feet to the end of the Blue Summit Trail.

To the left, the Lookout Rock Trail leads uphill to the site of the former Sky Line Inn, the upper end of the toll road, and the summit of Equinox Mountain (2.7 miles), with some of the finest views in southern Vermont. To the right, the Lookout Rock Trail takes you to Lookout Rock, with the same views from northeast to southeast as from the summit, but without the building and television repeater. This trail continues down to Beartown Road, a trail that is described in the Green Mountain Club's publication *Winter Hiking Guide to Vermont*.

To get back to your car, return along the same route.

3

White Rocks/Ice Beds Trail

Total distance: 2.0 miles (3.2 km)

Hiking time: 1½ hours

Vertical rise: 460 feet (140 meters)

Rating: Easy

Map: USGS 7.5' Wallingford

Trailhead GPS Coordinates: N43° 27.05', W72° 56.6'

This relatively easy hike offers wonderful views of the White Rocks Cliff and the "Ice Beds," where ice, formed beneath the rocks during the previous winter, chills a meltwater stream.

HOW TO GET THERE

Drive east on VT 140 from its US 7 junction in Wallingford to Sugar Hill Road at 2.2 miles. Turn right, drive about 150 yards on Sugar Hill Road, and turn right onto Forest Road 52 (FR 52). Continue to the White Rocks Picnic Area at 2.8 miles. The picnic area has ample parking for 30 cars, along with picnic facilities and outhouses. The picnic area is also the trailhead for a different trail—the Keewaydin Trail—leading 0.4 mile to the Long Trail.

THE TRAIL

Near the entrance to the picnic area, a trailhead sign marks the beginning of the blue-blazed Ice Beds Trail. You immediately pass through a small wet area on bridges and turnpiking. Large rock outcrops appear on your left, and boulders dot the area as you hike up the hillside. The trail swings to your right and climbs through boulders and softwoods. Hike along switchbacks, then ascend more steeply to a trail junction at 0.3 mile.

From this point, the White Rocks Trail leads left to a spectacular view of the White Rocks Cliff and the Otter Creek Valley to the southwest. A talc mine in South Wallingford on US 7 is also visible.

Because peregrine falcons have returned to the area and may be nesting on the cliffs,

Fun scrambling on the boulders

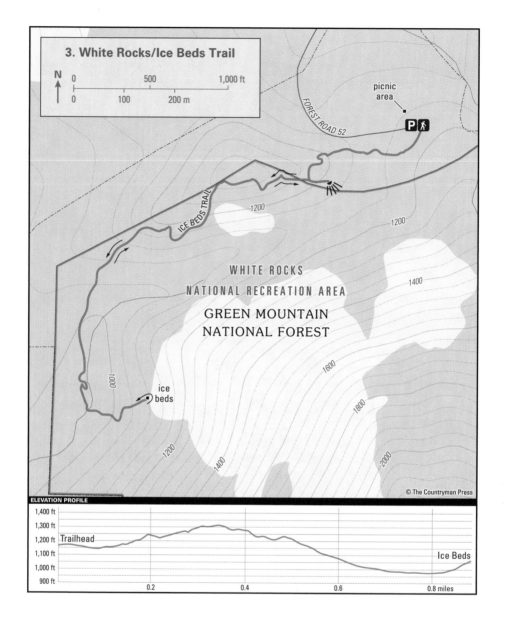

3. White Rocks/Ice Beds Trail

N

| 0 | 500 | 1,000 ft |
| 0 | 100 | 200 m |

FOREST ROAD 52

picnic area

P 🚶

1200

1200

ICE BEDS TRAIL

WHITE ROCKS
NATIONAL RECREATION AREA

GREEN MOUNTAIN
NATIONAL FOREST

1400

1600

1800

1000

ice beds

1200

1400

2000

© The Countryman Press

ELEVATION PROFILE

| 1,400 ft |
| 1,300 ft |
| 1,200 ft | Trailhead |
| 1,100 ft |
| 1,000 ft |
| 900 ft |

Ice Beds

0.2   0.4   0.6   0.8 miles

the White Rocks Trail may be closed during their nesting season; these beautiful endangered birds are easily disturbed from above. Please obey all posted signs, and refer to the introduction for more information about the falcons.

Return to the junction, and continue up-hill along the Ice Beds Trail. *Watch carefully for the blue blazes as there are many "herd" trails in this area.* Enjoy the good view back to White Rocks before you hike behind the ridge and have only limited views

View on Ice Beds Trail

to the north. The trail is quite rocky in this section, so watch your step. The trail soon levels before descending toward, then away from, the base of White Rocks Cliff. At the double blaze, turn right, and begin a rocky descent. Follow the blazes along a series of small switchbacks as the trail becomes less steep and more wooded. You begin to hear a brook to your left, and the air feels cool and damp.

After descending a few steps, you reach a junction with an old road, where you go left and downhill. Cross a brook on a small bridge, and follow along the valley floor. You soon cross the brook again, ascend slightly, and at 1.0 mile reach the Ice Beds, where the brook you have been following emerges from the base of the White Rocks Slide.

A shattering of cheshire quartzite rock probably occurred during the ice age to create this rock slide. During the winter, ice and snow accumulate in the depths of the rock crevices. A continual downdraft of cold air in the shaded canyon helps preserve the ice and snow during the summer. The stream flowing from the rocks is fed by the melting ice. This keeps the water temperature at approximately 40 degrees throughout the summer.

After enjoying this cool, refreshing retreat (especially on a hot summer day!), hike back via the same trail to the picnic area.

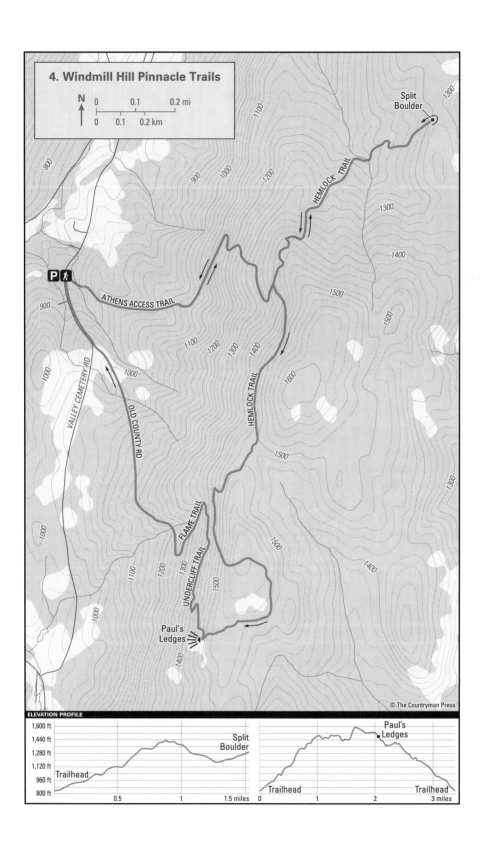

4. Windmill Hill Pinnacle Trails

N

| 0 | | 0.1 | | 0.2 mi |
| 0 | 0.1 | | 0.2 km | |

Split Boulder

HEMLOCK TRAIL

1100
1200
1300
1400
1500
1500

800
900
1000

P

ATHENS ACCESS TRAIL

900

VALLEY CEMETERY RD

OLD COUNTY RD

1000

1000

1100
1200
1300
1400

1600

1500

HEMLOCK TRAIL

1500

1300

FLAME TRAIL

UNDERCLIFF TRAIL

1200
1300
1500

1500

1400

Paul's Ledges

1400

© The Countryman Press

ELEVATION PROFILE

1,600 ft
1,440 ft
1,280 ft
1,120 ft
960 ft
800 ft

Split Boulder

Trailhead

0.5   1   1.5 miles

Paul's Ledges

Trailhead

Trailhead

0   1   2   3 miles

4

Windmill Hill Pinnacle Trails

Total distance:
Athens Access Trail to Split Boulder and return, 3 miles (4.8 km)
Athens Access Trail to Paul's Ledges Loop, Old County Road return, 3.4 miles (5.5 km)

Hiking time:
Athens Access Trail to Split Boulder and return, 2 hours
Athens Access Trail to Paul's Ledges Loop, Old County Road return, 2½ hours

Vertical rise: 500 feet (152 meters)

Rating: Easy

Map: USGS 7.5' Westminster West

Trailhead GPS Coordinates: N43° 6.2', W72° 34.55'

With lovely, moderate hikes through a variety of forests, this area also has signs of former human habitation and geologic interest. It is uncrowded and peaceful.

Pick up a map at the trailhead, as it will help you with the trail choices you will encounter, and check for the latest trail additions.

The Windmill Hill Pinnacle Association's website contains full trail maps, and some new trail additions are planned. Check for updates at www.windmillhillpinnacle.org.

HOW TO GET THERE

From the junction of VT 121 and VT 35 in Cambridgeport, follow VT 35 south 1.3 miles and bear left onto Brookline Road. Follow Brookline Road 1.7 miles and turn left onto Valley Cemetery Road. The Athens Access Trailhead (37 Valley Cemetery Road) is 0.4 mile up this road on the left.

From VT 30 north of Newfane, at the sign for Brookline, follow Radway Hill Road—which becomes Grassy Brook Road at the West River Bridge, soon turns left (do not take the Putney Mountain turn to the right), and eventually becomes unpaved, becoming Brookline Road at the Athens town line. From VT 30 it is 9.1 miles to Valley Cemetery Road (unsigned) just after two large beaver ponds on the left. Turn right here and in 0.9 mile pass Old County Road (also unsigned, appears as a dirt driveway with three mailboxes). The trailhead is another 0.2 mile on the right (small entrance) and has a kiosk with maps.

Above the clouds on Windmill Hill

THE TRAIL

Leaving the parking lot, follow small red blazes along a gentle, pine needle–carpeted trail that winds uphill through mixed forest. The woods gradually turn to hemlock, and the trail switchbacks across a steep, shady hillside. Returning to deciduous forest, the trail meets the white-blazed Hemlock Trail at 0.8 mile.

Straight ahead at the intersection (north), the Hemlock Trail passes through ferny (and brambly) open woods, past old stone walls, over some small dips and climbs to a spur trail on the right leading to a large, split, glacial erratic boulder at 0.7 mile. The trail extends a further 0.3 mile to a small view. (If you take this section, return the way you came.)

To the right, the Hemlock Trail south continues to climb through hemlock woods, passing a small west view at 0.3 mile and the Undercliff Trail junction at 0.6 mile. It then follows the ridge through northern hardwood forest until reaching a grassy clearing. A short spur path south through the field leads to Paul's Ledges, where there is an expansive western view toward Stratton Mountain. A plaque commemorates Paul R. Sternfels, who was instrumental in cleaning and preserving this beautiful spot.

Retracing your steps through the field,

follow the old drive 100 feet and look for the Hemlock Trail dropping to the right just as you enter the woods. (Do not follow the old drive left and down.) Follow the trail downhill 0.1 mile to the blue-blazed Undercliff Trail, which goes along a ledged hillside for 0.3 mile before reaching the orange-blazed Flame Trail. Go straight, downhill, on the Flame Trail and soon (0.2 mile) join the grassy, gravelly Old County Road, which descends moderately to Valley Cemetery Road, which you will follow back to the parking lot. (For a longer walk with no road walk, stay on the Undercliff Trail by turning right and going uphill to rejoin the Hemlock Trail and retrace your steps.)

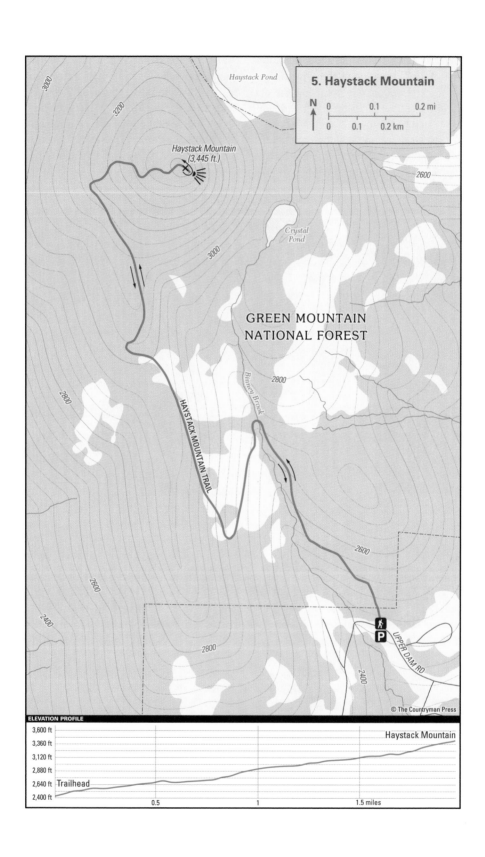

Haystack Pond

5. Haystack Mountain

N

| 0 | | 0.1 | | 0.2 mi |
| 0 | 0.1 | | 0.2 km | |

Haystack Mountain
(3,445 ft.)

2600

Crystal
Pond

GREEN MOUNTAIN
NATIONAL FOREST

2800

Binney Brook

HAYSTACK MOUNTAIN TRAIL

2800

2600

2800

2600

2400

2400

UPPER DAM RD

© The Countryman Press

ELEVATION PROFILE

| | | | | Haystack Mountain |
3,600 ft
3,360 ft
3,120 ft
2,880 ft
2,640 ft Trailhead
2,400 ft

0.5   1   1.5 miles

5

Haystack Mountain

Total distance: 4.2 miles (6.8 km)	
Hiking time: 3 hours	
Vertical rise: 1,020 feet (311 meters)	
Rating: Moderate	
Map: USGS 7.5' Mount Snow	
Trailhead GPS Coordinates: N42° 53.98', W72° 54.64'	

Rock outcroppings on the summit of Haystack Mountain provide beautiful views of southern Vermont and southwestern New Hampshire.

HOW TO GET THERE

Care is needed to find the trailhead, which is in the Chimney Hill development northwest of Wilmington. From the traffic light in Wilmington, drive 0.1 mile west on VT 9. Turn right (north) onto Haystack Road, and at 1.4 miles bear right, continuing to follow paved Haystack Road. At 2.35 miles, you reach an intersection where you turn left at a large CHIMNEY HILL sign pointing the way to the clubhouse and Chimney Hill Road. At 2.5 miles, turn right onto unpaved Binney Brook Road. Continue uphill on Binney Brook Road by bearing left at the next three intersections. At 3.5 miles, turn right onto Upper Dam Road. Continue for a short distance to a T-intersection at 3.6 miles where you turn left. At 3.8 miles you reach the trailhead, marked on your right with a brown sign with orange lettering. Parking for about 10 cars is available along the road just beyond the trailhead. Please do not block driveways or park on private property.

THE TRAIL

Your pathway, which follows an old road on easy-to-moderate grades, is sporadically marked with blue plastic diamonds. A sign indicating the Haystack Mountain Trail points up a road surfaced in crushed stone. At 0.1 mile you pass by a yellow gate that blocks vehicles from driving up the road. Listen on your left for Binney Brook, which is the outlet for Haystack and Crystal ponds.

At 0.6 mile, just after crossing Little Binney Brook, the trail turns left and follows the Deerfield Ridge Trail. This intersection is identified by signs marking the Wilmington Watershed Protection Area and prohibiting snowmobiles from continuing on the road, which eventually leads to Haystack and Crystal ponds.

Descend slightly, and pass over some wet ground. The trail then curves right and ascends moderately on a rocky route for a short way before climbing more gradually along the ridge. You may notice that many beech and yellow birch trees in this area sport contorted trunks and broken limbs. This is evidence of the harsh growing conditions found on this north-south ridge, which is nearly 3,000 feet in elevation. The trees here are subject to ice and high winds. Continue on a gentle ascent through a boggy section where the forest becomes increasingly evergreen. Pass a large rock outcrop on your left, and look for a blue-blazed trail leading uphill to the right. There is another watershed protection area sign at this intersection. Turn right and follow this winding trail as it ascends through a dense spruce-fir forest to the summit of Haystack Mountain at 2.1 miles.

Climb up and over two rock outcrops to a view overlooking the Deerfield Valley. Mount Monadnock in New Hampshire is straight ahead. Below is Haystack Pond, and to your far left is the summit of Mount Snow and its ski trails at the north end of the Deerfield Ridge. Just to the right of Mount Snow, on the far horizon, Killington Peak and the Coolidge Range may be visible to the north.

By walking to the right and negotiating a small cleft in the rock, you will come to two more vistas. One looks to the southeast, where you can spot Mount Wachusett, a rounded bump on an otherwise level horizon 60 miles away near Leominster, Massachusetts. The other vista, to the south, includes a view of Harriman Reservoir, or Lake Whitingham, the second-largest body of water completely within the state of Vermont. To its right are the 11 turbines of the Searsburg Wind Power Facility. The turbines are nearly 200 feet tall and generate enough electricity to power 1,700 homes. The Searsburg facility, when constructed in 1997, was the largest of its kind in the East. Mount Greylock, with its Veterans War Memorial Tower, rises above the turbines. At 3,491 feet (1,064 meters), Greylock is the highest point in Massachusetts. After enjoying the view, hike back down the same trail to your car.

6

Bald Mountain

Total distance: 3.8 miles (6.1 km)	
Hiking time: 3 hours	
Vertical rise: 1,160 feet (354 meters)	
Rating: Moderate	
Map: USGS 7.5' Townshend	
Trailhead GPS Coordinates: N43° 2.47', W72° 41.56'	

Bald Mountain, located in Townshend State Park, offers excellent views of the surrounding area. The trail starts in Townshend State Park, which offers camping and picnicking. Nearby is the U.S. Army Corps of Engineers' Townshend Lake Recreation Area, where you can swim and picnic before or after your hike. On your way to the trail, you pass the Scott Covered Bridge, which spans the West River. The bridge, built in 1870, is composed of three separate spans. The northern span, a town lattice truss that was later strengthened, though unsuccessfully, with laminated wooden arches, is 165.7 feet long—the longest single span of any covered bridge in Vermont.

HOW TO GET THERE

From the north take VT 30 south to the Townshend Lake Recreation Area; turn right over the dam, then left at a T-intersection. The park is 2 miles ahead on the right.

From the south take VT 30 north from Newfane to State Forest Road on the left, marked by a state highway sign. The park is 2 miles ahead on the left.

Parking is available in a small lot just before the park building. Walk to the building, where a day-use fee is charged.

THE TRAIL

You begin your hike in Townshend State Park, the site of a Civilian Conservation Corps (CCC) camp during the Great Depression. The CCC constructed the picnic area and campground at the park and built the stone caretaker's dwelling and attached

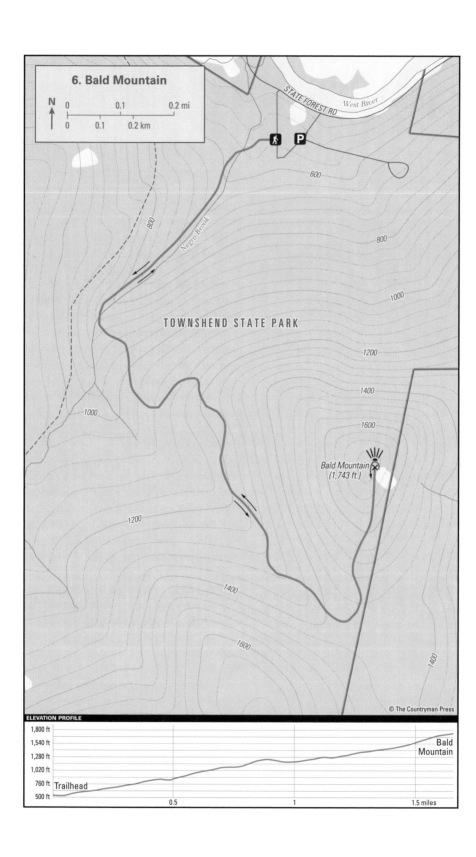

picnic shelter. This structure was placed on the National Register of Historic Places in 2001.

Cross the road to the right of the park building. Descend on a short spur trail to campsite 25, where the trailhead is marked with a sign and blue blazes. Take the trail over Negro Brook on a bridge constructed by the Vermont Youth Conservation Corps in 1990, and turn left. Begin climbing on an old truck road built by the CCC in the mid-1930s. Floodwaters from the 1938 hurricane caused extensive damage to the road and its four bridges, and the road was never rebuilt.

The road closely follows Negro Brook as it tumbles down the side of Bald Mountain, and you should take time to enjoy the brook's pretty cascades and pools. Watch for a double blue blaze, which signals a turn to the left. Here, at the remains of an old bridge abutment, you cross the brook on stepping-stones. The trail soon bears left and ascends away from the brook. Ascend along the hillside, covered with small boulders, into an open hemlock forest. Follow the blazes carefully in this area, as the lack of vegetation on the forest floor makes the trail difficult to discern. The trail bears sharply right and continues on easy grades through several wet areas.

The trail, now nearly level, joins an old road that leads up a wet, rocky draw. At 1.1 miles you pass a large rock outcrop on the left. Cross a brook and soon cross the brook again. Turn left at the edge of a swamp where red spruce and speckled alder are found, and begin a steep ascent up the peak. The dry soils, coarse-grained and shallow, result in a forest of stunted red oak and white pine with a lovely, open, grassy understory. Rock outcrops are scattered across the forest floor. Continue on the steep but quite open trail to the 1,740-foot summit. A sign directs you to a southeastern view that includes Mount Monadnock in New Hampshire and the West River Valley below you. The western view includes Stratton and Bromley mountains. Look for foundation footings of an old fire tower between the two overlooks. A fire station was established on Bald Mountain in 1912. This spot was one of the earliest sites in Vermont used as a forest fire lookout. The CCC built a steel tower on the summit in the early 1930s. In 1950 the tower was relocated to Mount Olga in Wilmington (see hike 1).

After enjoying the views, return via the same route to your car.

Note: In 1996, the eastern return leg of the old loop trail, which continued over the summit and down the north side of the mountain, was closed because of severe erosion.

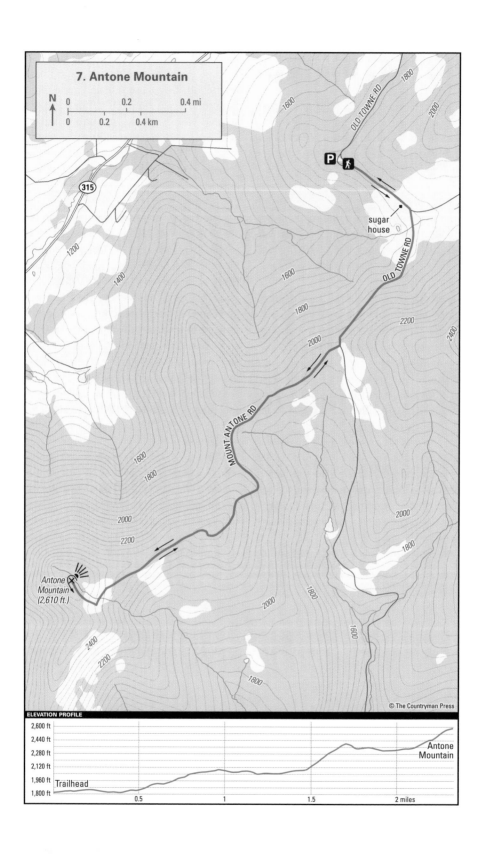

7

Antone Mountain

Total distance: 5.0 miles (8.0 km)
Hiking time: 3 hours
Vertical rise: 890 feet (721 meters)
Rating: Moderate
Map: USGS 7.5' Pawlet
Trailhead GPS Coordinates: N43° 16.45', W73° 10.37'

This hike in southwestern Vermont follows some of the 26 miles of trails at the Merck Forest and Farmland Center, a nonprofit outdoor educational facility with a small diversified farm, hardwood forests, and several small ponds and streams. It offers a variety of educational programs, including astronomy, sustainable farming, forest management, wildflower and bird identification, and low-impact camping.

HOW TO GET THERE

The center can be reached from East Rupert. From the intersection of VT 30 and VT 315, follow VT 315 west 2.4 miles to the height-of-land and a MERCK FOREST sign on your left. Look carefully for the sign as it is hard to see. Turn left onto the dirt road, and continue to a visitors center and a parking area at 2.9 miles. An information board adjacent to the visitors center includes area rules (no mountain bikes, no unleashed dogs) as well as trail maps that are available with a donation to help cover the center's expenses.

THE TRAIL

The unblazed trail, which follows old roads, starts from the information board. Follow the dirt road on level grades until you reach a field with a sugarhouse on your right. There are picnic tables on the deck of the sugarhouse. There is also an interesting natural history museum in the sugarhouse building. The caretaker's cabin is on your left.

Continue your hike on the Old Towne Road by going straight at the intersection. This is the oldest road in Merck Forest, built

Picturesque southwest Vermont from Antone Mountain

by Ebenezer Smith in 1781 to provide access between his home on the mountain and the town highway. The most recent roads are used for logging and sugaring, which help support the educational center. Old Towne Road passes several fields, descends for a short distance, and then ascends on easy grades. Enjoy the nice views of New York's Adirondack Mountains to the north and northwest, best seen during leaf-off season.

Stay on Old Towne Road through the Gallup Road intersection on your left and then the McCormick Trail intersection on your right at 0.5 mile. Hike up a short, steep grade, and pass a small clearing on your right as the road levels again. The Old Towne Road turns left, and you come to a well-marked junction with Lodge Road on your left and Mount Antone Road on your right. Turn right onto Mount Antone Road along easy grades on top of the ridge, and then descend to Clark's Clearing, a log

landing, at 1.3 miles. You pass the McCormick Trail junction on your right and a small lean-to for firewood on your left. Look for berry bushes in two small clearings, where you can feast on ripe berries in late July while enjoying views of Antone Mountain.

Follow the trail into the woods until you come to Clark's Clearing shelter and trail intersection. The Clark's Clearing Road bears left, and a spur trail bears right. Continue straight on the Mount Antone Road up a steep grade to the top of the ridge. The road levels and starts an easy, winding descent. At 1.9 miles you reach the Wade Lot Road junction on your left. Continue on Antone Road and hike past the Lookout Road junction, again on your left, and climb the mountainside on moderate grades past the Beebe Pond Trail and Masters Mountain Trail junction. The Mount Antone Trail continues to the right up a steep grade to the summit (elevation 2,610 feet) at 2.5 miles.

There are views to the east and northeast of the visitors center's barn, Dorset Peak, Woodlawn Mountain, and the Pawlet area. A trail beyond the summit leads downhill to another lookout, with good views of the Adirondack Mountains, eastern New York, and the Rupert and Pawlet areas.

After enjoying the views, hike back to the summit and retrace your steps to the parking area.

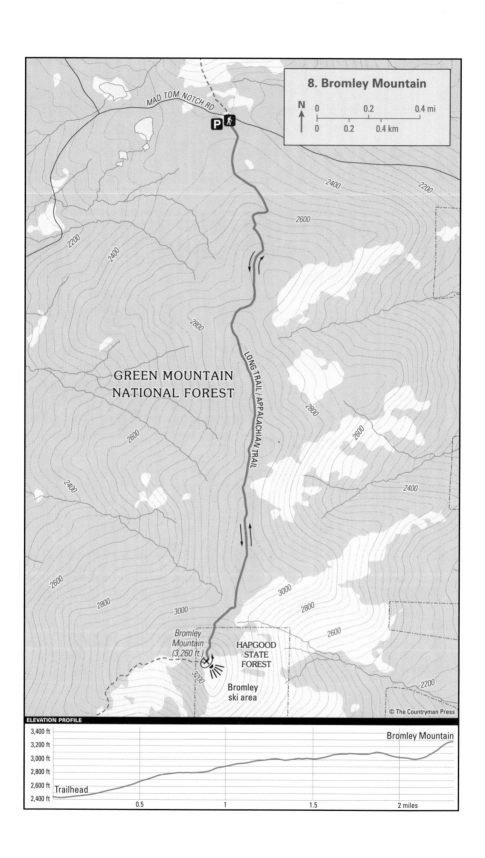

8. Bromley Mountain

N

| 0 | | 0.2 | | 0.4 mi |

| 0 | 0.2 | | 0.4 km |

MAD TOM NOTCH RD

P

2400

2200

2600

2200

2400

2800

GREEN MOUNTAIN
NATIONAL FOREST

LONG TRAIL / APPALACHIAN TRAIL

2600

2600

2600

2400

2600

2400

2800

3000

3000

2800

2600

Bromley
Mountain
(3,260 ft.)

HAPGOOD
STATE
FOREST

3200

Bromley
ski area

2200

© The Countryman Press

ELEVATION PROFILE

3,400 ft				Bromley Mountain
3,200 ft				
3,000 ft				
2,800 ft				
2,600 ft	Trailhead			
2,400 ft				

| | 0.5 | 1 | 1.5 | 2 miles |

8

Bromley Mountain

Total distance: 5.0 miles (8.0 km)

Hiking time: 3½ hours

Vertical rise: 1,075 feet (328 meters)

Rating: Moderate

Maps: USGS 7.5' Danby; 7.5' Peru

Trailhead GPS Coordinates: N43° 15.45', W72° 56.29'

Bromley Mountain is a ski area mountain, with chairlifts and buildings and other facilities associated with downhill skiing on its summit. None of this should keep you from walking up Bromley, however. The Long Trail/Appalachian Trail (LT/AT) from Mad Tom Notch south to the 3,260-foot summit is an extremely pleasant route. Except for two short sections, the trail is never steep or particularly rocky. Any climbing you do alternates with level sections of trail, and your route is punctuated with attractive stretches of forest filled with spruce and fir. The observation tower has been removed from the summit, but efforts are underway to replace it. In the meantime, the cleared ski slopes permit good views in several directions.

HOW TO GET THERE

From VT 11 between Londonderry and Manchester, follow signs to the village of Peru. In the center of the village, at the Congregational Church, turn north onto Hapgood Pond Road. At 0.9 mile after this, turn left onto North Road, which soon becomes gravel. Turn left again at 1.7 miles onto Mad Tom Notch Road, and follow it to the top of the hill and the LT/AT crossing at 3.9 miles. A parking area for a dozen cars is just past the trail on the left. The last 1.1 miles of Mad Tom Notch Road are not plowed in winter. There is a winter parking lot 1.1 miles before the trailhead that can be used in the winter.

THE TRAIL

Follow the white blazes of the LT/AT south through a wet area in a mixed forest. At 0.3

mile the trail begins climbing gently through a hardwood forest of birch, beech, and maple. Make several turns as you follow overgrown woods roads for short distances on your ascent of the ridge.

After passing a large boulder on the right at 0.7 mile, the trail levels out before ascending gently at 1.0 mile. Another flat section is reached at 1.4 miles. While climbing look for a good northeastern view behind you during leaf-off season. The hardwood forest here has shorter trees, a more open canopy, and a brushy understory. The trail then enters a lovely section filled with spruce and fir. Mosses, ferns, and wood sorrel carpet the forest floor, with some puncheon (log bridges) and stepping-stones to help with some of the boggy areas.

Several sections of gradual ups and downs bring you to one short, steep uphill that tops out next to a small, flat-topped rock on Bromley's north peak at 2.0 miles. The rock, partially moss covered and with room for three, is a perfect height for sitting upon. You may wish to rest here before continuing on over the only truly steep portion of your hike.

Break time on the trail to Bromley

Ski trail near the summit of Bromley Mountain

The trail now suddenly drops over rocks and stone steps toward a col at the base of Bromley's summit. You descend through several brushy openings in the forest before the trail becomes level at 2.2 miles. Look to your left for an orange stake and paint blazes that mark the property boundary between U.S. Forest Service land, which you have been on since the beginning of your walk, and the Hapgood State Forest, which encompasses the top of Bromley Mountain.

Now begin a short, steady ascent to the grassy summit of Bromley Mountain at 2.5 miles.

While you're looking out from the summit, consider what the area was like two hundred years ago. It must have been a tough existence in the mountain town of Peru. The original name of the town, like the mountain today, was Bromley, but residents felt the name was rather dull sounding and indicative of poverty. In 1804, the people of Bromley voted to change the name of their town to Peru, hoping the new name would be associated with the wealth and treasures of that South American country and would bring prosperity to the area. Interestingly, it is the original name Bromley, as in the mountain and the ski area, that has brought change and opportunity to the area unimaginable to the early 19th-century residents.

Return to the 21st century, and follow the LT/AT north back to your car.

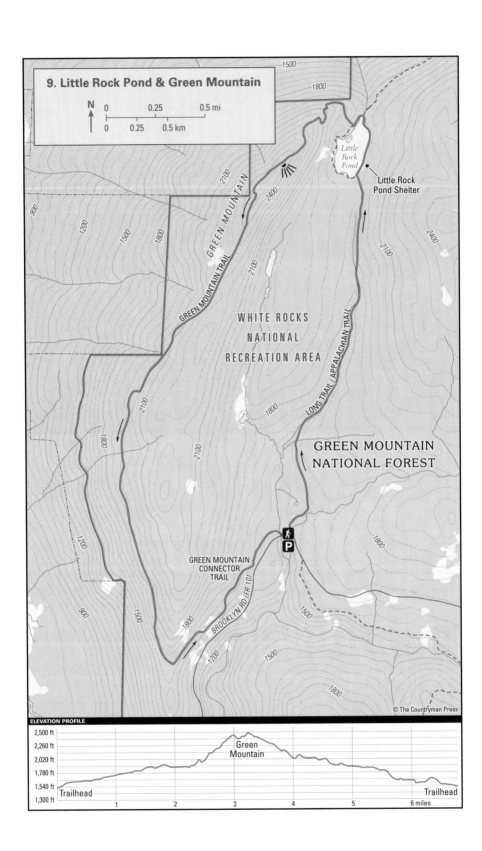

9. Little Rock Pond & Green Mountain

N

0   0.25   0.5 mi

0   0.25   0.5 km

1500

1800

Little Rock Pond

Little Rock Pond Shelter

2100

2400

900

1200

1500

1800

GREEN MOUNTAIN

GREEN MOUNTAIN TRAIL

2100

2400

2100

WHITE ROCKS NATIONAL RECREATION AREA

LONG TRAIL/APPALACHIAN TRAIL

1800

GREEN MOUNTAIN NATIONAL FOREST

2100

1800

1800

1200

900

1500

GREEN MOUNTAIN CONNECTOR TRAIL

BROOKLYN RD (FR 10)

1800

1200

1500

1500

1800

© The Countryman Press

ELEVATION PROFILE

2,500 ft			Green Mountain		
2,260 ft					
2,020 ft					
1,780 ft					
1,540 ft	Trailhead				Trailhead
1,300 ft	1	2	3	4	5 6 miles

9

Little Rock Pond and Green Mountain

Total distance: 7-mile loop (11.2 km)

Hiking time: 4¼ hours

Vertical rise: 1,236 feet (377 meters)

Rating: Moderately strenuous

Map: USGS 7.5' Wallingford

Trailhead GPS Coordinates: N43° 22.37', W72° 57.75'

This hike, which provides a nice variation from the usual out-and-back trail, allows you to enjoy both mountain trails and a beautiful pond. Leave a full day for this journey to give yourself adequate time to enjoy the pond, as well as some wonderful views.

HOW TO GET THERE

To reach the trail, take US 7 to its junction with Forest Road 10 (FR 10) in Mount Tabor. Turn east onto FR 10, also called Brooklyn Road. Cross the railroad tracks, and go by the U.S. Forest Service Mount Tabor Work Center. Follow the road uphill, passing a fountain of water spouting from a pressure relief fitting on a water line serving the village of Mount Tabor before entering the Green Mountain National Forest. Pass a sign at 0.9 mile that indicates you have entered the White Rocks National Recreational Area. Cross the silver bridge, and follow the road up the mountain, passing beautiful stone culverts built by the Civilian Conservation Corps (CCC) crews from the camp where the Mount Tabor Work Center now sits. At 2.7 miles, you reach Big Branch Overlook. The road turns to dirt at 3.0 miles. You soon reach the paved Long Trail/Appalachian Trail (LT/AT) parking area at 3.2 miles, where there is space for approximately 20 cars.

THE TRAIL

Cross the road, and follow the white-blazed LT/AT north to Little Rock Pond. The sign-post at the trailhead indicates a distance of 2 miles to the pond, your first stop on this hike. The beginning of this trail, which starts

View from Green Mountain Trail

as a gradual climb, passes through a substantial historical industrial site that includes the remains of several charcoal kilns and is strewn with bricks and black soot. Enter some mixed hardwood, and start to leave the brook behind. Follow an old roadway parallel to the brook on your left, and soon cross the brook on a steel I-beam bridge, set in the 1940s, at 0.6 mile.

The trail swings right after the bridge and continues to follow the brook, then crosses the brook again on rocks. By 1.0 mile, the brook is considerably smaller as you cross a wet area on puncheon. The trail then switches from a roadway into a more rugged path with numerous slippery wet areas and significant erosion from the heavy rains over the last few years, so be sure to watch your step.

At 1.9 miles you reach a trail junction. The left turn takes you around the west side of Little Rock Pond. (You can go this way as an alternate route to the start of the Green Mountain Trail. It is 0.9 mile to the junction with the Green Mountain Trail, which is a left turn if approached from this alternate route.) Turn right, staying on the LT/AT. At 2.2 miles you reach the camping area at the southeast end of the pond.

Little Rock Pond, up to 60 feet deep in places, is one of the most popular day- and overnight-use areas on the LT/AT. A good fishing spot, the pond is annually stocked with brook trout. Beavers frequent the area, and moose have occasionally been sighted along the pond shore. Careful management is required to preserve the area's natural beauty and fragile shoreline environment. Because of the area's popularity, a Green Mountain Club caretaker is stationed at the site during the hiking season to assist hikers, maintain the local trails and campsites, and compost sewage to protect water quality. A small camping fee is charged. In 2009 a new Little Rock Pond Shelter with room for eight was built by volunteers led by Erik and Laurel Tobiason. This shelter replaced both the old Little Rock Pond Shelter and the Lula Tye Shelter, bringing overnight campers much closer to the pond.

Continue along the east side of the pond on the LT/AT to the junction with the Little Rock Pond Trail. Turn left onto this, while the LT/AT continues on straight. Cross the bridge over the pond outlet, noting the beaver dam under the bridge. At the fork bear left on the Little Rock Pond Trail while the Homer Stone Brook Trail goes off to the right. Continue several hundred yards to the junction with the Green Mountain Trail (at 2.8 miles), onto which you turn right and go sharply uphill. (If you have taken the alternate route around the pond you will have turned left to go sharply uphill here.)

Switchback up the ridge and climb to the right of a long, pointed rock outcrop that resembles a dinosaur back. Occasional views along the trail remind you how far you have climbed above the pond. At 3.4 miles, you reach and continue on a wooded ridge walk, climb over a steep rock face, and reach the signed VIEW junction. Hike straight ahead for 100 yards to spectacular views of the pond and valley below.

From the junction, the trail takes a sharp right into a spruce forest, with minor ascents and switchbacks. Pass through a series of rock shelves with several short side trails to the left for views; note especially a spur at 4.1 miles. Back on the main trail, which now resembles an old road, descend through some mixed hardwoods. The trail is quite wide in this section. Descend and ascend short distances through two saddles, continuing through spruce forest and then a mix of spruce and white birch. There is a signed spur to the left for a second vista. Continue

Reflection in Little Rock Pond

Skipping rocks after a nice swim in Little Rock Pond

trending downhill through evergreens and, after a while, mixed hardwoods and lots of ferns. Throughout your hike, note the spring wildflowers—clintonia, bunchberry, jack-in-the-pulpit, trillium, and lady slipper.

The end of the first major descent is reached at 4.9 miles, where you turn left and continue through mature hardwoods. Be careful to watch for blazes in this area. Continue your descent, then travel through a level area and descend again until you cross a brook at 5.6 miles. Enter a much younger hardwood forest, climb briefly again, and then level off. You soon reach a very unusual old road cut out of the hillside. During leaf-off seasons enjoy views of the valley through the trees along the road. Traverse the side of the mountain, mostly on a gentle downhill, but with one steeper section. As you cross a rockslide, take time to notice that the area uphill is predominantly hardwood, whereas the valley below is all softwood. The road forms the dividing line. The trail then swings around the edge of the ridge, and you begin to hear Big Branch Brook. The trail now is fairly level, following the old road.

At 6.4 miles you reach another trail junction, where you bear left onto the Green Mountain Connector Trail to return to your car. There is a sign pointing to the trail going to the right downhill to the picnic area, but no sign for the trail to the left, which is the Connector Trail to bring you back to your car. As you turn left and return to the woods, pass among some beech trees and descend along an old road. At the bottom of the hill you begin to see FR 10 on the right as you cross a wet overgrown area parallel to it. At 7.0 miles, cross a gravel road, pass through another wet overgrown area, and descend to the road. Turn left, and return to the parking lot.

10

Okemo Mountain

Total distance: 6.0 miles (9.6 km)
Hiking time: 4 hours
Vertical rise: 1,950 feet (594 meters)
Rating: Moderate
Maps: USGS 7.5' Ludlow; 7.5' Mount Holly
Trailhead GPS Coordinates: N43° 25.95', W72° 45.71'

Okemo is a mountain of contrasts, with a ski area on one side and a wilderness hiking trail on the other. Built in the summers of 1991 to 1993 by the Youth Conservation Corps, this blue-blazed trail ascends 3.0 miles from the village of Healdville (named for its first post-master) to the 3,343-foot summit of Okemo Mountain. On the summit you will find a fire tower, complete with a 360-degree view of the surrounding region.

HOW TO GET THERE

From its junction with VT 140 in East Wall-ingford, follow VT 103 east until reaching the gravel Station Road at 6.4 miles. (The Wright Construction building and sign is on the cor-ner and easier to see than the Station Road sign.) Turn right onto Station Road, and fol-low it until reaching a grade crossing of the Green Mountain Railroad near the hamlet of Healdville at 7.2 miles. A signed parking lot with room for 10 cars is located just past the tracks on the left, at the former site of the Healdville Station. Be sure to check out the trailhead information board.

From the east, follow VT 103 west from its junction with VT 100 north of Ludlow. Reach Station Road at 2.8 miles. Turn left onto Station Road to the railroad crossing and the trailhead parking lot at 3.5 miles.

THE TRAIL

From the parking lot, follow the blue-blazed trail parallel to the railroad tracks, following an old woods road across a small bridge in 50 feet. Turn right from the railroad, and climb gently. Cross a bridge over a brook

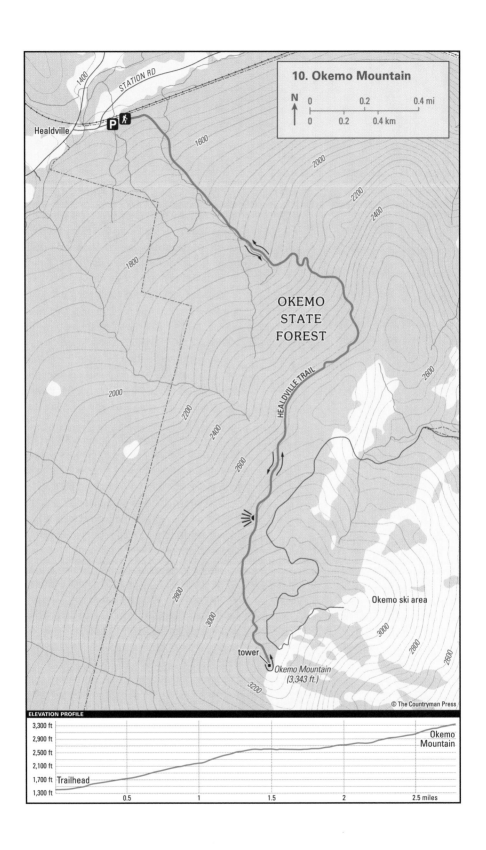

10. Okemo Mountain

N
0   0.2   0.4 mi
0   0.2   0.4 km

STATION RD

1400

Healdville

1600

2000

2200

2400

OKEMO
STATE
FOREST

HEALDVILLE TRAIL

2600

1800

2000

2200

2400

2600

Okemo ski area

2800

3000

3000

2800

2600

3200

tower
Okemo Mountain
(3,343 ft.)

© The Countryman Press

ELEVATION PROFILE

3,300 ft
2,900 ft
2,500 ft
2,100 ft
1,700 ft
1,300 ft

Trailhead

Okemo
Mountain

0.5   1   1.5   2   2.5 miles

Beautiful day on Okemo

at 0.2 mile, pass a cascade at 0.6 mile, and cross a small brook at 0.7 mile as you ascend, gently with occasional short steep pitches, on the old woods road. (There are also Catamount Trail (CT) cross-country ski trail blue diamonds with a catamount print on the first 0.3 mile going up, and again further up the trail coming down. You are watching for the 2-by-6-inch painted blue blazes that denote a hiking trail.) The mix of dense, small hardwood that surrounds you is an indication of past logging in this area. Leave the woods road and brook you have been following, ascend on moderate to easy grades on some switchbacks, and pass glacial boulders and rock outcrops. At 1.5 miles, the grade levels as you reach a plateau. You have climbed about 1,100 feet, more than half the climb, and have gone half the distance to the top. Notice how much more mature the forest is now. Maple begin to yield to yellow birch and occasional hemlock and spruce.

A sign at 1.9 miles indicates you are 1 mile from the summit. A small split boulder with embedded quartz is just right of the trail. Descend gradually, cross a rock-filled gully, and pass by glaciated rock outcrops as the trail gets steeper and you pass through a grove of white birch. At 2.3 miles, you reach an overlook to the west with VT 103 below you and (right to left) Salt Ash Mountain, Shrewsbury Peak, Killington Peak, Little

Stone chimney on the trail up Okemo Mountain

Killington, Mendon Peak, and the Taconics in the distance. Beyond the overlook, ascend again as the forest changes to spruce and fir (with ferns and wood sorrel on its floor) and the trail becomes rockier. Pass 20 feet right of a tiny marsh at 2.7 miles, enjoy a short level stretch in evergreens and striped maple, and then climb steeply. At 2.9 miles take a sharp left turn through a switchback

to a northern view of Killington Peak. You can also see most of what you could see at the lower lookout, plus Lake Ninevah and Echo Lake (which locals call Plymouth Pond) near the village of Tyson.

Isaac Tyson Jr., originally from Baltimore, Maryland, discovered iron in this region in 1835. He developed the Tyson Furnace into what was once one of the most productive iron regions in New England.

After enjoying the view, continue on the now nearly level trail to an overgrown area where you will find the chimney, foundation, and wood remains of a forest ranger's cabin. Just beyond the cabin site, look for a sign on a tree that points right to the summit fire tower. Follow the fire tower trail 100 feet to the tower, still complete with a roof, at 3.0 miles.

The tower gives a 360-degree view of southern Vermont. Below you is the Okemo Mountain Resort, east is Mount Ascutney with its antennae, north is Killington Peak, directly south are Stratton and Bromley mountains, and southwest are Dorset Mountain and the Taconic Mountains. After resting and enjoying the beautiful view, return via the same trails to your car. Alternatively, you may choose a summit loop leading past several fine views. This is especially worthwhile if you don't want to climb the tower or want to find a scenic picnic spot out of the wind.

11

Stratton Pond

Total distance: 7.4 miles (11.9 km)
Hiking time: 4½ hours
Vertical rise: 201 feet (61 meters)
Rating: Moderate
Map: USGS 7.5' Stratton Mountain
Trailhead GPS Coordinates: N43° 3.71', W72° 59.2'

This long but almost level hike leads to Stratton Pond. The route is easy walking. Much of the path you follow is devoid of rocks and tree roots, thanks in part to the careful trail work that has been done. The trip can be extended by 1.2 miles by following the Lye Brook Trail along the south shore to the bridge at the west end of the pond for a fine view of the pond and the entire Stratton Mountain ridge line, and then returning back on the Lye Brook Trail on the south shore. Stratton Pond is located just east of the 15,680-acre Lye Brook Wilderness. There are few trails through this heavily forested wilderness, but several lakes, streams, and bogs dot the landscape. The wilderness contains beautiful waterfalls and meadows, as well as the remnants of old logging railroads and sawmills. "The Burning," the site of a large fire around the turn of the 20th century, is located in the western portion of the wilderness. It is a popular spot for wildlife, such as wild turkey, white-tailed deer, and black bear.

HOW TO GET THERE
The trail is located on the north side of the Stratton-Arlington Road (also known as the Kelley Stand Road). From VT 100 in West Wardsboro, drive 8.2 miles west on the Stratton-Arlington Road to a parking area on the right side of the road. This is just before the intersection with Forest Road 71 (FR 71). A wooden U.S. Forest Service (USFS) sign and information board marks the trailhead.

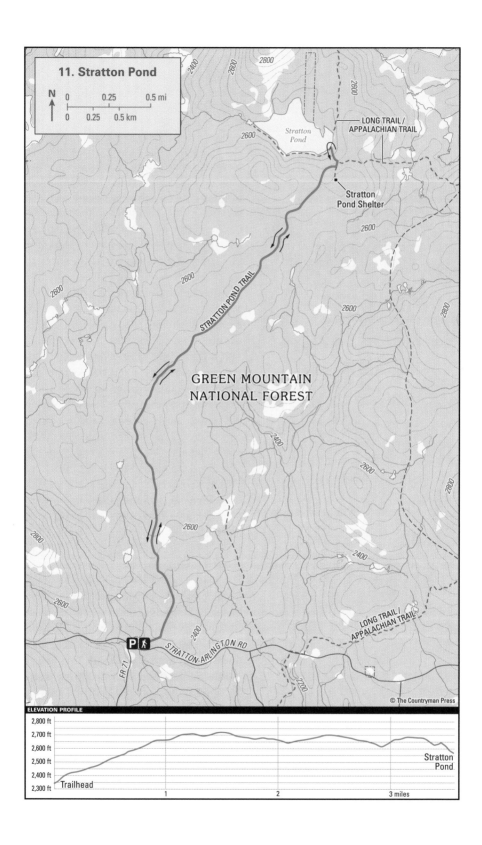

11. Stratton Pond

N

| 0 | 0.25 | 0.5 mi |
| 0 | 0.25 | 0.5 km |

Stratton Pond

LONG TRAIL /
APPALACHIAN TRAIL

Stratton
Pond Shelter

STRATTON POND TRAIL

GREEN MOUNTAIN
NATIONAL FOREST

LONG TRAIL /
APPALACHIAN TRAIL

STRATTON-ARLINGTON RD

FR 71

© The Countryman Press

ELEVATION PROFILE

2,800 ft	
2,700 ft	
2,600 ft	
2,500 ft	Stratton
2,400 ft	Pond
2,300 ft	Trailhead

1   2   3 miles

THE TRAIL

This blue-blazed trail follows the former route of the Long Trail/Appalachian Trail (LT/AT). Note the extensive trail work—including water bars, puncheon, and turnpiking—along your route. Puncheon are plank walkways constructed to span wet or boggy areas. Turnpiking involves creating a hardened, slightly elevated trail bed over soft ground by piling soil between logs or rocks placed along both sides of the trail. Water bars are found on steeper sections of trail, where logs or shingled stones are laid diagonally across the trail to support ditches that divert rainfall runoff from the trail to prevent erosion.

Signpost showing the way

Begin your hike across puncheon and over turnpiking through a young beech and softwood forest, and ascend alternately moderately and gently for 0.9 mile. The trail, now resembling a boardwalk through the woods, ascends slightly and crosses several wet areas on puncheon. Pass through a section of white birch, and come to an open area with ferns. At 1.5 miles, follow puncheon across another wet area, and enter a birch forest. This area is quite beautiful on a sunny day, with sunlight filtering through the trees.

After a long stretch of puncheon, you cross an old road at 2.1 miles. The Catamount Trail (CT), a cross-country ski trail running the entire length of Vermont, follows this road from the Kelley Stand Road to this point and then turns north to share the Stratton Pond Trail the rest of the way to the pond. The previous route of the CT was lost to a wind shear that dropped trees like pickup sticks along the CT for 0.5 mile. Some of the CT's most remote sections are in the Stratton and Somerset areas.

Enter a dark, dense softwood forest with more puncheon before returning to a sunnier, more open hardwood forest. As you begin a gradual ascent, notice the large stumps that

indicate the size of the trees that once grew in this area. Cross another wet area on puncheon, and look to your right for a large birch with roots engulfing a boulder. Continue your hike through a small softwood forest, across more puncheon, and then through a forest now composed of white birch and a spruce understory. The forest becomes dominated by hardwoods once again before you pass a large moss-covered boulder.

At 3.5 miles you cross a small brook on stepping-stones. At 3.6 miles you come to a trail junction. Your route, which continues on the Stratton Pond Trail, bears left, but you may wish to take a short detour by turning right and walking 200 feet up the side trail to see the Stratton Pond Shelter. This two-story post-and-beam shelter was built in 1999 and can sleep 24 people. From the trail junction, descend a rocky, wet, old logging road to the junction of the LT/AT. A USFS sign indicates that Stratton Mountain is 2.6 miles east (a right turn) from this junction.

Turn left, and follow the LT/AT north to the shore of Stratton Pond at 3.7 miles. The pond, where you can swim and fish, is 30 feet deep at its deepest point and averages 10 feet deep overall. Most of the pond and surrounding lands were acquired by the USFS in 1985. Stratton Pond, the largest body of water on the LT, is one of the heaviest overnight-use areas on the trail. There are more than two thousand overnight hikers at the pond between Memorial Day and Columbus Day. Until recently, two shelters at the pond's shoreline focused much of the overnight use at the water's edge. Trampling of shoreline vegetation, degradation of water quality as a result of poor waste disposal, and the loss of a sense of solitude on the pond caused the land and trail managers to reexamine camping at Stratton Pond.

Today, a tenting area with tent platforms is located away from the pond's edge, as is the new shelter. Composting toilets are used at both sites to protect water quality. A Green Mountain Club caretaker is stationed at the site during the hiking season to assist hikers, maintain the trails and campsites, and compost sewage. Please follow the caretaker's instructions to help protect this valuable natural area.

The clearing where the LT reaches the pond shoreline is the legacy of a popular backcountry lodge, Willis Ross Camp, which burned in 1972. If time permits, you may wish to walk along the south shore of the pond to

Stunning sunset at Stratton Pond

Break time at Willis Ross Clearing at Stratton Pond

the bridge over the outlet at the west end for the view of the pond and Stratton Mountain. You cannot circle the pond, though you can continue on to the tent sites. Either way, you then return the way you came back to the Willis Ross clearing. You may also wish to walk north on the LT for 0.1 mile, then turn left on the North Shore Trail and walk the 200 feet to the wide bridge just before the flooded part of the North Shore Trail. This bridge affords great viewing of the wetlands and all three sides. After exploring the pond area, return to Kelley Stand Road via the LT south from the pond and Stratton Pond Trail.

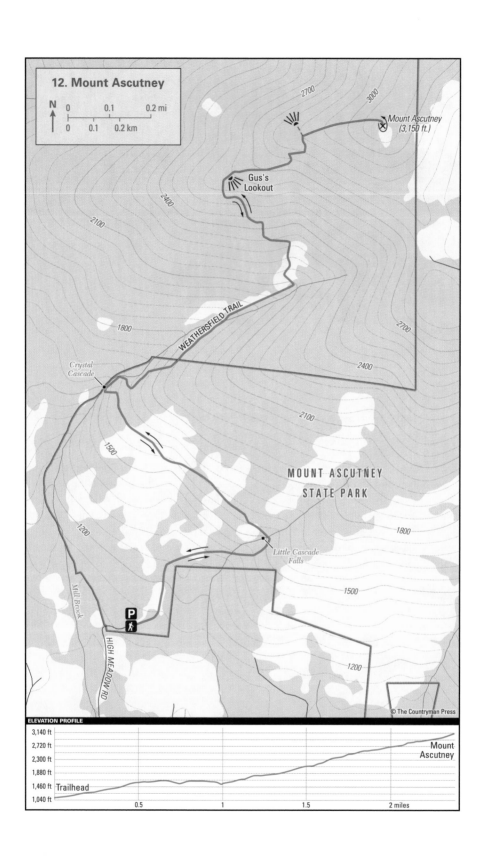

12. Mount Ascutney

N

| 0 | 0.1 | 0.2 mi |
| 0 | 0.1 | 0.2 km |

Mount Ascutney
(3,150 ft.)

Gus's
Lookout

2700

3000

2700

2400

2400

2100

2100

1800

1800

WEATHERSFIELD TRAIL

Crystal
Cascade

1500

1500

1200

1200

1200

Little Cascade
Falls

MOUNT ASCUTNEY
STATE PARK

Mill Brook

HIGH MEADOW RD

P

© The Countryman Press

ELEVATION PROFILE

3,140 ft				Mount
2,720 ft				Ascutney
2,300 ft				
1,880 ft				
1,460 ft	Trailhead			
1,040 ft				

0.5　　　1　　　1.5　　　2 miles

12

Mount Ascutney

Total distance: 5.8 miles (9.3 km)

Hiking time: 4½ hours

Vertical rise: 2,250 feet (686 meters)

Rating: Strenuous

Map: USGS 7.5' Mount Ascutney

Trailhead GPS Coordinates: N43° 25.61', W72° 27.97'

Mount Ascutney is an unusual monadnock (a hill or mountain of resistant rock standing by itself rather than in a range) located near Windsor. The mountain's granite and related gabbro-diorite and syenite rock is the remains of an underground upswelling of molten White Mountain magma through the native metamorphic rock. This monadnock has withstood the erosion and glaciation that has worn away the softer rocks of the surrounding piedmont peneplain, an area near the foot of a mountain that has been almost reduced to a plain by erosion.

Mount Ascutney is the predominant feature in southeastern Vermont, visible for miles in every direction. The mountain derives its name from the word *Ascutegnik,* meaning "meeting of the waters," which was originally the name of an Abenaki settlement where the Sugar River joins the Connecticut River. The Abenaki words for the mountain itself were *Cas-Cad-Nac,* meaning "mountain of the rocky summit."

As a monadnock, Mount Ascutney stands alone, not as part of a mountain range. There are five primary trails which ascend the mountain; the Weathersfield, Brownsville, and Windsor trails (each named for the village closest to their respective trailheads); the Futures Trail (which begins in the Mount Ascutney State Park); and the Bicentennial Trail (which starts in the West Windsor Town Forest on the western slope of the mountain). There is also a road which starts at the Mount Ascutney State Park on the eastern slope of the mountain.

The first trail on Mount Ascutney may

have been opened in 1825. In 1858, a trail that was almost a road was opened along much of the route of the present Windsor Trail. In 1883, a summer-long forest fire burned away stretches of this trail. Great boulders lined the trails, and charred tree trunks and ash were everywhere. The Ascutney Mountain Association was formed in 1903 to relocate the damaged part of the Windsor Trail and rebuild the destroyed stone hut on top of the mountain. In 1898, the Brownsville Trail was opened, followed by the Weathersfield Trail in 1906.

In 1920, a ranger cabin and summit fire tower were constructed on the mountain. Around 1940, the Civilian Conservation Corps (CCC) built a new steel tower, which was abandoned as a fire tower in the 1950s. The tower remained standing until the mid-1980s. In 1989, the original fire tower, about 300 feet north of the summit, was converted into an observation tower.

The building of a road in 1934 by the CCC, as well as the great hurricane of 1938, created so much debris and so many trail problems that by 1966 only the Weathersfield Trail could easily be found. In that year the Herbert Ogden (junior and senior) located, cleared, blazed, signed, measured, and mapped the Windsor Trail. In 1967, the Ascutney Trails Association (ATA) was formed to continue their work; it still maintains the trails on the mountain. Its interesting 47-page *Mount Ascutney Guide* describes the four trails up Ascutney that the ATA maintains (all but the Bicentennial Trail), their history, and more. It is available from the Ascutney Trails Association, P.O. Box 147, Windsor VT 05089, for $5. You can also visit their website at www.ascutneytrails association.org. Please consider joining the ATA after benefiting from its work. Dues are $10 for families, $2 for people younger than 18, and $5 for people 18 and older.

Because of several antennae, the summit is not as interesting as the west peak, which is more secluded and used as a hang glider launching site.

The hike described below is the Weathersfield Trail, which is the most popular route up the mountain. This is a 5.8-mile round-trip ascent that passes Cascade Falls, traverses the West Peak, and accesses the summit from the southern slope of the mountain. Hikers can also traverse the mountain, from one side to the other by spotting a car at either the Windsor or Brownsville trailheads, and utilizing these trails on the descent. The Windsor Trail descends much more steeply, with a 2,500-foot vertical drop. The Brownsville Trail passes over the North Peak, where there are several lookouts, and an old quarry where there are massive blocks of granite and the remnants of the quarrying operation.

HOW TO GET THERE

Take exit 8 (Ascutney) off I-91 to VT 131 west. Drive 3.3 miles to Cascade Falls Road, and turn right (north). Bear left at the fork, and continue to a right turn at 3.6 miles. Drive up the short, steep hill to the 15-car parking lot and the information board. The state of Vermont and the ATA built the trailhead and parking area in 1989.

THE TRAIL

From the information board at the left rear end of the parking lot, take the white-blazed Weathersfield Trail, which ascends some small stairs and enters the woods. Swing right along easy grades, cross a small brook, ascend moderately, and cross just above Little Cascade Falls. In tall evergreens, continue your ascent to a deep, mossy rock cleft into which a little brook falls. This flume is 0.5 mile from the trailhead. Hike out the other side on rock and a metal and wood staircase obtained from the fire tower when its upper

Taking in the view on the way up Mount Ascutney

levels were removed during the conversion to today's observation tower. Now on easier grades, pass several overlooks at 0.6 mile. The trail crosses an old logging road and proceeds almost level for a while. This break is a rarity on this mountain, where most trails climb ceaselessly. Descending slightly through spruce and hemlock, the trail leads to the top of Crystal Cascade at 1.1 miles, where there is a good view to the south.

The geology of Crystal Cascade is unusual. This 84-foot, nearly sheer cliff is a rare example of a ring dike, formed by the upward flow of magma into a somewhat circular fissure. The molten rock made its way through overlying sedimentary rocks; however, the fledgling volcano lacked the thrust necessary to reach the surface, and all the White Mountain magma cooled underground. Erosion and glaciation wore away much of the overlying bedrock, exposing the igneous edge of the ring dike. The rocks at

the border of the newly formed pluton (any body of igneous rock solidified far below the Earth's surface) were metamorphosed by the extreme heat of the magma. This contact zone is clearly visible at the base of Crystal Cascade, where a second bedrock shows as a gray mass. Evidence of the ring dike formation can also be found at the top of the Cascades. Chunks of the surrounding bedrock were constantly consumed by the magma as it moved upward. However, pieces that were only partially absorbed when the magma cooled are visible in the little cascades above the cliff.

At the top of the cascade, the trail turns right and follows the brook upstream a short distance before ascending a series of switchbacks through an attractive stand of conifer. The trail then contours along the side of the brook's ravine and then dips down to cross the bottom of the ravine and the brook. The trail then climbs a bank and turns right onto

Evergreens in winter on Mount Ascutney

an old woods road. You are now on the original 1906 route of the Weathersfield Trail.

Continue on the road past several rock outcrops to Halfway Brooks at 1.7 miles. Turn left from the old route, and follow the sign's instructions to stay on the trail and not take shortcuts as you ascend the steep ridge. Erosion here is a serious problem that you can help control by staying on the trail. Still climbing, you pass exposed rock outcrops, where you can rest and enjoy the views. Swing right through some stunted birch, and return to the woods on easier grades.

At 2.3 miles, make a sharp right turn at Gus's Lookout (elevation 2,690 feet), a series of large rock outcrops with views of the Connecticut River Valley and the summit ridge. The lookout was named for Augustus Aldrich, a charter ATA member and trail worker, who died in 1974 on Mount Katahdin at age 86. Below and above the lookout are two bypasses to avoid the slippery rocks in wet weather.

Return to the woods, pass a large boulder on a switchback through a fern-filled white birch grove, and reach West Peak Spring. Climb moderately on switchbacks to a trail junction at 2.6 miles. A spur leads a short distance to a hang glider takeoff ramp, which provides a splendid view of Brownsville and the hills beyond. Back on the main trail, climb moderately and then steeply to the ridge. To the right, the antennae-covered 3,150-foot summit is reached at 2.9 miles. To the left, a white-blazed trail leads past the observation tower and then splits. The right fork descends to a parking lot at the top of Ascutney Road. The left fork continues north to the Stone Hut, 0.2 mile north of the summit. There are several short summit trails connecting points of interest on the mountaintop, described and mapped in the ATA's *Mount Ascutney Guide*.

Return to the junction south of the observation tower, and hike back down the trail to your car.

13

Baker Peak

Total distance: 8.1 miles (13.0 km)
Hiking time: 5¼ hours
Vertical rise: 2,230 feet (680 meters)
Rating: Strenuous
Map: USGS 7.5' Danby
Trailhead GPS Coordinates: N43° 18.76', W72° 59.21'

The first 3.5 miles of this strenuous hike follow the Lake Trail over an old road that was once a carriage road to the Griffith Lake House, owned by Silas L. Griffith, on the west side of Griffith Lake, then known as Buffum Pond. Silas Griffith, Vermont's first millionaire, lived in Danby and operated a sawmill camp, or job, that became known as the village of Griffith. That site is now called Old Job.

HOW TO GET THERE

Drive 2.0 miles south of the Danby–Mt. Tabor crossroad on US 7, or 5.7 miles north of East Dorset, to South End Road. Follow this road east, crossing a set of railroad tracks. Pass a small cemetery on the right, cross Otter Creek, and in 0.5 mile reach a small parking lot for five to six cars on the left.

THE TRAIL

Your path starts at the right rear corner of the lot and ascends on easy grades through tall evergreens. Note the occasional barbed wire remnants on the left side: this land was once farmed. You soon cross a brook, hike parallel to the brook, passing a lot of stinging nettles, and cross a smaller brook. At 0.75 mile the old roadway widens through a hemlock grove but quickly narrows and begins a sweeping switchback to your left, leaving the brook sounds behind. Pass a sign indicating the boundary of the Big Branch Wilderness Area at 0.9 mile, and continue climbing past a steep ledge on your right.

Imagine the labor required to construct

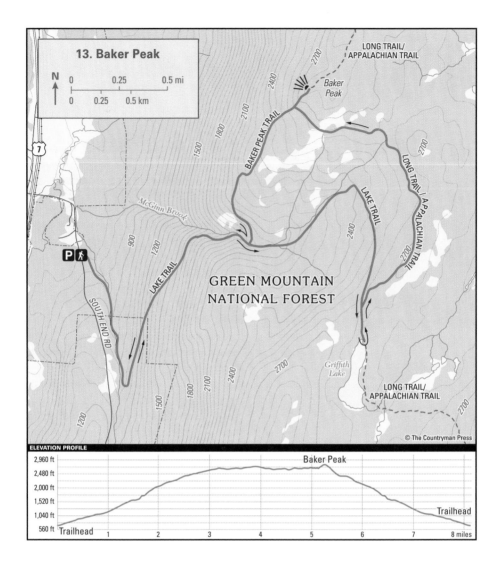

13. Baker Peak

N

0   0.25   0.5 mi
0   0.25   0.5 km

LONG TRAIL/
APPALACHIAN TRAIL

2700

2400

Baker
Peak

BAKER PEAK TRAIL

2100

1800

1500

LONG TRAIL / APPALACHIAN TRAIL

2700

LAKE TRAIL

2400

2700

McGinn Brook

900

1200

LAKE TRAIL

GREEN MOUNTAIN
NATIONAL FOREST

SOUTH END RD

2700

Griffith
Lake

1500   1800   2100   2400

LONG TRAIL/
APPALACHIAN TRAIL

2700

1200

© The Countryman Press

ELEVATION PROFILE

| | | | | | Baker Peak | | |
2,960 ft
2,480 ft
2,000 ft
1,520 ft
1,040 ft   Trailhead
560 ft Trailhead
         1   2   3   4   5   6   7   8 miles

the old road. At 1.5 miles you cross a rock slab on a narrow bridge. Through the trees on the left, there are glimpses of Dorset Peak and the Danby Imperial marble quarry across the valley. Look below in the rock for the metal pins that once held the carriage road bridge in place. A notch in the mountain ridge is visible ahead as the trail swings right and ascends along McGinn Brook—on your left, flowing out of the notch. At a small

cairn, an unmarked spur leads 0.1 mile up to a ledge with a fine vista up and down the Great Valley of Vermont. At 1.9 miles, cross McGinn Brook on rocks (this can be tricky when the water is high), and reach the junction with the Baker Peak Trail, on which you will return.

The Lake Trail bears right, continues upstream on easy grades, and crosses a brook as the trail becomes quite wet and rocky.

Numerous small brooks cross the trail in this section. The trail bears right into the woods to avoid a very wet part of the old roadway. You soon return to the old road and pass through a maple forest on easy grades. The trail leaves the road at an obscure junction, crests a small knob, and reaches the Long Trail/Appalachian Trail (LT/AT) junction at 3.3 miles.

If you turn right on the white-blazed LT/AT you will reach Griffith Lake in 0.1 mile. A high, 16-acre mountain lake, Griffith Lake was originally called Buffum Pond. This warm-water lake averages 10 feet deep and, although stocked with brook trout, is not a particularly good fishing site. All camping at the lake is restricted to designated sites on the east shore, and a small fee is charged for overnight use. A Green Mountain Club caretaker is stationed at the lake during hiking season to assist hikers, maintain the local trails and shelters, and compost sewage at the tenting area and at Peru Peak Shelter, 0.8 mile south of the Lake Trail junction with the LT/AT. A small camping fee is charged.

From the Lake Trail junction (3.3 miles), follow the LT/AT north along a relatively level grade to Baker Peak. Hike up, down, and over wet areas on puncheon until you reach a large boulder. Continue over several rock shelves with occasional views along the birch-lined hillside. At 5.1 miles, you reach the Baker Peak Trail Junction. Follow the LT/AT up the exposed rock slab to the summit at 5.2 miles. Be careful of your footing along the slab. If it is wet, consider using the bypass that begins near the Baker Peak Trail junction and ends in the woods just north of the bald peak. From the summit of Baker Peak, you have great views of the Taconic

Celebrating a sunny day on Baker Peak

Range, including Dorset Peak directly across the valley and Mount Equinox to the south. To the southeast lies Stratton Mountain with its ski trails and tower. Otter Creek meanders through the narrow Great Valley of Vermont below.

From the summit, return to the junction and descend the ridge along the blue-blazed Baker Peak Trail. Turn first steeply and then more gradually along a rock outcrop through mixed hardwoods. The trail soon bears right and begins a steep descent until you enter a fern-filled maple forest, where the trail levels slightly and resembles an old road. You begin to hear water as you reach the Lake Trail Junction at 6.2 miles. Turn right, cross the brook, and return along the old carriage road to your car at 8.1 miles.

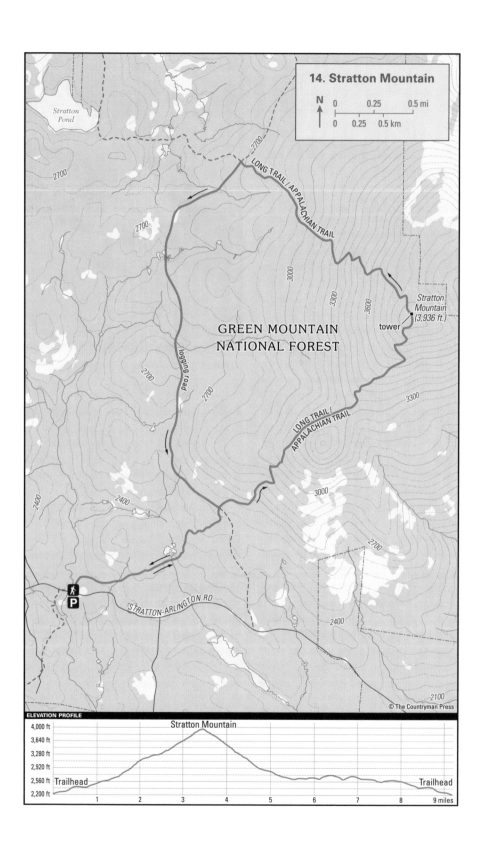

Stratton Pond

14. Stratton Mountain

N

| 0 | 0.25 | 0.5 mi |
| 0 | 0.25 | 0.5 km |

2700

LONG TRAIL / APPALACHIAN TRAIL

2700

2700

3000

3300

3600

Stratton Mountain (3,936 ft.)

tower

GREEN MOUNTAIN NATIONAL FOREST

logging road

2700

2700

3300

LONG TRAIL / APPALACHIAN TRAIL

2400

2400

3000

2700

3000

2400

STRATTON-ARLINGTON RD

2400

2100

© The Countryman Press

ELEVATION PROFILE

4,000 ft			Stratton Mountain						
3,640 ft									
3,280 ft									
2,920 ft									
2,560 ft	Trailhead								Trailhead
2,200 ft									
	1	2	3	4	5	6	7	8	9 miles

14

Stratton Mountain

Total distance: 9.3-mile loop (15.0 km)	
Hiking time: 6 hours	
Vertical rise: 1,910 feet (582 meters)	
Rating: Moderately strenuous	
Map: USGS 7.5' Stratton Mountain	
Trailhead GPS Coordinates: N43° 3.67', W72° 58.06'	

This long, beautiful loop hike visits a fire tower on the summit of Stratton Mountain. At 3,936 feet in elevation, it is the highest point in southern Vermont. The fire tower offers views that overlook Somerset Reservoir and Stratton Pond as well as the many mountains in southern Vermont and beyond. You can also hike to the fire tower and back on the same trail for a shorter trip of 7.6 miles. This out-and-back route up moderate grades to the mountaintop makes a fine, day-long snowshoe trip in winter.

Stratton Mountain played an important role in the conception of both the Long Trail (LT) and the Appalachian Trail (AT). On Stratton Mountain in 1909, James P. Taylor thought about a "long trail" that would link the summits of the Green Mountains. Several years later, on the same mountain, Benton MacKaye was inspired to develop an entire trail system along the Appalachian Mountains from Georgia to Maine.

HOW TO GET THERE
Take VT 100 to the junction of Stratton-Arlington Road (or Kelley Stand Road) in West Wardsboro. Drive 7.1 miles west on Stratton-Arlington Road to the LT/AT parking lot on the north side of the road. There is parking space for 8 to 10 cars. A U.S. Forest Service (USFS) sign marks the trailhead. In winter, the Stratton-Arlington Road is not plowed west of the trailhead.

THE TRAIL
Begin your hike north along the white-blazed LT/AT up the bank behind the parking area.

Stratton Mountain from the west side of Stratton Pond

You immediately cross a grassy logging road, veer right, and climb onto a small knob. Numerous old, fading logging roads intersect the trail, and at times you follow them for a short distance while crossing several wet areas on puncheon. At 0.7 mile you pass below an old beaver dam. Walk uphill through a mixed hardwood and softwood forest, and at 1.1 miles pass by an old farm site with apple trees, a stone wall, and several foundations and continue through a birch stand. Cross the gated, gravel Forest Road 341 (FR 341; or International Paper [IP] Road) at 1.3 miles. Make a note of this junction, because you will be completing your return loop along this road, which is also a designated bicycle route.

Option: You can shorten the hike slightly by parking at the junction of the IP road 1 mile east of the AT/LT parking lot. Watch out for the ditches and do not block access to the gate.

Beyond the road, the trail crosses a small brook and passes by several faint old logging roads. The trail begins to ascend, and gets steeper as it climbs over uneven rocks. Continue your ascent up the ridge through a mixed hardwood forest with numerous birch. At 2.5 miles, intersect the original route of the Stratton Mountain Trail, visible faintly on the right.

In 1985, the Nature Conservancy acquired 12,000 acres of the western slope of Stratton Mountain, including the summit, and held it in trust until the USFS received the allocated money. In 1986, after years of negotiation with the property owner, International Paper Company, the USFS obtained funding to make the purchase final. The relocation of the LT/AT over Stratton Mountain, which involved 8.7 miles of new trail, was completed in 1989.

Continue your hike parallel to the ridgeline as the trail becomes nearly level. Climb again among higher-elevation spruce and birch, and come to a partially overgrown view at 2.75 miles of Somerset Reservoir and Mount Snow. Beyond the overlook, ascend past a spring on your left. This is the only reliable water on the ascent. You now hike primarily through balsam fir trees along several switchbacks until you reach the fire tower at 3.8 miles.

Stratton Mountain was one of the earliest fire tower sites in Vermont. A steel tower was constructed in 1914. In the early 1930s, the Civilian Conservation Corps (CCC) built a new cabin and a steel lookout tower. This tower, abandoned as a fire tower around 1980, was renovated by the USFS in 1988. It is one of two fire towers remaining on USFS Vermont lands and was nominated to the National Register of Historic Places in 1989.

A summit caretaker, supported by the Green Mountain Club, Appalachian Trail Conservancy, and Green Mountain National Forest, is stationed on the summit during the hiking season. No camping is permitted on the summit. A trail leading 0.6 mile north along the ridge connects to the top of the Stratton Mountain ski area.

From the tower you can enjoy spectacular views: to the south, Somerset Reservoir and Mount Snow; to the southwest, Glastenbury Mountain; to the west, Mount Equinox and the Taconic Range; to the northeast, Mount Ascutney; and to the southeast, New Hampshire's Mount Monadnock. Unless you decide to take the shorter 7.6-mile total route back down the same trail to your car, continue north on the LT/AT and begin to descend. There is a water source on the right at 3.9 miles. At 4.3 miles you reach a small overlook of Stratton Pond on your left with Mount Equinox in the distance. In the upper section, the trail uses stone steps, water bars, and turnpiking to cross a wet area.

At 4.4 miles you steeply descend over rocks and roots in the trail and begin a series of long switchbacks through a softwood forest. As the trail passes through mixed hardwoods, continue your descent, and cross a brook at 5.1 miles. The trail soon intersects several faint old logging roads, descends for a short distance, and crosses a wet area on puncheon.

After a more moderate descent, you reach the gravel IP Road at 5.8 miles. The LT/AT goes 1 mile straight ahead to Stratton Pond. Turn left, and follow the grassy logging road south to the LT/AT intersection at 8.3 miles, which you passed earlier in your hike. Turn right, and follow the LT/AT south back down the trail to your car at 9.3 miles.

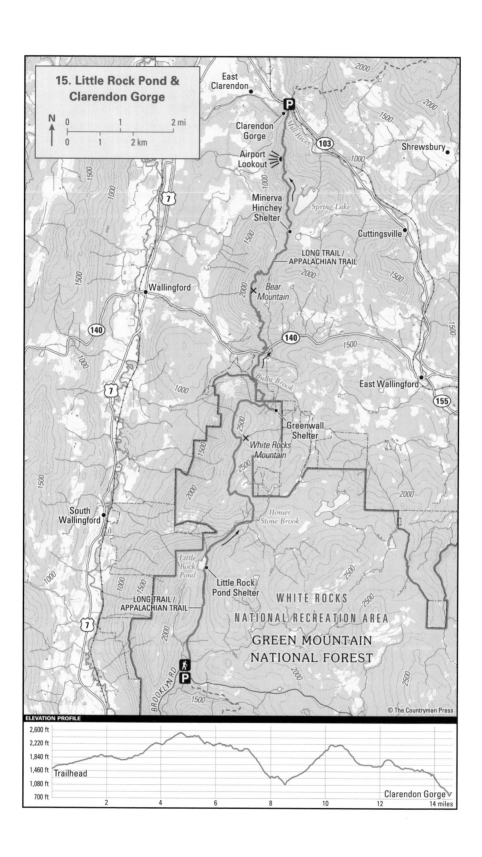

15. Little Rock Pond & Clarendon Gorge

N
0 .... 1 .... 2 mi
0 .... 1 .... 2 km

East Clarendon

P

Clarendon Gorge

Mill River

103

Shrewsbury

Airport Lookout

7

Minerva Hinchey Shelter

Spring Lake

Cuttingsville

LONG TRAIL / APPALACHIAN TRAIL

Wallingford

140

× Bear Mountain

140

East Wallingford

155

Bully Brook

Greenwall Shelter

× White Rocks Mountain

7

South Wallingford

Homer Stone Brook

Little Rock Pond

Little Rock Pond Shelter

WHITE ROCKS NATIONAL RECREATION AREA

LONG TRAIL / APPALACHIAN TRAIL

GREEN MOUNTAIN NATIONAL FOREST

7

BROOKLYN RD.

P

© The Countryman Press

ELEVATION PROFILE

2,600 ft
2,220 ft
1,840 ft
1,460 ft
1,080 ft
700 ft

Trailhead

Clarendon Gorge

2 .... 4 .... 6 .... 8 .... 10 .... 12 .... 14 miles

15

Little Rock Pond and Clarendon Gorge

Total distance: 15.0 miles (24.2 km)

Hiking time: 2 days, 1 night

Vertical rise: 3,100 feet (945 meters)

Rating: Day 1—moderate; Day 2—easy

Maps: USGS 7.5' Wallingford; 7.5' Rutland

Trailhead GPS Coordinates: N43° 22.37', W72° 57.75'

This enjoyable hike along the Long Trail/Appalachian Trail (LT/AT) is appropriate for even a novice backpacker. The trail crosses valleys, passes mountain ponds, follows ridgelines, crests mountains, offers swimming and scenic vistas, and concludes across a suspension bridge over Clarendon Gorge.

The first day, you hike past Little Rock Pond and over White Rocks Mountain to Greenwall Shelter, where you spend the night. Little Rock Pond is one of the most popular day-use and overnight-use areas on the LT. The pond is a good fishing spot and is annually stocked with brook trout. Beavers frequent the area, and moose have occasionally been sighted along the pond shore. Careful management is required to preserve the area's natural beauty and fragile shoreline environment. Because of the area's high use, a Green Mountain Club (GMC) caretaker is stationed at the site during the hiking season, and an overnight-use fee is charged.

The second day, you cross VT 140, traverse Bear Mountain, hike through overgrown farmlands and pastures, continue along a rocky ridge with an overlook, and finish by crossing the suspension bridge at Clarendon Gorge. The suspension bridge over the gorge was built in 1974. For several years, until the mid-1950s, an old timber bridge spanned the gorge, but it was removed when it decayed and became unsafe. The GMC's Killington Section planned a new bridge in 1955 and completed construction in the spring of 1957. The bridge held strong until the flood of 1973 washed it away. Four days later, tragedy struck when

17-year-old Robert Brugmann, attempting to cross the still-swollen river on a fallen tree, slipped, fell into the stream, and drowned.

A subsequent relocation made such a long detour to reach the bridge in East Clarendon that the GMC planned a new bridge. With a design from GMC member Allan St. Peter, major technical assistance from the Vermont Department of Highways, and memorial gifts from Robert Brugmann's family and friends, construction started in the spring of 1974. The bridge cost almost $8,000, quite a difference from the $700 bridge constructed in 1957! Highway engineers, U.S. Forest Service (USFS) personnel, and GMC volunteers worked together to complete the bridge in July 1974.

HOW TO GET THERE

Spot a car on the south side of VT 103 at the Clarendon Gorge parking area, 2.1 miles east of US 7, approximately 5.0 miles south of Rutland. Avoid the temptation to explore the gorge so that it remains the reward at the end of your journey. Vandalism can be a problem at this parking area; see "Situational Awareness" in the introduction for specific precautions to follow.

To reach the trail where you begin your journey, take US 7 to Danby, where a sign points east to Mount Tabor and Forest Road 10 (FR 10). The turn is also signed Brooklyn Road. Turn east onto FR 10, and drive 3.5 miles to the Long Trail Parking Area at Big Black Branch. Because this trailhead is popular with hikers traveling to Little Rock Pond, there is an outhouse as well as a trailhead information board.

THE TRAIL

Day One

Total distance: 7.0 miles (11.3 km)
Hiking time: 4½ hours
Vertical rise: 1,275 feet (389 meters)

Begin your hike over easy terrain along the Little Black Branch on an old road. At 0.6 mile cross the brook on a single I-beam bridge and bear right along the brook. Notice that the brook gets smaller as you cross it again. Continue up the rocky hillside, occasionally on puncheon.

You approach the south end of Little Rock Pond at 2.2 miles. Nestled among the mountains at an elevation of 1,854 feet, Little Rock Pond is a scenic place to swim, rest, and cool off. An overnight-use fee is charged. A sign indicates the Little Rock Pond Loop Trail is to your left. Bear right to continue north on the LT/AT. A tenting area is immediately on your right, set back at the end of a short path. Continuing your hike around Little Rock Pond, you see to your right the tent of the GMC caretaker. Just up the hill behind the caretaker's tent is Little Rock Pond Shelter.

Hike parallel to the stony shore among dense conifer to the pond outlet at 2.4 miles, where the Green Mountain and Homer Stone Brook trails bear left. Continue straight and descend away from the pond to a spur on the right to the Little Rock Pond Group Tenting Site.

Follow easy grades until you reach an old clearing. This is the site of an abandoned 1880s lumber town named Aldrichville. The USFS spent several years with local high school students researching and excavating artifacts from this site. According the USFS website, "At the time of its peak operation the village consisted of a steam-powered mill, a store, school, blacksmith shop, boarding house, and roughly a dozen households." The remnants of an interpretive sign stand near an old stone foundation to your right as you leave the clearing. Ascend from the clearing, listening to the Homer Stone Brook babble to the left. Soon cross Homer Stone Brook on a bridge, and at 3.3 miles meet

Stepping stones on the LT/AT

Little Rock Pond and Clarendon Gorge

Campsite sign

up with the old South Wallingford–Wallingford Pond Road. Turn left to begin a steady and generally rocky ascent of White Rocks Mountain through dense red spruce, passing just west of the summit at 5.6 miles. Arrive at a blue-blazed spur on the left leading 0.2 mile downhill to a fantastic view from the top of White Rocks Cliff. Continue on the LT/

AT, descending to the Greenwall Spur junction at 6.8 miles. Follow the spur downhill to Greenwall Shelter, where you end your day at 7.0 miles. The shelter, a frame lean-to for eight, was built by the USFS in 1962. There are a few tenting sites behind the shelter as well as two composting outhouses. A blue-blazed trail leads 600 feet northeast to a spring, which may fail in very dry weather.

Day Two

Total distance: 8.0 miles (12.9 km)
Hiking time: 5 hours
Vertical rise: 1,825 feet (556 meters)

Pack up and return up the spur to the LT/AT on the slope of White Rocks Mountain. Proceed north, descend to an old road, and follow it downhill to a junction with the Keewaydin Trail at 0.9 mile. Turn right and walk upstream to the crossing point over Bully Brook. Follow Bully Brook downhill, then bear right and traverse the slope through a shady hemlock grove. Continue your descent to the graveled Sugar Hill Road at 1.6 miles, and then drop steeply down rock stairs to cross Roaring Brook Bridge, built in 2000 by GMC's Volunteer Long Trail Patrol. Cross VT 140 carefully at 1.7 miles, and climb gently to the trailhead parking lot.

Cross the parking lot and ascend the old road to an old pasture. Turn right to enter the pasture between old stone walls and continue uphill through open forest, passing an old foundation, before turning right to join another abandoned road at 2.3 miles. Turn left to leave the road, and begin to climb Bear Mountain on switchbacks. A spur to the west leads to a nice view south down the Valley of Vermont, flanked by White Rocks Mountain to the east and Dorset Peak to the west. Continue uphill, join an old road to ascend steeply through an oak forest, and reach the height-of-land just west of the main ridge of Bear Mountain. Follow gentle

Enjoying the view of Clarendon Gorge

grades to parallel the ridge. Ascend briefly and then descend on large stone stairs, now moving through open and ferny woods. Descend to a clearing known as Patch Hollow at 4.4 miles.

Descend further on an abandoned road, which is also used locally as a cross-country ski trail. Turn left at the signpost (the ski trail continues straight along the road) and then cross a brook, pass under a power line, and turn right onto a dirt road. Straight ahead at 5.3 miles is the spur trail to Minerva Hinchey Shelter. This three-sided frame structure is named for the GMC's corresponding secretary for 22 years (1955–1977). The shelter is a nice spot to eat lunch and rest before the final leg of your journey.

Standing on the LT/AT facing the spur, bear left/west on an old road and then take

Suspension bridge over Clarendon Gorge

an immediate right heading north into the woods and up the ridge. Follow the hardwood ridge through a massive patch of stinging nettle and down toward Spring Lake, which you can just make out through the trees. What has been known as Spring Lake Clearing is now being reclaimed by the forest after years of prescribed USFS burns which maintained the openness.

Continue hiking along the ridge until you reach Airport Lookout at 7.2 miles, with a good western view of the Otter Creek Valley, Rutland, and the Taconic Range. Descend steeply from the outcrop, following signs carefully to avoid further erosion at this popular day-use area. You reach Mill River and Clarendon Gorge at 7.9 miles. Cross the suspension bridge over the gorge. As you look down into the deep gorge, picture the river during floods, when the water can get high enough to nearly touch the bridge! Ascend to the parking lot at 8.0 miles to complete your hike. After dropping off your gear at your car, you may wish to further explore and enjoy this scenic area and popular swimming hole.

View of Lake Dunmore from Rattlesnake Point (hike 23)

16

Robert Frost Trail

Total distance: 1.0-mile loop (1.6 km)	
Hiking time: ¾ hour	
Vertical rise: 120 feet (37 meters)	
Rating: Easy	
Map: USGS 7.5' East Middlebury	
Trailhead GPS Coordinates: N43° 57.48', W73° 0.67'	

Robert Frost (1874–1963) spent 23 summers in a small cabin in the Ripton area. He considered himself a Vermonter by preference and was considered by his community to be Ripton's First Citizen. Frost located here seasonally because of his involvement with the Middlebury School of English and its writers' conference. This trail, constructed in 1976 by the Youth Conservation Corps, commemorates his poetry in a location near his summer residence. Prepare yourself; this may be the most poetic hike you'll ever take—literally. Many of Frost's best-loved poems, and some not so well known, are mounted on plaques along the loop trail. Walkers will also find many signs identifying plants and trees and labeling features of the natural environment. Visitors may wish to stop at the Robert Frost Wayside, with picnic tables and information boards, 0.2 mile east of the trailhead on VT 125.

HOW TO GET THERE

The trail is located on VT 125, 2.1 miles east of Ripton (itself 2.0 miles east of VT 116), or 9.8 miles west of VT 100 in Hancock. There is a U.S. Forest Service trailhead parking area for 10 to 20 cars. One trail map signboard at the parking area shows the location of the trail system within the region and lists significant dates and facts about Robert Frost; a second signboard offers a trail description and ecological information. The trail system is comprised of two loops: a wheelchair-accessible loop closest to the parking lot, and a second, nonaccessible

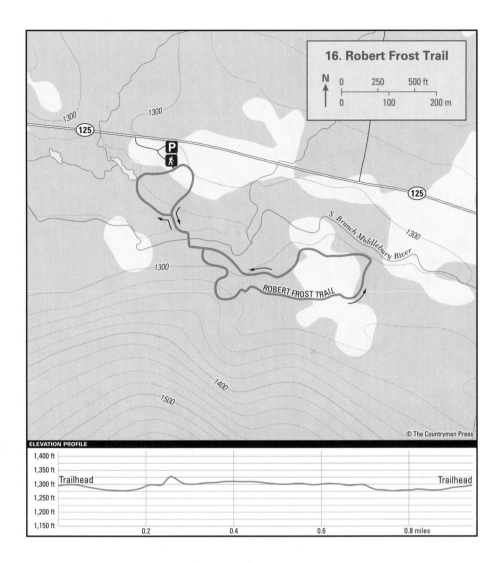

16. Robert Frost Trail

N 0   250   500 ft
   0   100   200 m

ELEVATION PROFILE

1,400 ft
1,350 ft
1,300 ft Trailhead   Trailhead
1,250 ft
1,200 ft
1,150 ft
          0.2   0.4   0.6   0.8 miles

© The Countryman Press

loop through the woods and meadow. A modern privy is located at the trailhead.

THE TRAIL

The walk described below follows blue trail markers and blazes and is essentially a figure eight, taking full advantage of both hiking loops described above. Although a sign located across from the signboard indicates that the trail starts to your right, instead head left, following the smooth gravel path past thick meadow growth. You arrive at a junction where Frost's poem, "Stopping by Woods on a Snowy Evening," is posted next to a bench. Turn left here, and just ahead cross a bridge over the South Branch of the Middlebury River. After the bridge, curve left and ascend to a grove of red spruce overlooking the river. You soon come to a fork in the trail, with another bench from which

Bench on the Robert Frost Trail

to consider Frost's poem, "The Road Not Taken." Follow the arrow to the right (both paths look equally well-trod). The trail swings through hay-scented ferns following an easy grade through the forest, over a footbridge, and up a small hill to its junction with Water Tower Trails.

Turn left and descend to another footbridge and through a birch grove at 0.5 mile, after which the trail becomes more gravelly and open. You soon enter a meadow full of blueberry bushes.

A sign here provides profiles of area mountains including Firetower Hill, Bread Loaf Mountain, Battell Mountain, Kirby Mountain, and Burnt Hill. The trail becomes a narrow, grassy path through the meadow, gently curving until you are heading in the opposite direction by the time you again reach the river.

The trail now parallels the river, cutting through thick field growth. Prescribed burning practices have been used to keep the meadow open and encourage the growth of blueberries and huckleberries. Signage describes the transition from field to woods which would naturally occur without these practices. Leaving this open environment, the trail reenters the woods, where another bench and poem await, this time with a distant view of the mountains. Continuing on, you soon arrive back at "The Road Not Taken." Turn right, retracing your steps to the bridge you crossed earlier. At the junction ("Stopping by Woods on a Snowy Evening"), bear left, passing through a large blackberry patch. The trail now rises onto a large wooden boardwalk leading over a swamp, and then swings to the right, arriving back at the trailhead at 1.0 mile.

17

Thundering Falls

Total distance: 0.5 mile (0.8 km)

Hiking time: ½ hour

Vertical rise: Minimal

Rating: Easy

Map: USGS 7.5' Pico Peak

Trailhead GPS Coordinates: N43° 40.83', W72° 46.93'

This short section of trail in the town of Killington takes visitors to one of Vermont's tallest and most beautiful cascades. It is also one of very few sections of the Appalachian Trail (AT) (and the only one in Vermont) that is accessible to people using wheelchairs. The trail crosses the upper Ottauquechee River floodplain on 1,000 feet of boardwalk, and then climbs through two gentle switchbacks on a wide gravel path to a viewing platform perched before the 140-foot cascade. The trail opened in 2008 after three years of work by crews from the Green Mountain Club and the Vermont Youth Conservation Corps. After 300 feet of the boardwalk was washed away by the remnants of Tropical Storm Irene in 2011, the club rebuilt it in 2012.

Thundering Falls is part of Kent Brook, which flows east out of Kent Pond. The cascade, said to be the sixth tallest in Vermont, is a roaring torrent in the spring and after rainstorms. At times of low water, it multiplies into countless miniature waterfalls braiding the steep face of a huge rock slab.

Small platforms and pullouts along the length of the trail provide opportunities to pause or rest. The time needed to reach the falls and return will depend on how long you spend observing your surroundings.

HOW TO GET THERE

The parking area and start of the trail are on the west side of River Road, north of US 4. To reach it from the south, go east on US 4 from its westernmost junction with VT 100. At 2.0 miles, turn north onto River Road.

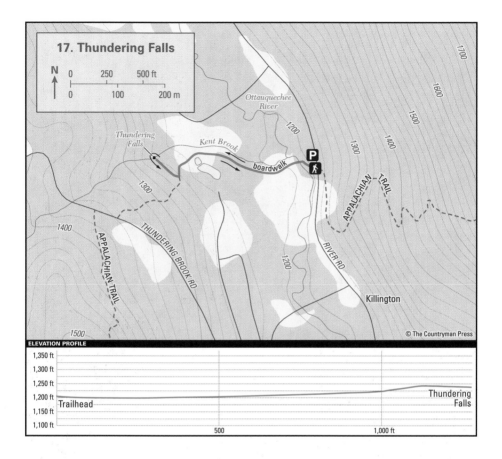

17. Thundering Falls

N

| 0 | 250 | 500 ft |
| 0 | 100 | 200 m |

Ottauquechee River

Thundering Falls

Kent Brook

boardwalk

P

APPALACHIAN TRAIL

THUNDERING BROOK RD.

APPALACHIAN TRAIL

RIVER RD.

1200

1300

1400

1500

1600

1700

1200

1300

1400

1500

1200

Killington

© The Countryman Press

ELEVATION PROFILE

Trailhead

Thundering Falls

Continue on this road for 1.6 miles to the parking area. To reach it from the north, turn east onto River Road from VT 100 about 2.5 miles north of US 4 or 5.5 miles south of the green and gazebo in Pittsfield. Continue on River Road for 2.4 miles.

THE TRAIL

From the parking area, the boardwalk passes through thickets of alder and willow and crosses the headwaters of the Ottauquechee River, which will flow through the village of Woodstock and tumble through Quechee Gorge many miles downstream. As the trail emerges into more open floodplain, it is bordered in summer by many varieties

of wildflower, including aster and meadowsweet. Tuft sedge grows in its characteristic large clumps.

Beavers are busy in the floodplain, and their pools can be seen on either side of the boardwalk, although their location changes as the animals pursue their ceaseless work.

After about 700 feet, you will pass a dry, gravelly clearing on the left, where a hole in the ground indicates a snapping turtle nest. Crows are attracted to the nests to feed on the eggs and young.

At the end of the boardwalk, the surface switches to gravel for the final 300 feet. The trail makes its first gentle switchback around a large clump of thimbleberry on the left; the

Thundering Falls

area is also thick with blackberry, raspberry, and blueberry bushes.

Across Kent Brook stands a house and a building housing a 100-kilowatt hydroelectric generating station. A pipe draws in water from above the falls, and smaller pipes emerging from the power station return the water to the brook.

At the second switchback, the southbound AT splits off to the left; a far narrower path that soon climbs the side of a fern-filled hollow. The Thundering Falls Trail doubles back and passes through a very mature hemlock forest to the platform at the falls. Even in times of low water, the water's plunge through this narrow cleft in the hillside creates a roar that requires visitors to raise their voices to be heard. At high water, mist kicked up by the falls envelops viewers. The power of the water is a marked contrast to the sense of serenity in this mossy, shady wood.

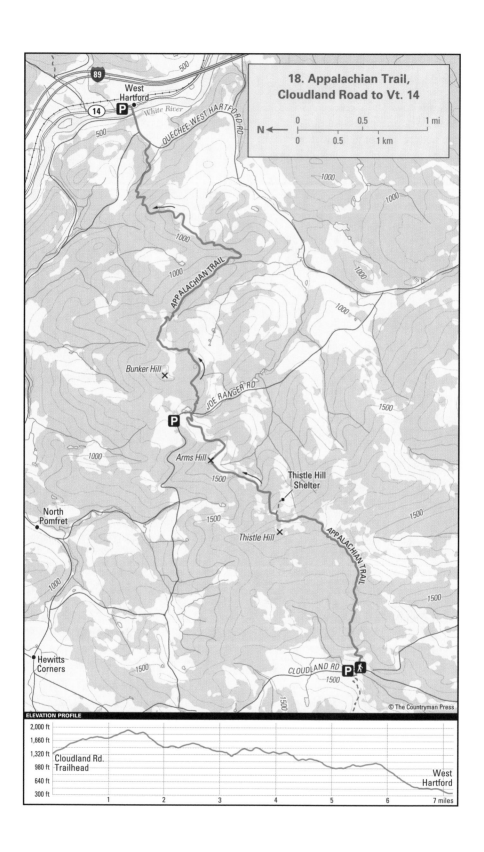

18. Appalachian Trail, Cloudland Road to Vt. 14

West Hartford

OUECHEE-WEST HARTFORD RD

White River

APPALACHIAN TRAIL

JOE RANGER RD

Bunker Hill

Arms Hill

Thistle Hill Shelter

Thistle Hill

North Pomfret

APPALACHIAN TRAIL

Hewitts Corners

CLOUDLAND RD

© The Countryman Press

ELEVATION PROFILE

Cloudland Rd. Trailhead

West Hartford

18

Appalachian Trail (Cloudland Road to VT 14)

Total distance: 7.1 miles (11.4 km)
Hiking time: 4½ hours
Vertical rise: 1,317 feet (401 meters)
Rating: Moderate
Map: USGS 7.5' Quechee
Trailhead GPS Coordinates: N43° 41.2', W72° 30.01'

This section of the Appalachian Trail (AT) can be done in two short out-and-back day hikes—Cloudland Road to Joe Ranger Road, 3.8 miles (6.1 km), and Joe Ranger Road to VT 14, 3.3 miles (5.3 km.)—or one longer day hike with a car spot, 7.1 miles (11.4 km). This hike is characterized by ups and downs over hills; scenic woodland; stone walls, apple trees, old foundations, and other evidence of past settlement; and vistas from former hilltop pastures, now kept open by the Green Mountain Club. The footpath is generally smooth, without a lot of protruding rocks and roots, making for relatively easy walking. You

Bunker Hill Burying Ground

will meet AT thru-hikers (someone trying to hike the entire AT in one hiking season) on this section in summer, especially in July.

HOW TO GET THERE

To the western trailhead: From VT 12 just north of Woodstock, turn right onto River Road. At 0.8 mile turn left onto the gravel Cloudland Road. Reach the AT crossing (4.3 miles) and park in a pullout on the right (east) side of Cloudland Road, at the bottom of a dip, south of Cloudland Farm (which has a farm store) and north of a red house. In the spring and fall, check the parking area before parking to be sure it is not too muddy. The AT generally goes west–east in this section, with the northbound AT heading east.

To the eastern trailhead: Take VT 14 north 6.9 miles from US 4 and US 5 in White River Junction to the bridge over the White River in West Hartford. Parking is available on the west side of VT 14 just north of a bridge on a side road on the left, *opposite* the general store. The general store welcomes hikers, and has a special box outside for packs, but please do not park at the store. Hiker parking is across the road.

To the Joe Ranger Road trailhead: From VT 14 in West Hartford, go west on Quechee–West Hartford Road. In 3.0 miles turn right onto the gravel Joe Ranger Road. Reach the AT trail crossing at 4.8 miles. Park at the Bunker Hill Cemetery, unmarked and on the right (east) side of the road, 0.2 mile beyond the trail crossing; there is no roadside parking at the trail crossing.

Field near Cloudland Road

Central Vermont

Red Baneberry along the trail

THE TRAIL

From Cloudland Road, go south on the road, then left into a field north of a stream and red house. Follow the footpath uphill along the right edge of the field before entering the woods. Pass through a power line cut. Shortly, pass the sign for the spur trail to Cloudland Shelter (no longer part of the official AT Shelter System). Climb gradually through a hardwood forest of sugar maple and beech, with scattered yellow birch, hophornbeam, red oak, white ash, and black cherry. Look for a stone wall visible on the left. Cross several woods roads. Hike up and down over rolling terrain of rocky knolls with ledge outcrops, some with veins of white quartz. Cross several wet areas and small streams. Climb up and over Thistle Hill (2.0 miles) and descend a long downhill stretch paralleling the ridge to the left through a rich northern hardwood forest, with clumps of maidenhair fern, blue cohosh, and slivery glade fern (indicators of rich soils). Reach a blue-blazed spur trail on your left (2.3 miles),

which leads 0.1 mile south to Thistle Hill Shelter. A three-sided log lean-to, Thistle Hill Shelter has bunk space for eight and was built by the Dartmouth Outing Club in 1995. Water is available nearby.

From the spur, continue downhill to cross a small brook. Climb gradually toward the top of Arms Hill, crossing a couple of woods roads, and following a stone wall through young woods with paper birch and old apple trees to an open field, with views east into New Hampshire. Descend Arms Hill through young woods (former pasture) with a few scattered large sugar maple that probably provided shade for the cows or sheep. Emerge in a hillside meadow with views of wooded hills to the north and northeast. Bobolinks (an uncommon bird) can be seen here in spring and early summer. Follow wooden posts and a stone cairn through the field. Enter the woods again for the steep descent to the gravel Joe Ranger Road (3.8 miles).

Approximately 0.2 mile to the left (north) is the interesting and picturesque Bunker Hill Burying Ground, with gravestones dating from the early 1800s. Parking is possible beside the cemetery. There are no parking pullouts near the trailhead on Joe Ranger Road.

Cross Joe Ranger Road by a small pond with a stone dam (where pink water lilies bloom in summer), and ascend through deciduous woods and a pine plantation to the wooded summit of Bunker Hill. Descend Bunker Hill to a stream valley and traverse more rolling terrain. Cross an old road (4.5 miles) lined by a stone wall and look for the old foundations of a former farmstead to your right. Traverse several openings (overgrown hilltop pastures) with views to the southeast. Cross a woods road in a hardwood forest, then hike through mixed forest with huge sugar maple and hemlock. Climb to another hilltop pasture with views of the White River

Soaking in the view along the Appalachian Trail

Valley (an Adirondack chair has been placed here for you to rest and enjoy the vista). Follow rock cairns through the field (6.1 miles), then descend steadily through hardwoods with large clumps of maidenhair fern to cross a stream. Cross a small wetland on puncheon, and turn left onto the paved Quechee–West Hartford Road (6.8 miles). No parking is available here. Follow this road to cross an iron bridge over the White River to VT 14 (7.1 miles) in the village of West Hartford. This part of the river is a popular local swimming hole on a hot day. Turn left on VT 14 to reach your car.

19

Mount Horrid's Great Cliff

Total distance: 1.4 miles (2.3 km)
Hiking time: 1 hour
Vertical rise: 600 feet (183 meters)
Rating: Moderate
Map: USGS 7.5' Mount Carmel
Trailhead GPS Coordinates: N43° 50.4', W72° 58.1'

This short, steep hike takes you to the top of Mount Horrid's Great Cliff, a geologic feature as rare in Vermont as it is ecologically significant. Being one of only a handful of "boreal calcareous" cliff types found in Vermont (others being in Smugglers' Notch and along Mount Pisgah), its combination of rock type, cooler climate, available groundwater, and vertical face supports several species found in few to no other locations in the state.

One of these supported species is the peregrine falcon, which was wiped out from the eastern United States and Canada in the 1960s due largely to use of the pesticide DDT. The state of Vermont successfully reintroduced peregrines following a ban on DDT, and was the first state in the nation to remove the falcons from its endangered species list. Even today, peregrine falcons are extremely sensitive to human disturbance, especially from above, and may abandon their nest or even attack humans if approached too closely. Please obey all posted trail signs, and be aware that the trail may be closed entirely during nesting season any time from April through August. Reference this book's introduction for more information on peregrine falcons.

According to Green Mountain National Forest literature, "The rock that makes up the exposed face of this cliff was formed during earliest geological times. Freezing and thawing have wedged off fragments which have accumulated over time on the mountain slope." These fragments are known as talus and, in the case of Mount Horrid, make for

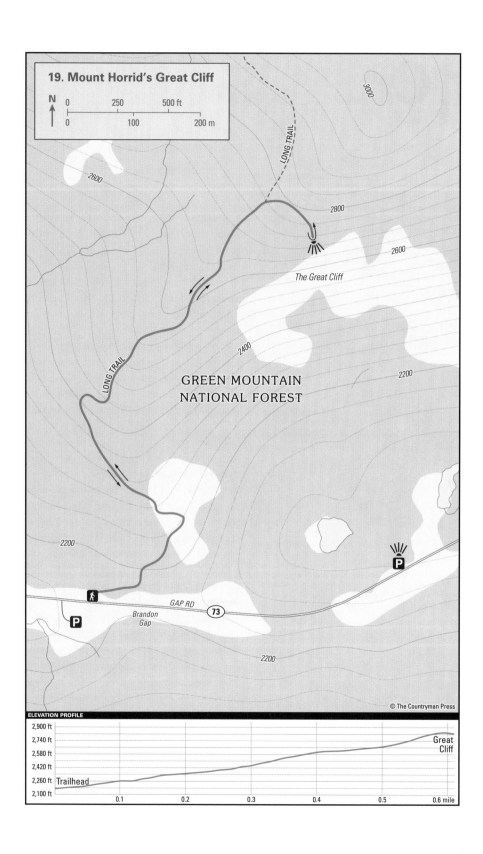

19. Mount Horrid's Great Cliff

N

| 0 | 250 | 500 ft |
| 0 | 100 | 200 m |

LONG TRAIL

3000

2600

2800

2600

The Great Cliff

2400

2200

LONG TRAIL

GREEN MOUNTAIN
NATIONAL FOREST

2200

P

GAP RD 73

Brandon
Gap

2200

2200

© The Countryman Press

ELEVATION PROFILE

2,900 ft							
2,740 ft							Great
2,580 ft							Cliff
2,420 ft							
2,260 ft	Trailhead						
2,100 ft							
	0.1	0.2	0.3	0.4	0.5	0.6 mile

View of Brandon Gap from Mount Horrid's Great Cliff

interesting boulders and rock formations to view along the hike. It also makes for a tricky descent at times, especially in wet conditions when the rocks can be quite slippery.

HOW TO GET THERE
Follow VT 73 to the top of Brandon Gap. Just west of the gap summit, there is a large parking lot on the south side of the road. However, before parking your car, stop at the pullout area just east of the gap summit for a view of the cliffs and a beaver pond as well as information describing the cliffs and pond ecology. After enjoying the views, drive to the parking lot at the top of the gap.

THE TRAIL
Carefully cross VT 73 and climb the embankment to a U.S. Forest Service signboard offering further information on the area. Begin

Mount Horrid's Great Cliff

hiking north on the white-blazed Long Trail (LT). You cross a small raspberry patch buzzing with insects and ascend to a Green Mountain National Forest registration box and sign indicating a distance of 0.7 mile to the Great Cliff overlook.

After the sign, ascend steeply to a ridge at 0.2 mile. Birch line the trail and boulders dot the woods along the ridge. You ascend more steps, sometimes rock, sometimes root. The trail swings to the western side of the ridge, passes through mixed hardwoods, and becomes much rockier and steeper. Watch your step, particularly in wet conditions, and stay on the trail to limit erosion in this high-use area. Through the trees to your right, the Great Cliff towers above you. Climb an extensive staircase, built by U.S. Forest Service and Green Mountain Club trail crews, and at the top of the stairs reach a trail junction at 0.6 mile. To the left, the LT continues north to the summit of Mount Horrid, and to the right a blue-blazed spur leads uphill 500 feet to the cliff overlook. As you step out into the opening, you are on top of the 2,800-foot Great Cliff you saw earlier from the parking area—now 700 feet below. Also below is the beaver pond you saw from the pullout.

After enjoying the views, including Bloodroot Gap to the south, hike back down the same trail to Brandon Gap.

20

Deer Leap Overlook

Total distance: 2.0 miles (3.2 km)
Hiking time: 1¼ hours
Vertical rise: 520 feet (158 meters)
Rating: Easy
Map: USGS 7.5' Pico Peak
Trailhead GPS Coordinates: N43° 39.84', W72° 49.94'

The Deer Leap Trail is a unique introductory day hike that includes portions of the former Long Trail (LT) and Appalachian Trail (AT), as well as a side trail that leads to a spectacular view from the top of Deer Leap Cliffs. The cliffs are a popular climbing area, so be sure to look for rock climbers.

In southern Vermont, the AT coincides with the LT from the Massachusetts border to Maine Junction in Willard Gap, 1 mile north of where both trails cross US 4. From there the AT continues east through Vermont and across the White Mountains in New Hampshire to Maine. The LT heads north to Canada.

Built by volunteers between 1921 and 1937, the AT extends 2,100 miles from

Deer Leap Overlook

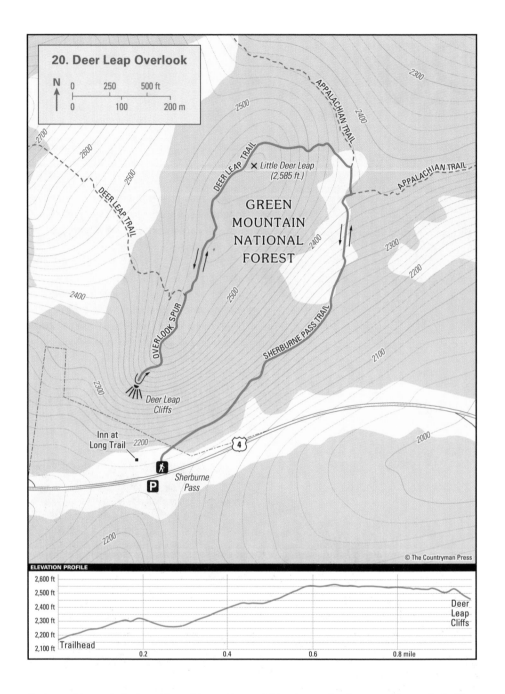

N

| 0 | 250 | 500 ft |
| 0 | 100 | 200 m |

2300

APPALACHIAN TRAIL

2500

2400

2700

2600

2500

DEER LEAP TRAIL

× Little Deer Leap
(2,585 ft.)

APPALACHIAN TRAIL

DEER LEAP TRAIL

GREEN
MOUNTAIN
NATIONAL
FOREST

2400

2300

2200

2400

2500

OVERLOOK SPUR

SHERBURNE PASS TRAIL

2100

2300

Deer Leap
Cliffs

Inn at
Long Trail

2200

4

2000

Sherburne
Pass

P

2200

© The Countryman Press

ELEVATION PROFILE

2,600 ft					
2,500 ft					
2,400 ft					Deer
2,300 ft					Leap
2,200 ft					Cliffs
2,100 ft	Trailhead	0.2	0.4	0.6	0.8 mile

Springer Mountain in Georgia to Mount Katahdin in Maine. Benton MacKaye, a forester, author, and philosopher, first proposed the AT in 1921. On Stratton Mountain in Vermont, MacKaye conceived the idea of connecting the high peaks of the east after

View to Pico from Dear Leap Overlook

construction of the LT had already begun. Today, nearly 30 local nonprofit trail groups such as the Green Mountain Club; individual volunteers; community groups; and more than 80 local, state, and federal agencies in 14 states (all coordinated through the Appalachian Trail Conservancy) maintain, manage, and preserve this valuable recreational resource.

Deer Leap is a popular area and sees many hikers in all seasons. To prevent trail expansion and further degradation of the vegetation along the trail, stay on the main trail and do not cut switchbacks.

HOW TO GET THERE

Take US 4 to the top of Sherburne Pass, 9.1 miles east of US 7 in Rutland. Park in the lot opposite the Inn at Long Trail on the south side of the highway, where there is ample parking.

THE TRAIL

Carefully cross US 4, where traffic travels at high speeds, and begin your hike on the north side of US 4 to the east (right) of the inn. Follow the blue-blazed Sherburne Pass Trail over the first set of boulders. Be careful to avoid the old Deer Leap Lookout Trail on your left, which has been closed and relocated because of severe erosion and hazardous footing. You soon pass over more boulders. They provide the roughest footing of the hike, but also make some interesting little caves where they are jumbled. The trail descends to your right to avoid a steep rock face, levels out, and then ascends until you reach a trail junction at 0.5 mile. Be sure not to take a right turn, which would take you on the AT (blazed in white) to Maine. This was Maine Junction from 1966 until 1999, when the LT/AT north of Pico Peak was moved west to

Sherburne Pass from Deer Leap

avoid possible ski area expansion and the former LT/AT became the Sherburne Pass Trail. (Before 1966, Maine Junction was at Sherburne Pass, and the LT went west around Deer Leap Mountain on its way to Canada.)

Continue straight ahead "southbound" toward Georgia (actually heading north here) on the white-blazed AT, and in 200 feet reach the junction of the blue-blazed Deer Leap Trail. The U.S. Forest Service constructed this trail in 1994 to replace the eroded and unsafe Deer Leap Lookout Trail.

Turn left onto the Deer Leap Trail, and ascend mostly through white birch until you crest a series of small spruce- and fir-covered knobs beginning at 0.8 mile. Look for the trail sign at the junction of the Overlook Spur near a boulder on your right at 0.9 mile, just beyond the 2,585-foot west summit of Little Deer Leap. (To the right, the Deer Leap Trail continues over Big Deer Leap and

reaches the AT in another mile, 0.7 mile from where you left it.) Keep left at this junction to remain on the Overlook Spur, and continue along the spruce- and fir-lined ridge of Little Deer Leap until it opens onto a small but long rock shelf. Keeping to the left side, descend the shelf face. Just beyond the shelf, the trail opens onto the Deer Leap Cliffs at 1.0 mile. The rocks can be slippery, and the overlook is quite steep, so use caution.

Enjoy the views of Pico Peak directly across Sherburne Pass and the sweeping views to the east and west. The remains of the old Long Trail Lodge are in the woods just south of US 4 and west of the parking lot. You may also see some technical rock climbers, as this is a popular rock-climbing area. After resting and enjoying the views, return to your car along the same trails, exercising caution that you keep to the south and west back to Sherburne Pass.

21

Mount Independence

Total distance: 4.1 miles (6.6 km)
Hiking time: 3½ hours
Vertical rise: 200 feet (61 meters)
Rating: Easy
Map: USGS 7.5' Ticonderoga
Trailhead GPS Coordinates: N43° 49.11', W73° 23.1'

No ordinary hiking site, this National Historic Landmark offers 6 miles of well-marked trails (1.6 miles of which are accessible by wheelchair) steeped in history. Mount Independence was Vermont's major Revolutionary War fortification and is one of the least disturbed Revolutionary War sites in the United States. With its north-facing orientation, steep cliffs, and 300-foot elevation above Lake Champlain, it was an important strategic defense component against a British attack from Canada.

When American General Philip Schuyler ordered troops to begin clearing land on what was then Rattlesnake Hill or East Point in 1776, his plan was to prevent the British fleet from sailing down Lake Champlain and dividing New England from the rest of the colonies. On July 28th of that summer, after a reading of the Declaration of Independence, the soldiers renamed their fortification Mount Independence. In October, General Guy Carleton, fresh from his victory over Benedict Arnold and the fledgling American fleet at Valcour Island, sailed south toward Mount Independence and Fort Ticonderoga. But Arnold's fleet had bought the time necessary for the Americans to upgrade their fortifications. Carleton was so impressed with the two American fortifications and the twelve to thirteen thousand troops stationed there that he turned north, retreating to Canada before the onset of winter, thus delaying the British invasion for another year. Twenty-five hundred troops then spent a hard winter on the mount, with seven or eight soldiers freezing to death each night.

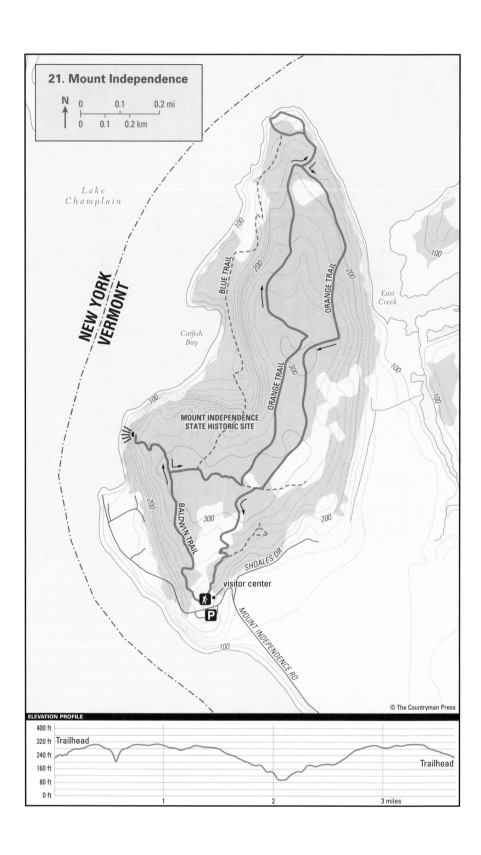

21. Mount Independence

N

| 0 | 0.1 | 0.2 mi |
| 0 | 0.1 | 0.2 km |

Lake Champlain

NEW YORK
VERMONT

Catfish Bay

BLUE TRAIL

ORANGE TRAIL

ORANGE TRAIL

East Creek

100

200

300

100

MOUNT INDEPENDENCE STATE HISTORIC SITE

200

300

BALDWIN TRAIL

200

100

SHOALES DR

visitor center

P

MOUNT INDEPENDENCE RD

100

© The Countryman Press

ELEVATION PROFILE

400 ft	
320 ft	Trailhead
240 ft	
160 ft	
80 ft	Trailhead
0 ft	

1   2   3 miles

Mount Independence historic site

In the summer of 1777, the British returned, and the Americans, under the command of General Arthur St. Clair, retreated southward with the enemy close at their heels. British General John "Gentleman Johnny" Bourgoyne left troops to guard the fort. After the British defeat at Saratoga, these soldiers burned most of Mount Independence's buildings and hightailed it back to Canada.

After the war, Mount Independence was used to pasture livestock, its historical significance largely forgotten.

In 1911, the Pell Family purchased the northern half of Mount Independence and began working to preserve the site. The Pell land was deeded to the Fort Ticonderoga Association in the 1950s and the state of Vermont purchased an additional 108 acres in 1961 and 1973. These two institutions

jointly manage the site today. Mount Independence is open from Memorial Day to Labor Day. When you arrive, stop at the award-winning bateau-shaped visitors center and museum, built in 1996, to pay the entry fee, which includes trail use, a site map, and access to the museum. Although trails are well-marked, the site map is highly recommended both for its overview of the trail system and for the self-guided historical tour it provides.

HOW TO GET THERE

Mount Independence lies 6 miles west of the junction of VT 22A and VT 73 in Orwell. From VT 22A, turn west onto VT 73. At 0.3 mile, head straight onto Mount Independence Road, leaving VT 73 (making sure to yield to oncoming VT 73 traffic). After a few miles the paved road turns to gravel. In the distance ahead you can see the mount rising above the farmland, its location clearly advantageous for anyone keeping watch over the lake. At 5.2 miles, you come to the junction with Shoales Drive. Turn left, up the steep road. The visitors center is tucked into the hill on your right and a large parking lot is across the road on your left.

THE TRAIL

Although there are many ways to explore the trails at Mount Independence, this description follows the entirety of the Baldwin Trail—a wheelchair-accessible trail completed in 2007—and the Orange Trail. Some time is allowed for reading the signage. For a faster hike you could skip the spur trails, stick to the Baldwin Trail, or resist—if you are able—the urge to read the interpretive signage. Follow the stone steps just west of the visitors center to the trailhead kiosk. Turn left from the kiosk, following signs for the Baldwin Trail. The well-groomed crushed gravel surface winds through a field. In the woods to your left is the first of several picnic areas, this one next to an informational bronze plaque embedded in a "sentry rock." Continue north along the field, and then into the cooler woods, reading interpretive signs along the way, until you reach a side spur to the left. After exploring the spur, its site markers, and the view it offers across the lake to Mount Defiance, retrace your steps to the main trail and turn left. Shortly you arrive at the site of a former field hospital, sheltered by a small stand of white pine. Standing in this peaceful spot, it's hard to imagine the suffering that took place in the winter of 1776–77. Follow the boardwalk to the end—its length indicating the approximate length of the hospital—and stay straight, continuing on the Baldwin Trail. You enter a clearing, the site of the Third Brigade Encampment, and soon arrive at the West Leg of the Orange Trail. Turn left here to enjoy what is now a pleasant grassy stroll, noticing how your pace changes once you're off the wider gravel path. You reenter the woods, following the orange trail markers, and soon come to a small clearing. Catfish Bay is briefly visible through the trees to the west. Duck back into the woods and head up a small hill to a clearing, the site of the old Star Fort and the highest point on the mount. Head west back into the woods and pass a well; the trail becomes rocky here. A spur trail on the left leads to the site of the crane used to hoist cargo from ships floating down below to the fort on the hill above. Continue on the Orange Trail through the woods, and then enter a field as you begin your descent north to the point.

Spurs along the point lead to several important historical sites: the remains of two batteries, a masting point (where masts for Benedict Arnold's boats were stepped), and the site from which, amazingly enough, a 350-foot-long floating bridge was built between 1776 and 1777, connecting Mount Independence with Fort Ticonderoga across the lake. You will also pass a prominent obelisk commemorating the soldiers buried on Mount Independence, as well as the terminus of the Blue Trail—an alternate and slightly faster route back to the visitors center, with its own set of historical site markers numbered 1 through 7. After visiting the point, retrace your steps to the last junction and turn left on the trail marked RETURN TRAIL. This is the East Leg of the Orange Trail. The return trip has a completely different feeling than the rest of the hike; in the wake of all the historical site markers, groomed trails, and frequent clearings, moving through the consistently cool, dark woods suddenly feels a bit wild, with ample time for contemplation on the long and sometimes troubled history of the area. You pass foundations at sites 8 and 9, the first thought to be perhaps a lookout shelter, and the second possibly a block house. Below site 9 is an outcropping of black chert, described by the trail map as being "used by Native Americans for thousands of years to make tools and weapons, and by Revolutionary War soldiers to make gun flints." Following the orange markers, you return to the packed gravel surface of the Baldwin Trail.

Turn left to explore a Baldwin Trail spur leading to the old Southern Battery; turn right to go directly to an information kiosk just down the trail. The kiosk directs you left down the hill to the visitors center, 0.7 mile away. There will be one more kiosk and spur trail halfway down the hill, and then one more site marker before arriving back at the original kiosk next to the visitors center.

22

Mount Tom

Total distance: 3.6 miles (5.8 km)

Hiking time: 2¼ hours

Vertical rise: 600 feet (183 meters)

Rating: Moderate

Maps: USGS 7.5' Woodstock North; 7.5' Woodstock South

Trailhead GPS Coordinates: N43° 37.9', W72° 31.02'

Marsh-Billings-Rockefeller National Historic Park in Woodstock is Vermont's second national park; the Appalachian Trail is its first. The estate was donated by the Rockefeller family and features historic buildings, a carefully managed forest landscape, and plenty of opportunities for walking and exploring the grounds. Mount Tom is but one of many wild destinations close to the heart of Woodstock. If time permits, the Billings Farm and Museum is well worth the visit. The trail system is operated as a cross-country ski touring center, with a fee, in winter.

HOW TO GET THERE

From US 4 in Woodstock, follow VT 12 north 0.5 mile to the parking lot for Marsh-Billings-Rockefeller National Historic Park and Billings Farm and Museum on your right.

THE TRAIL

Cross the road using the crosswalk between the Billings Farm and Museum and the Marsh-Billings-Rockefeller Park. Start up the hill on the path. If you want to pick up the park service map of the carriage roads and all the trails through the park, at the fork take the left fork to the carriage barn, which serves as the park's visitors center (the carriage road is well-signed, the trails in the historical park are unmarked). If you want to develop your own variations of hikes in this area, this is a useful map. There are also restrooms, an interesting exhibit on the history of the park and on land stewardship, a small library, and the park ranger at the information

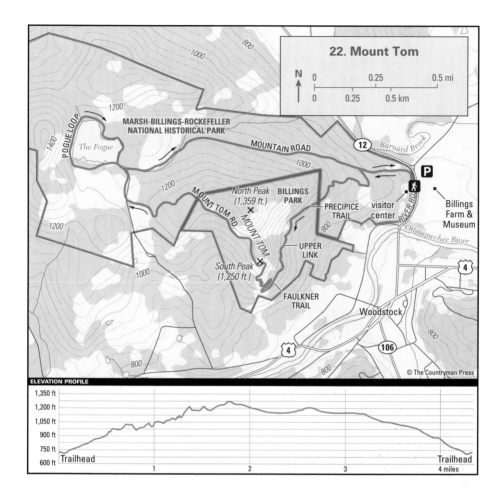

ELEVATION PROFILE

desk. If you visit the Carriage Barn, return to this fork to start the hike.

To begin the hike, at the fork bear right toward CARRIAGE ROAD AND TRAILS. Follow this wide dirt carriage road around the gate, passing a large, fancy woodshed on the right as you climb gently but steadily. Spring hikers should look for the wild ginger, jack-in-the-pulpit, and trillium. Take the first sharp left turn (0.3 mile) onto a narrow carriage road, again going gently uphill. Reach a T intersection (0.35 mile), and turn right onto another narrow carriage road near the horse shed's clearing. At the next T intersection

(0.4 mile.), turn right again onto a wide carriage road that leads away from the clearing. Take the first left (0.45 mile) (sign To THE MOUNTAIN RD AND THE POGUE) onto a wide but less-worn carriage road that goes uphill and curves off to the left. Reach a T-intersection (0.5 mile) (sign To NORTH PEAK AND PRECIPICE TRAIL), and go right uphill. This road will rapidly diminish into a narrow trail. This area is in the historical park. You will be walking through mixed hardwoods and evergreens of varying ages, up to 80 to 100 years old. The trail contours across the south side of Mount Tom. You will start to see yellow blazes (0.8 mile) as you come around from the east to the southeast side of Mount Tom and pass into the town of Woodstock's Billings Park; all the trails within the town park are marked with yellow paint. You'll find a sign marked UPPER LINK with arrows pointing to a trail going left; bear left downhill on the Upper Link Trail (straight continues on the Precipice Trail, which can also be used to go to the summit).

Go downhill with several switchbacks, cross an intermittent stream, go uphill about 30 feet, and reach a junction (0.9 mile). Go straight on this trail, staying on the Upper Link Trail (left will take you downhill into the town of Woodstock's Faulkner Park and out

to Mountain Avenue), continuing to circle Mount Tom on a generally level trail. Look for lots more jack-in-the-pulpit, as well as jewelweed, wild parsley, and blue cohosh.

Bear right, and go gently uphill. Cross a wet area on rocks, noting the rock jumble on the right. Continue trending around the mountain as you begin very gently going uphill. The woods change from tall hardwoods to tall evergreens. Pass two green railing posts on the right, and reach the junction (1.0 mile) of the Link Trail and the Faulkner Trail. Bear right slightly uphill (left will again take you downhill to Faulkner Park and Mountain Avenue).

The trail now ascends Mount Tom in

Woodstock, Vermont, from Mount Tom

long, very gentle switchbacks with many benches; views of Woodstock that can be caught through the trees (especially when the leaves have fallen); occasional remains of fencing; a short, low-rising rock staircase (1.2 miles); and an alternation of types of trees, with a large number of oak. You will come to an area with two split log benches together (1.3 miles). There is a good view here looking east into New Hampshire and southeast through the trees to Mount Ascutney.

The trail takes a short dip, and then climbs moderately uphill, with some rock steps and some wire handrails to the top. Here you meet the carriage road (Mount Tom Road) on top of the south peak of Mount Tom (1.4 miles). There are several benches, with views to the east into New Hampshire, southeast to Mount Ascutney, and south to Woodstock in the valley (note the town green and the Woodstock Inn and Resort). There is also a huge pair of wooden posts with lights in a star that is visible in Woodstock.

Turn left onto the carriage road, and follow it to a crossroad (2.3 miles). Turn left at a sign, THE POGUE, after 0.1 mile. When you reach the Pogue you can add 0.75 mile to your hike by circling this artificial pond on a carriage road (Mountain Road). To return to the visitors center from here via carriage road, just follow the signs east for the visitors center for 1.3 miles, for a total of 3.6 miles.

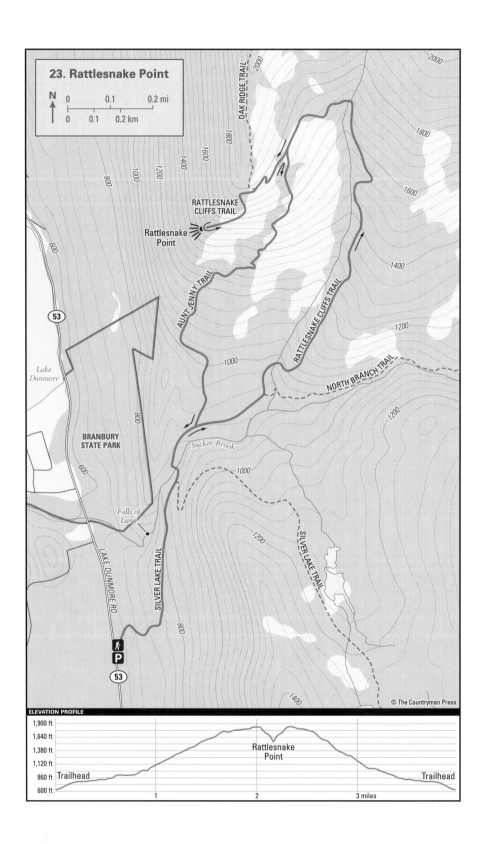

23. Rattlesnake Point

N 0   0.1   0.2 mi

0   0.1   0.2 km

OAK RIDGE TRAIL

2000

2000

1800

1800

1600

1600

1400

1400

1200

1200

1000

1000

800

600

RATTLESNAKE CLIFFS TRAIL

Rattlesnake Point

AUNT JENNY TRAIL

RATTLESNAKE CLIFFS TRAIL

NORTH BRANCH TRAIL

53

Lake Dunmore

BRANBURY STATE PARK

Sucker Brook

Falls of Lana

1000

1200

1200

800

SILVER LAKE TRAIL

SILVER LAKE TRAIL

LAKE DUNMORE RD.

1400

53

© The Countryman Press

ELEVATION PROFILE

1,900 ft	
1,640 ft	
1,380 ft	Rattlesnake
1,120 ft	Point
860 ft	Trailhead
600 ft	

1   2   3 miles

Trailhead

23

Rattlesnake Point

Total distance: 3.9 miles (6.3 km)
Hiking time: 2½ hours
Vertical rise: 1,160 feet (354 meters)
Rating: Moderate
Map: USGS 7.5' East Middlebury
Trailhead GPS Coordinates: N43° 54.02', W73° 3.85'

Curious creature along the trail

Rattlesnake Point, a large rock outcrop at the southern end of Mount Moosalamoo, provides spectacular views of Silver Lake and Lake Dunmore and the expansive Champlain Valley beyond. This trail, which begins on Green Mountain National Forest land, was completed in 1977 by the Youth Conservation Corps and rebuilt in 1983 by a crew from the Rutland Community Correctional Center. This blue-blazed U.S. Forest Service (USFS) trail begins a loop that links the Falls of Lana Picnic Area, Rattlesnake Point, Mount Moosalamoo, and the Moosalamoo Campground.

Hikers should be warned that peregrine falcons are known to nest on the steep cliffs. When they do, the USFS will close the trail to the cliffs, usually from April to August. Signs will be posted just before the spur trail to the cliffs at the terminus of the trail. The rest of the trail will remain open. Hikers may wish to call the USFS (Middlebury Ranger District) ahead of time if planning to hike during this period.

HOW TO GET THERE

The trail is located on VT 53, 5.7 miles north of VT 73 in Forest Dale or 3.8 miles south of US 7 (7 miles south of Middlebury). A USFS sign indicating Silver Lake Trail designates the parking area on the east side of the road.

THE TRAIL

The trailhead is marked by a sign that reads MOOSALAMOO NATIONAL RECREATION AREA–TRAIL, located behind the parking area. It climbs a rocky bank and quickly reaches the

Sucker Brook as it approaches the Falls of Lana

USFS access road to Silver Lake. Turn right, and follow the road uphill on easy grades. You soon reach a signpost indicating motorized vehicles are prohibited beyond this point. At this point it is 0.5 mile to the Falls of Lana and 1.5 miles to Silver Lake.

Ascend the wide dirt road along switchbacks until you enter a clearing where a power line and penstock descend from Silver Lake to a power station on VT 53 below. (A penstock is a pipe that carries water, usually downhill, to a turbine to generate power.) Through the clearing are views down to Lake Dunmore, and following the penstock downhill a short distance there is a great view of the Falls of Lana to the right.

Beyond the power-line cut, the road begins a gentle ascent and soon reaches a small wooden NO TENTING sign on your left where you will hear Sucker Brook and the Falls of Lana. Take a minute to enjoy the views from the top of the falls, which you can access from a number of short, unmarked trails in the area. The Falls of Lana were discovered in 1850 and named by a party of soldiers for their commander, General Wool, who, during a tour of duty in Mexico, was known as General Lana, the Spanish word for wool.

Continue your hike along the road parallel to Sucker Brook until you reach the Silver Lake Trail junction at 0.5 mile. Keep left, parallel to the brook, and then cross a wooden bridge over the brook less than 100 yards from the junction. Just beyond the bridge the trail swings to the right, passing the Falls of Lana Picnic Area along the brook. You'll soon reach another trail junction, which leads straight ahead to the Rattlesnake Cliffs Trail.

Hike along Sucker Brook on the intermittently blue-blazed Rattlesnake Cliffs Trail. You soon reach a junction with the lower end of the Aunt Jenny Trail on your left, which will be your return route. Past this junction, continue on the Rattlesnake Cliffs Trail to a clearing filled with fireweed, a tall perennial willow-herb with pink flowers in midsummer, at 0.8 mile. A signpost in the clearing indicates the junction with the North Branch Trail on your right.

Keep left, following the Rattlesnake Cliffs Trail at this junction and back into the woods.

Note the marker in the ground indicating the Youth Conservation Corps constructed this trail in 1977. After crossing a small wooden bridge over a brook, follow the trail as it rises steadily. After perhaps 0.5 mile of steady climbing, the trail crosses a small, steep brook, and swings along the face of a large, bowl-like ravine. The trail soon reaches the upper end of the Aunt Jenny Trail at 1.75 miles. Note this intersection, because the Aunt Jenny Trail will be your return route.

Beyond the junction, the climb continues steeply up the mountain following a series of diagonally placed wood steps designed to help control erosion. At 2.0 miles, the Oak Ridge Trail, which leads to other trails and the summit of Mount Moosalamoo, enters on your right. Bear left at this junction, and continue along the Rattlesnake Cliffs Trail,

Silver Lake in autumn from the Rattlesnake Cliffs Trail

Admiring the view of Lake Dunmore from Rattlesnake Point

enjoying occasional views of the lake below for 0.1 mile until you reach the junction of the West Cliff Overlook Trail at 2.1 miles, marked by a sign that simply says CLIFFS, with arrows pointing both left and straight ahead. The trail to the left leads gently down and around to the ledges of Rattlesnake Cliffs and multiple overlooks with spectacular views of Lake Dunmore below, Silver Lake higher in the hills to the left, the Otter Creek watershed, and the Adirondacks in the distance.

Return to the junction and the CLIFFS sign following the same trail back. At the junction,

take a left to continue on the Rattlesnake Cliffs Trail to the South Lookout, which descends to an open rock overlook of Silver Lake and Lake Dunmore at 2.3 miles. (Note: The cliffs may be closed to hikers between April and August if peregrine falcons are nesting. Signs will be posted before you reach the cliffs alerting hikers of closure.)

After enjoying the view, reverse your route along the same trail to the junction with the Aunt Jenny Trail at 2.8 miles. In the early 1900s, hikers used to enjoy stopping at Aunt Jenny's Tea Room, a favorite resting spot and refreshment stand. Mrs. Jenny Dutton

Rickert operated the tearoom, located just south of the Silver Lake Power Station.

Turn right at the junction and follow the Aunt Jenny Trail—descending steeply and steadily, passing through a beautiful oak forest. The trail is easy to follow and marked occasionally with blue markers, though you may see a few pale yellow ones as well. At the trail junction with the Rattlesnake Cliffs Trail near the brook at 3.4 miles, turn right, and follow the trail over the bridge and back to the access road. From here, follow the road downhill past the Falls of Lana Overlook and back to the parking area at 3.9 miles.

24

Snake Mountain

Total Distance: 4.6 miles (7.4 km)

Hiking time: 2¾ hours

Vertical Rise: 1,087 feet (331 meters)

Rating: Moderate

Map: USGS 7.5' Port Henry

Trailhead GPS Coordinates: N44° 3.12', W73° 15.36'

Hiking Snake Mountain is an adventure. Not only will you find a beautiful summit view, you will also enjoy oak forests, rare plants, old foundations and roads, and an area rich in Vermont folklore and history. While enjoying the views from the summit, consider that fourteen thousand years ago you would have been standing on an island in Lake Vermont! Lake Vermont covered this region from the Adirondacks to the Green Mountains except for a serpentine ridge—from which Snake Mountain derives its name.

Please respect other trail users you may encounter along your journey. Because the trail and summit of Snake Mountain are part of the 999-acre Snake Mountain Wildlife Management Area, hikers, skiers, mountain bikers, and hunters all use these multipurpose trails.

HOW TO GET THERE

From the junction of VT 17 and VT 22A in Addison follow VT 17 east for 2.8 miles to a right turn onto VT 23. Follow VT 23 to the junction with Snake Mountain Road (3.4 miles) and bear right. At 5.2 miles a Vermont Fish and Wildlife Department parking area and the trailhead will be on your right.

Alternatively, from the junction of VT 125 and VT 23 in Middlebury, follow VT 23 west 4.3 miles to a left turn on Prunier Road. Follow Prunier Road to a T-intersection with Snake Mountain Road (5.4 miles) and turn right. At 5.8 miles a Vermont Fish and Wildlife Department parking area and the trailhead will be on your left.

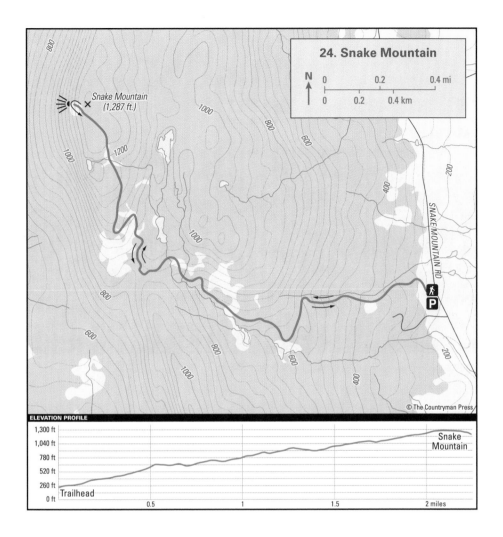

N

| 0 | | 0.2 | | 0.4 mi |
| 0 | | 0.2 | 0.4 km | |

© The Countryman Press

ELEVATION PROFILE

Snake Mountain

Trailhead

THE TRAIL

From the parking area, begin a steady ascent on an old road. Pass through a field, over a culvert, and around a gate (0.3 mile). Reach an area of former beaver activity and a SUMMIT sign with an arrow (0.7 mile), and an area of current beaver activity just beyond (0.9 mile). Pass another SUMMIT sign with an arrow (1.0 mile) where a side trail branches to the left. Continue straight ahead, ascending steadily, then leveling off. Pass a side trail on the left

(1.4 miles) and 75 feet beyond reach the former carriage road that ascends the mountain from the west. (Take note of this point as you will need to bear left off the carriage road here on your hike back to your car.)

Bear right along the carriage road, which begins to get steep and has deep water bars to control erosion. At 1.7 miles, the road swings right, then sharply left onto a switchback along the steep bank. Please stay on the main road—the switchbacks are used to control erosion.

Champlain Valley farms and Lake Champlain from Snake Mountain

Above the switchback the grade moderates. Cross a small valley, and continue through an oak forest, where you will likely see an abundance of squirrels and chipmunks. Old roads continue to intersect the main route, so be sure to stay on the main road, which gets rockier and then levels off at 2.2 miles. As you near the summit, numerous old roads continue to intersect the main carriage trail. Reach a concrete pad near the site of the former Grand View Hotel (2.3 miles). From the concrete pad you can enjoy 180-degree views of Addison County and Lake Champlain, and a view of Dead Creek below. Dead Creek, a spidery body of water surrounded by rich farmland, is part of the Dead Creek Wildlife Management Area and a favorite spot for canoers, duck hunters, and birders. The area maintains restricted and important waterfowl nesting areas.

If you choose to explore the summit area looking for old foundations and building remains, be sure not to get lost. After resting, enjoying the views, and possibly exploring, return to your car via the same route.

The abundance of roads on Snake Mountain originated in the 1800s, when the mountain was the site first of a sawmill and then the Grand View House, which opened on the summit in 1874. The Grand View Hotel was a popular destination for summer outings. In fact, for a time the name of the mountain was changed to Grand View Mountain because the founder of the summit house, Jonas Smith, thought the name Snake Mountain would discourage people from visiting his hotel. Smith also built two towers on the summit, first a wooden one and then a replacement made of steel; he charged his guests a fee to climb and see the view.

Life on the mountain changed a great deal in the early 1920s and 1930s. The Grand View Hotel was permanently closed in 1925, the road to the summit was washed away in the flood of 1927, the hurricane of 1938 destroyed the tower, and the hotel eventually burned. The old foundation is well hidden but still visible if you explore the summit.

The concrete pad on the summit overlook is not, as many think, the foundation of the old hotel but rather the foundation of a house a young man attempted to build on the summit before he died overseas in a car crash. The state of Vermont eventually acquired the summit land in 1988.

Return using the same route, taking care to bear left off the carriage road 0.9 mile down from the summit.

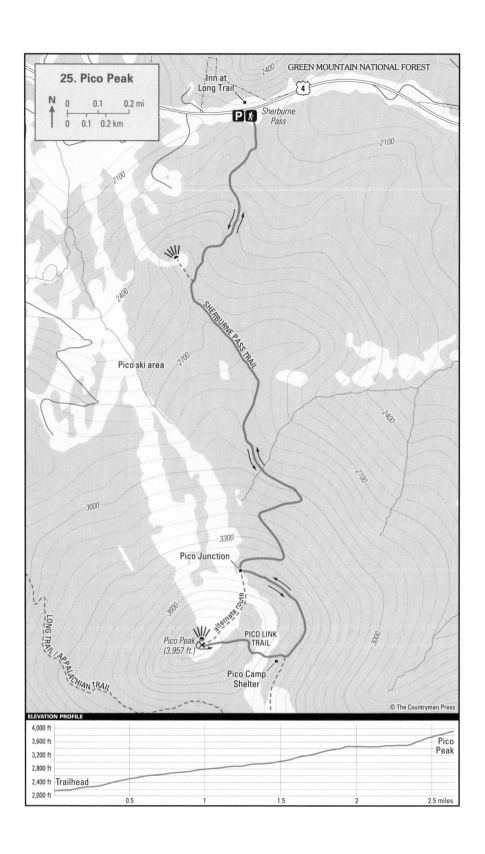

25. Pico Peak

N
0   0.1   0.2 mi
0   0.1   0.2 km

GREEN MOUNTAIN NATIONAL FOREST

Inn at
Long Trail

2400

4

Sherburne
Pass

2100

2100

Pico ski area

SHERBURNE PASS TRAIL

2700

2400

2700

3000

3300

Pico Junction

alternate route

PICO LINK
TRAIL

3600

Pico Peak
(3,957 ft.)

LONG TRAIL / APPALACHIAN TRAIL

3000

Pico Camp
Shelter

© The Countryman Press

ELEVATION PROFILE

4,000 ft
3,600 ft
3,200 ft
2,800 ft
2,400 ft
2,000 ft

Pico
Peak

Trailhead

0.5   1   1.5   2   2.5 miles

25

Pico Peak

Total distance: 5.8 miles (9.3 km)
Hiking time: 4 hours
Vertical rise: 1,800 feet (549 meters)
Rating: Moderate
Map: USGS 7.5' Pico Peak
Trailhead GPS Coordinates: N43° 39.81', W72° 49.96'

Pico Peak is a popular hike because of the fairly short, albeit sometimes steep and eroded trail that leads to an open summit with excellent views. The trail's proximity to a major road, however, means you may have plenty of company on your hike. The trail from Sherburne Pass to Pico Camp was the route of the Long Trail (LT) from 1913 until 1999, when it was moved west to avoid possible ski area expansion. It even predates the LT, showing up on an 1893 map. It was used to reach the fire watchman's tower atop Pico Peak until that was moved to Killington Peak around 1965. Wooden posts for long-gone glass insulators that once held the watchman's telephone line can still be seen on at least four trees 1.0 to 1.4 miles south of Sherburne Pass.

The Inn at Long Trail, located directly across the road from where your hike begins, is an expansion of the annex of the original Long Trail Lodge, the former headquarters of the Green Mountain Club (GMC), which was built in the early 1920s with a gift from the Proctor family. Standing on the south side of Sherburne Pass, the lodge was an intriguing structure—with a rock ledge wall, a huge stone fireplace, and the LT passing through the building. At one point in the late 1930s, skiers could actually ski from the annex across the road directly to the Pico Peak ski tow. Although the GMC survived the Great Depression in fairly good financial shape, restoring the trails and shelters after World War II was not so easy. In 1954, the club needed additional funds and decided to sell the lodge. Unfortunately,

Pico Peak from Killington Peak

the lodge was destroyed by fire in 1968.

In 1992, almost 40 years after the lodge was sold, the GMC established permanent headquarters on VT 100 in Waterbury Center. Once again, Vermonters, visitors, club members, and volunteers have a comfortable and central place to gather for hiking and outdoor recreation information and events. The GMC also opened the Marvin B. Gameroff Hiker Center, which annually responds to thousands of requests from around the country.

HOW TO GET THERE
Take US 4 to the top of Sherburne Pass (9.1 miles east of US 7 in Rutland; 1.4 miles west of the VT 100 northern junction with US 4). On the south side of the road, opposite the Inn at Long Trail, you will find ample parking.

THE TRAIL
Take the blue-blazed trail directly behind the parking lot. Walk south on an old road to Pico Pond (0.1 mile) until you reach a registration box where the Sherburne Pass Trail bears right and begins to ascend. You will soon reach a Killington Section sign from around 1966 that states that this section of the LT is "dumpless." This sign was erected because hikers used to bury their trash at a dump near each shelter. The sign now serves as a reminder of the GMC policy

of "pack it in, pack it out" that the Killington Section pioneered.

On a moderate grade, you ascend onto a ridge, and at 0.6 mile reach a spur leading right 0.1 mile to a view of Pico Ski Area from a 2,638-foot peak with a chairlift. The noise you may hear is the alpine slide, which operates during the summer. Bear left, and continue on easy grades. Enjoy occasional, although limited, views of Pico ahead from an almost level section of trail. In spring, before the trees leaf out, this is a lovely area full of wildflowers. At 1.1 miles, the trail passes a 7-foot-deep sinkhole and then a 15-foot-deep sinkhole. A permanent stream disappears into the latter. Both are part of a small cave that is not safe for amateur exploration.

The trail climbs gently in mixed hardwoods and evergreens and crosses several brooklets. The trail then takes a steeper grade and traverses the slope on three switchbacks until it reaches the Summit Glades ski trail at 2.1 miles. Turn left, and follow the ski trail uphill for about 50 yards, then turn left again and reenter the woods. From this point, known as Pico Junction, there are outstanding views north to Deer Leap, the Chittenden Reservoir, and (on a clear day) the Green Mountains as far north as Mount Mansfield. Make a special note of the junction location, because you may choose to return to this junction via the ski trail.

After reentering the woods, the trail is much rockier although fairly level. Watch your footing in this section. At 2.5 miles, pass a spring and reach Pico Camp. The Long Trail Patrol built this frame cabin, with bunk space for 12, for the Killington Section

in 1959. The camp is a snug place to take a break before continuing to the summit of Pico. There is a view to the east and southeast.

Continue your hike behind Pico Camp following the blue-blazed Pico Link. This trail is very steep, but quite short—only 0.4 mile to the summit. After crossing a wide swath cleared for an underground pipeline (2.6 miles), you climb more moderately through stunted evergreens to a service road. Bear left for about 25 feet, reenter the woods, and emerge in 100 feet on the 49er ski trail. Continue on the blue-blazed trail to the left of the top of a ski lift, cross the porch of a warming hut, and reach the 3,957-foot summit of Pico at 2.9 miles.

The summit offers two extensive viewing points. From the ski trails to the north you can see US 4, Deer Leap Mountain, and Kent Pond to the right; to the left of Deer Leap are the Chittenden Reservoir and part of the Green Mountain range. Watch Deer Leap carefully—you may spot some rock climbers. Near the radio towers (please heed the KEEP OUT signs; the towers operate under very high voltage) is a southern view of Killington Peak, Little Killington, Mendon Peak, and Parker's Gore.

After enjoying the views, you have two return options to Pico Junction. You could return via the route you followed up or, to create a small loop, descend along the 49er ski trail and then (at 0.2 mile north of the peak) bear right onto the Summit Glades ski trail. Descend steeply via this ski trail to Pico Junction at 3.3 miles. From Pico Junction, return via the Sherburne Pass Trail to the parking lot at 5.8 miles.

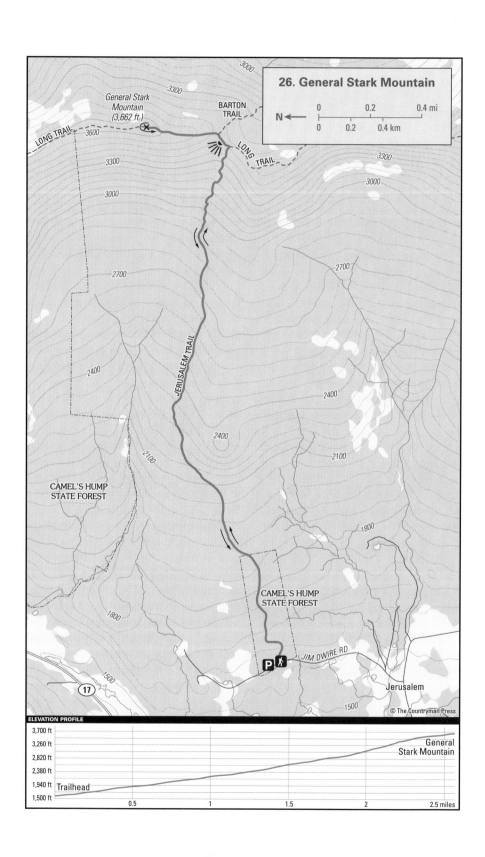

26. General Stark Mountain

N ←

| 0 | 0.2 | 0.4 mi |
| 0 | 0.2 | 0.4 km |

General Stark Mountain
(3,662 ft.)

BARTON TRAIL

LONG TRAIL

LONG TRAIL

JERUSALEM TRAIL

CAMEL'S HUMP
STATE FOREST

CAMEL'S HUMP
STATE FOREST

3000

3300

3600

3300

3000

2700

2400

2100

1800

1500

2700

3300

3000

2400

2100

1800

1500

2400

JIM DWIRE RD

Jerusalem

17

© The Countryman Press

ELEVATION PROFILE

3,700 ft				General
3,260 ft				Stark Mountain
2,820 ft				
2,380 ft				
1,940 ft	Trailhead			
1,500 ft				
	0.5	1	1.5	2	2.5 miles

26

General Stark Mountain

Total distance: 5.8 miles (9.3 km)
Hiking time: 4 hours
Vertical rise: 2,034 feet (620 meters)
Rating: Moderately strenuous
Map: USGS 7.5' Mount Ellen
Trailhead GPS Coordinates: N44° 10.6', W72° 58.1'

This trail is generally moderate in grade and traverses through a working sugarbush and forest management areas using a variety of old remnant logging roads, newer logging roads, and footpaths. Please respect the private landowner's generosity by staying on the marked trail! The trail is blazed in blue but caution is advised, as there are many crisscrossing logging roads and even some old trails here and there. Keep an eye out for blazes and turns and you should be fine. The trail is a mix of gentle and moderate grades with some short, steep sections to keep things interesting.

HOW TO GET THERE

Take the east branch of Jerusalem Road south from VT 17, 6.0 miles west of the Long Trail at Appalachian Gap and 3.5 miles east of VT 116. Follow this road 1.2 miles south and turn left onto Jim Dwire Road and follow it 0.5 mile to the trailhead on the right. Roadside parking space is limited to a widening of the road on the trailhead (right) side; please park considerately, on the trailhead side of the road.

THE TRAIL

Starting at Jim Dwire Road (elevation 1,628 feet) the Jerusalem Trail has an easy grade and quickly comes (125 feet) to a small brook crossing. Continue on this gentle terrain through mixed hardwoods with some conifer in the understory. The trail follows a remnant logging road on state land for about 0.5 mile or so before entering private property at the intersection with another old logging road

Out for an adventure on General Stark Mountain

Mad River Glen's single chair

(marked with orange boundary paint). You are now stepping immediately into a beautiful, working maple-sugaring operation! There are numerous lines, infrastructure, roads, and colored tubing in the surrounding forest. In winter and through the sugaring season, some lines may be attached across the trail; be careful not to disturb the equipment. The terrain is also punctuated by recent logging activity (selective thinning) with small open areas.

Continue following the blazes on moderate grades with occasional short, steep sections with the sap lines on both sides of the trail, eventually coming to a wider, more obvious work road. Follow this road through a beautiful open sugarbush with a fern-carpeted forest floor to an intersection. Turn right at the intersection, and soon you will come to a smaller path and the sugaring operation ends. The path again joins an old logging road briefly. Continue through some recently logged areas with moderate grade.

After the logging operation ends the grade picks up a bit in places and the path generally narrows and continues into the surrounding mixed hardwood forest. In this section the trail is lined by the common hobblebush (*Viburnum alnifolium*). Proceed through the hobblebush grove and watch for a sharp bend to the left following the less frequent blazes.

Soon the trail enters a beautiful white birch glade where it gets steeper for a short stretch and then backs off again to a moderate grade. All the while, the trail is tending left along the mountain. A flat spot is soon reached with a trail entering from the right. Bear left and continue on. Notice the beginning of the transition into the spruce and fir forest. After a brief level traverse a very small seasonal brook is crossed. Another short steeper pitch and another small seasonal brook follow. Here, notice the sound of a larger brook flowing somewhere off to the left. The forest is punctuated by some small openings and peeks out to the ridge above.

The woods transition to the higher alpine spruce-fir-dominated forest. Mossy rocks and herbaceous plants such as wood sorrel, starflower, and gold thread appear as the trail becomes steeper. Look for a large boulder on the immediate left of the trail. This signals the ridge and Long Trail (LT) are near! Ahead is the last and steepest pitch of the hike. The trail becomes rougher and rocky, but the pitch is short and quickly climbs the ridge to intersect the LT, which also marks the end of the 2.4-mile Jerusalem Trail.

Join the white-blazed LT and go left (north) along the ridge to continue to the summit of General Stark Mountain (0.4 mile). Within about 200 feet, a small unsigned spur leads off to the left to the Orvis Lookout. This small ledge affords pleasant views of the valley, Lake Champlain, and the Adirondacks in New York. Continuing north along the LT the grade is moderate and soon reaches the Barton Trail, which descends to the right down to the Green Mountain Club's Glen Ellen Lodge. Stay on the LT and begin a short, steep climb before the trail levels off again. This is a lovely, relaxing section rewarding the hiker with occasional views to the west (Champlain Valley) and east over the Mad River Valley. Eventually the nondescript summit of General Stark is gained. This is a forested summit but there is a small opening just north of the high point with views of the Mad River Valley and Camel's Hump, with the Worcester Range off to the right. Backtrack along the same route to return to your car.

Sun ray on Mount Roosevelt

Central Vermont

27

Mount Roosevelt

Total distance: 6.8 miles (10.9 km)
Hiking time: 4½ hours
Vertical rise: 2,100 feet (640 meters)
Rating: Moderate
Maps: USGS 7.5' Bread Loaf; 7.5' Lincoln
Trailhead GPS Coordinates: N43° 59.69', W72° 52.69'

Mount Roosevelt is a healthy hike up the verdant Clark Brook Trail. Although neither easy nor difficult, this hike offers a steady climb for the hiker keen to access one of the fine summits in the Breadloaf Wilderness. Roosevelt's peak is accessed via a short journey along the Long Trail (LT) at the summit of the Clark Brook Trail. The flat rocky summit has a largely undeveloped wilderness view to the north, and views as far as Killington Peak to the south.

VT 100 in Granville provides access to the eastern base of the wilderness, with a short ride into the national forest via Forest Road 55 (FR 55). The trailhead, off FR 55, is just south of the scenic Granville Gulf State Reservation. There are two exquisite waterfalls in the protected gulf and an ancient hemlock stand. Roadside stops along VT 100 can easily be fit into the itinerary for a day trip that includes the hike.

HOW TO GET THERE

From VT 100 in Granville, turn west onto West Hill Road, FR 55, marked with a wooden sign at the very north end of the settled area of Granville. From the north, it is the first right turn after emerging from the protected Granville Gulf. From the south, it is the last left turn before entering into the Granville Gulf.

Continue straight, and bear left onto a dirt road, which will be well-marked as FR 55. Continue for 1.7 miles, past three right turns, straight into a small dirt parking area—or continue driving left across a bridge for a short distance up the road to a second parking area past several hunters' cabins. The trail is well-marked on the right side, just past the cabins.

THE TRAIL

After a short walk along flat terrain past several informal campsites along Clark Brook, you will enter into the Breadloaf Wilderness. Register here.

For the first 1 mile, the trail meanders through the glades along the brook. Cross the brook twice, first at the site of a bridge washed away by Tropical Storm Irene in 2011 and then on a U.S. Forest Service bridge. The bridge offers fine views up and down the deeply forested valley where glacial pools are sculpted out of rock. (Although there are plans to replace the bridge that was washed away, the crossing is relatively easy except after a heavy rain.)

After the second bridge, the trail ascends away from Clark Brook and begins

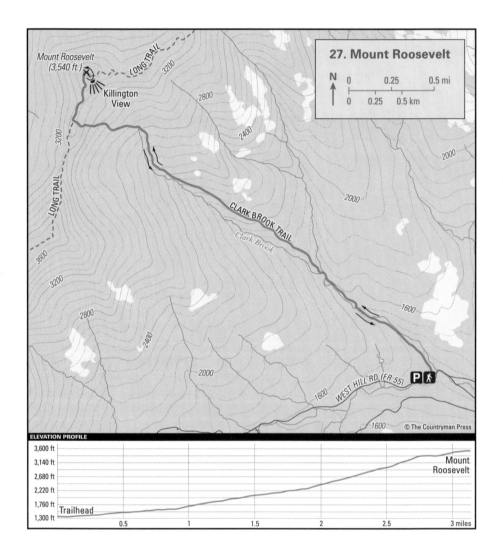

View from LT just north of Mount Roosevelt

the 2-mile climb to the LT. In the first mile of the climb, there are transitions of vegetation from the heavily shaded forest glade to the brighter fern and birch zones, where shamrocklike wood sorrel (oxalis) and other ground flowers can carpet the ground at the right time of year.

The second mile of the ascent is characterized by small, rocky creek bed crossings and a trail that narrows and steepens. Shortly before reaching the LT, well-built wooden steps help hikers reach the top.

The LT is a major intersection at the end of Clark Brook Trail. A sign at this intersection indicates the LT routes north and south and the Clark Brook Trail back to Granville.

Turn right (north) and follow the ridge that features low scrubby vegetation and stunted spruce and fir with bunchberries, typical of the northern peaks of Vermont. The ridge will feel notably cooler and the footpath appears obviously well worn. You are more likely to encounter backpackers and other overnight LT hikers here. It is always interesting to ask where they are heading and where they have hiked from.

After 0.4 mile, you reach the summit of Mount Roosevelt and, just beyond, the rocky outcrop known as Killington View. It is the first full view of the surrounding Green Mountains as you head north from the Clark Brook Trail intersection. The flat rocks provide a nice perch. The mountains are free of any development, and the view is of an undeveloped landscape of the northern mountains and forests of Vermont.

Return via the same route. As you descend the Clark Brook Trail, you can take more time to appreciate the ferns and silver birch and deep glades along the brook. The trail has given day hikers a solid 2 miles of healthy climbing, so on your return, be sure to relax and enjoy your hike.

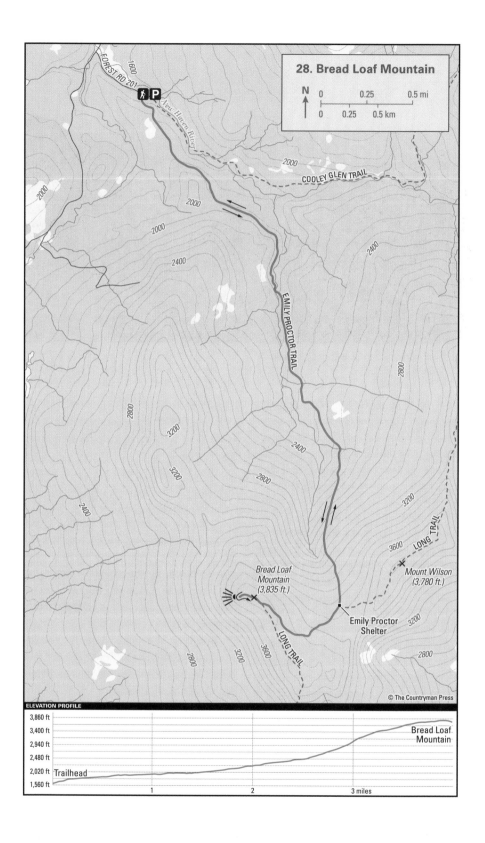

28. Bread Loaf Mountain

N

0   0.25   0.5 mi

0   0.25   0.5 km

FOREST RD 201

1600

New Haven River

COOLEY GLEN TRAIL

2000

2000

2000

2000

2400

2400

2800

2800

3200

3200

2400

2800

2400

EMILY PROCTOR TRAIL

2800

3200

3600

LONG TRAIL

Mount Wilson
(3,780 ft.)

Bread Loaf
Mountain
(3,835 ft.)

Emily Proctor
Shelter

3200

2800

2800

3200

3600

LONG TRAIL

© The Countryman Press

ELEVATION PROFILE

3,860 ft	
3,400 ft	Bread Loaf Mountain
2,940 ft	
2,480 ft	
2,020 ft	Trailhead
1,560 ft	

1   2   3 miles

28

Bread Loaf Mountain

Total distance: 8.6 miles (13.8 km)
Hiking time: 5½ hours
Vertical rise: 2,235 feet (681 meters)
Rating: Strenuous
Maps: USGS 7.5' Lincoln; 7.5' Bread Loaf
Trailhead GPS Coordinates: N44° 2.44', W72° 57.19'

Bread Loaf Mountain, so called because its long ridgeline profile resembles a loaf of bread, marks the halfway point along the 272-mile Long Trail (LT). An overlook near the wooded summit offers panoramic views to the west.

HOW TO GET THERE

From the center of Bristol, follow VT 17 east 1.6 miles to Lincoln Road. Follow Lincoln Road east 4.6 miles (it becomes West River Road and then East River Road) and turn right on South Lincoln Road (Forest Road 54 [FR 54]) and drive 4.1 miles to FR 201 on the left. Follow the road 0.4 mile to a primitive campsite and trailhead parking.

See the alternate route from VT 125 listed under the Mount Grant hike (see hike 29).

THE TRAIL

At the trailhead, note the Cooley Glen Trail, which continues along the gravel road. Take the Emily Proctor Trail on your right, which begins with a steep climb along an old road. At the top of the hill at 0.2 mile, you begin to notice an open area on your right. The trail bears to the left. A logging road enters on your right, and you soon reach a hiker registration box. The trail then follows a wide woods road and enters the Breadloaf Wilderness at 0.5 mile. Limiting the use of signs and trail blazes preserves the wild aspects of the Breadloaf Wilderness. Motor vehicles and chainsaws are prohibited. Continue along the trail on easy grades with occasional views of the ridge on your left

Emily Proctor shelter

across the valley. This is a good section to stretch your legs for the climb ahead, which is rocky—so watch your footing.

At 1.0 mile you reach a brook that is a branch of the New Haven River. The Long Trail Patrol rebuilt this section of trail in 2001, eliminating two brook crossings. At 1.3 miles, the trail crosses the brook. Be prepared to ford rather than rock hop if there has been a lot of rain in previous 24 hours. The quiet pools here provide a welcome respite on a hot day. At 2.0 miles, the trail begins to ascend. Look for views of Bread Loaf Mountain on your right. As the ascent gets steeper, you cross several small brooks, and at 3.2 miles, the character of the woods changes from birch to spruce and fir. During the steep ascent, occasional level spots offer you a chance to rest and enjoy views of the valley below. The steepness and rockiness of this section of the trail make hiking poles a welcome addition.

At 3.5 miles, you emerge from the woods at Emily Proctor Shelter and the LT, ready for a well-deserved rest. From the shelter there are excellent views of Mount Grant and Mount Abraham to the north. Named for an avid hiker and supporter of the Green Mountain Club (GMC) during the early 1900s, the shelter is a log structure built in 1960 by the Long Trail Patrol. The Youth Conservation Corps replaced the roof and foundation in 1983. The shelter was repaired again by the Long Trail Patrol in 2002. The Long Trail Patrol was founded in 1929 when the GMC decided it needed a summer patrol to help with trail maintenance. The patrol, which still exists today, helps maintain and blaze the trail and report on the condition of the trail.

Beyond the shelter, follow the white-blazed LT south across a brook and then along a gentle uphill. You will find this section of trail much easier than your climb up to the shelter. Wood sorrel (oxalis) covers the forest floor during summer months. Extensive trail work, including rock water bars and ditches to control erosion, has been done along the trail up the ridgeline of Bread Loaf Mountain. At 4.2 miles, the trail appears to double back on itself as you reach the now-unmarked halfway point of the 272-mile LT, a point very symbolic to end-to-end hikers. Take the blue-blazed trail that leads to your right. The wooded, unmarked 3,835-foot summit is a few yards along this spur trail. Continue to follow the blue blazes to the overlook at 4.3 miles.

This western overlook provides views of Lake Champlain and the Adirondacks beyond. The yellow buildings to the southwest are the Bread Loaf campus of Middlebury College, home to the Bread Loaf Writers' Conference. The Breadloaf Wilderness consists of land originally donated by early 1900s conservationist Joseph Battell. To the south lies the Middlebury Snow Bowl Ski Area and in the distance Killington Peak.

After you have rested and enjoyed the views, hike back down the same trails to your car, taking care to turn left on the white-blazed LT at the end of the blue-blazed spur trail.

Mount Grant

29

Mount Grant

Total distance: 8.0 miles (12.9 km)
Hiking time: 5½ hours
Vertical rise: 1,960 feet (597 meters)
Rating: Strenuous
Map: USGS 7.5' Lincoln
Trailhead GPS Coordinates: N44° 2.44', W72° 57.19'

The scenic Cooley Glen Trail up Mount Grant follows old logging roads along the New Haven River. The logging roads are dry and follow gradual grades, except for very steep sections near the top of the trail. Several swimming holes in the river provide the opportunity for a refreshing summer splash after (or maybe even before) your hike. Hikers will notice that the New Haven River is cutting deep into its banks in certain locations, requiring some trail relocations or adjustments. The bridge carrying Forest Road 54 (FR 54) over the river, just below the trailhead, was replaced in 2002.

HOW TO GET THERE

From the center of Bristol, follow VT 17 east 1.6 miles to Lincoln Road. Follow Lincoln Road east 4.6 miles (it becomes West River Road and then East River Road) and turn right on South Lincoln Road (FR 54) and drive 4.1 miles to FR 201 on the left. Follow FR 201 for 0.4 mile to a primitive campsite and trailhead parking.

Alternatively, from VT 125, 3 miles east of Ripton, follow gravel FR 59 (Steam Mill Road) north for 3.9 miles (passing the parking area for the Skylight Pond Trail at 3.8 miles). Turn right onto FR 54, and at 4.2 miles turn right again at a second junction. From here, keep to the right, and drive along the rough dirt road, passing an occasional residence. At the bottom of a moderately steep decline (8.0 miles) and just before the bridge over the New Haven River, turn right onto FR 201. Follow FR 201 for 0.4 mile to a primitive campsite and trailhead parking.

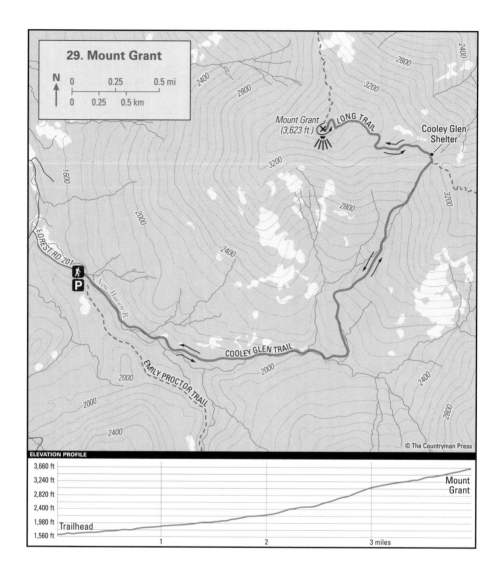

29. Mount Grant

N

| 0 | 0.25 | 0.5 mi |
| 0 | 0.25 | 0.5 km |

Mount Grant
(3,623 ft.)

LONG TRAIL

Cooley Glen
Shelter

FOREST RD 201

New Haven R.

COOLEY GLEN TRAIL

EMILY PROCTOR TRAIL

© The Countryman Press

ELEVATION PROFILE

3,660 ft
3,240 ft
2,820 ft
2,400 ft
1,980 ft — Trailhead
1,560 ft

Mount
Grant

1   2   3 miles

THE TRAIL

At the trailhead sign, note the Emily Proctor Trail, which turns right. Instead, take the blue-blazed Cooley Glen Trail that begins to follow an old lane along the New Haven River, but soon climbs above it to avoid serious river erosion below. Cross the river on a bridge at 0.3 mile (a trail register is here) and reach a clearing, once an old log landing.

The trail leaves the far end of the clearing and follows the river on almost level grades over a wide, overgrown old logging road. At 1.0 mile, you cross several deep water bars and tributaries as you move away from, and then return to, the river. No blazes are visible along this portion of the trail, except for occasional blue-blazed rocks in the grassy road.

At 1.5 miles, the road becomes quite wet and rocky. Enter the woods to avoid this wet area, and then return to cross a tributary. (There was once a bridge here, but this is revealed only to those who look closely at the opposite banks.) This point marks the entrance to the Breadloaf Wilderness, which was named for 3,835-foot Bread Loaf Mountain. Established in 1984, the 25,237-acre wilderness includes 17 miles of the Long Trail (LT), 11 major peaks (all more than 3,000 feet in elevation), and Vermont's Presidential Range (Mount Wilson, Mount Roosevelt, Mount Cleveland, and Mount Grant).

The trail now moves away from the river, ascends slightly, and swings left, still following an old road. Occasional blue blazes can be seen on the trees. At 1.9 miles, climb until you pass through a scenic, more mature forest. At 2.5 miles, the trail levels after a short ascent and you can see Mount Grant through the trees on your left. The trail ascends steeply along a gully, passes through a rocky stinging nettle patch (wearers of shorts may experience a temporary itching), then crosses the small brook you could hear during your climb up the gully. Now a steeper section of trail begins. You'll cross a small brook, pass a spur, and then reach the signed junction of the LT at 3.2 miles.

Turn left, and follow the LT north 50 feet to the Cooley Glen Shelter. The shelter, built by the U.S. Forest Service in 1965, is a frame lean-to with bunk space for six to eight hikers. Take time for a well-deserved rest.

Pass the shelter and continue north on the LT (the path just to the right of the LT is to the privy—recently rated five stars by a thru-hiker from Alaska!). The hike to Mount Grant's summit is comparable to the grade you just climbed. Look for southern views before the trail swings right and you continue your ascent. By 3.8 miles, the mixed forest turns to predominantly spruce. The trees become more stunted as you hike along switchbacks to the southern overlook. The 3,623-foot wooded summit of Mount Grant is reached at 4.0 miles. From the southern overlook, a small patch of open rock, you can see the New Haven River basin, Mount Cleveland, Mount Roosevelt, Mount Wilson, and Bread Loaf Mountain.

Follow the same trails back to your car at the parking area.

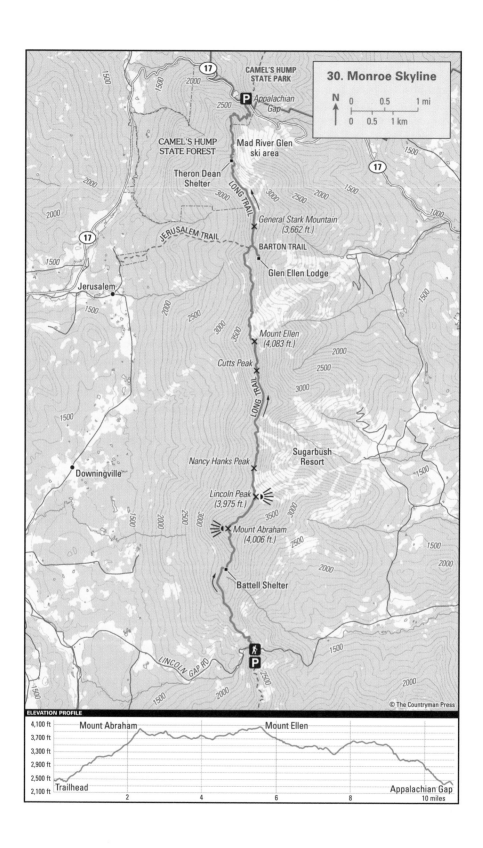

17

CAMEL'S HUMP STATE PARK

P *Appalachian Gap*

30. Monroe Skyline

N
0   0.5   1 mi
0   0.5   1 km

Mad River Glen ski area

17

CAMEL'S HUMP STATE FOREST

Theron Dean Shelter

LONG TRAIL

General Stark Mountain (3,662 ft.)

17

JERUSALEM TRAIL

BARTON TRAIL

Glen Ellen Lodge

Jerusalem

Mount Ellen (4,083 ft.)

Cutts Peak

LONG TRAIL

Downingville

Nancy Hanks Peak

Sugarbush Resort

Lincoln Peak (3,975 ft.)

Mount Abraham (4,006 ft.)

Battell Shelter

LINCOLN GAP RD.

P

© The Countryman Press

ELEVATION PROFILE

4,100 ft   Mount Abraham   Mount Ellen
3,700 ft
3,300 ft
2,900 ft
2,500 ft
2,100 ft   Trailhead   Appalachian Gap
                  2   4   6   8
                                         10 miles

30

Monroe Skyline

Total distance: 12.2 miles (19.6 km)
Hiking time: 1½ days, 1 night
Vertical rise: 2,535 feet (773 meters)
Rating: Moderate
Maps: USGS 7.5' Mount Ellen; 7.5' Lincoln
Trailhead GPS Coordinates: N44° 5.69', W72° 55.7'

The Long Trail (LT) between Lincoln Gap and Appalachian Gap (VT 17) is one of the most scenic ridge walks in Vermont. Named after professor Will S. Monroe, who was instrumental in locating this section of trail, the LT from Lincoln Gap north to the Winooski River is known as the Monroe Skyline.

Your first day is a short 1.8 miles. This gives you time to arrange equipment and place cars at both ends of the hike. You should allow two and a half hours to reach the Battell Shelter before dark. If you get there in the early afternoon, the 0.8 mile hike up to the summit of Mount Abraham to watch the sun set is definitely worthwhile.

Start early the second day. Right out of camp, you begin with a short but steep climb to the summit of Mount Abraham. After that, you spend the day hiking "high in the sky" along the relatively flat ridgeline. From several vantage points along the way, you can enjoy spectacular views of Vermont's Green Mountains, New York's Adirondack Mountains, and New Hampshire's White Mountains. After crossing Mount Abraham, Lincoln Peak, Nancy Hanks Peak, Cutts Peak, Mount Ellen, and (finally) General Stark Mountain, you finish your journey where VT 17 runs through Appalachian Gap.

HOW TO GET THERE

Park a car at the top of Appalachian Gap. This is the height-of-land on VT 17 that is 6.3 miles west of the junction of VT 100 in Waitsfield and 9.6 miles east of the junction of VT 116 just east of Bristol. This is the car that will be waiting for you at the end of your hike.

To get to the beginning of the hike, take VT 17 east into Waitsfield, where it intersects with VT 100. Follow VT 100 south to Lincoln Gap Road just outside Warren. Turn west onto Lincoln Gap Road. At 1.6 miles afterward, the road turns to gravel. At 2.8 miles, it turns back to pavement and ascends steeply to the top of Lincoln Gap at 4.3 miles.

THE TRAIL

Day One

Total distance: 1.8 miles (2.9 km)
Hiking time: 2 hours
Vertical rise: 840 feet (256 meters)

Take the white-blazed LT north from Lincoln Gap. Make sure to sign in at the Green Mountain National Forest registration box. Except for a short side trip to Glen Ellen Lodge on the second day, this hike stays on the LT, which is reliably blazed white. Keeping this in mind will help keep you off side trails, which are blazed blue, and ski trails, which are not blazed.

The trail from Lincoln Gap to Battell Shelter is quite steep in places as you ascend a series of plateaus. The trail starts in mixed hardwoods but quickly enters the boreal forest, characterized by a mix of red spruce and balsam fir that give the woods a pleasant fragrance. You should also keep your ears open for the numerous songbirds that make their home at high elevations. Prominent among these are the ever-present white-throated sparrow, tiny winter wrens, juncos, and blackpoll warblers.

At 1.7 miles you reach the Battell Trail junction. Joseph Battell, land conservator and former proprietor of the Bread Loaf Inn, cut a trail to Mount Ellen in 1901. This was possibly the first skyline trail in the Green Mountains.

Turn right at the Battell Trail junction and ascend on the LT to Battell Shelter, where you will spend the night. The shelter was constructed in 1967 by volunteers from Farm and Wilderness Foundation (a local summer camp) and is maintained by the U.S. Forest Service and the Green Mountain Club (GMC). The shelter has space for six to eight hikers.

From Memorial Day to Columbus Day, the GMC stations a caretaker at Battell Shelter. The caretaker is there to educate the public about the fragile alpine vegetation on the summit of Mount Abraham. He or she is also there to educate the public about low-impact camping techniques, protect water sources along the trail, maintain trails and backcountry campsites, and compost sewage to protect water quality. During the caretaker season, there is a six-dollar-per-person fee to stay at Battell Shelter. The GMC encourages all hikers, especially overnight visitors, to learn how they can minimize the impact that we have on the mountain environment. Please call the GMC Marvin B. Gameroff Hiker Center (802-244-7037) if you would like more information before beginning your trip.

Day Two

Total distance: 10.4 miles (16.7 km)
Hiking time: 7 hours
Vertical rise: 1,695 feet (517 meters)

Your second day begins with the ascent up Mount Abraham. This is a challenging 0.8 mile of climbing. Make sure you start at an easy pace so you have enough energy to enjoy the long ridge beyond. After 0.6 mile of increasingly exposed climbing, the trail descends briefly to a signed clearing before making the final ascent above tree line.

The trees are waist high as you ascend to the 4,006-foot open rock summit and one of

Staying on the trail on Mount Abraham

the best panoramic views in Vermont. To the east are New Hampshire's White Mountains; to the west, the Bristol Cliffs, Lake Champlain, and New York's Adirondack Mountains; to the south, the ridge of the Green Mountains as far as Killington Peak; to the north, Mount Mansfield peeks out from the east flank of Mount Ellen. The summit supports a small, rare arctic-alpine plant community. Please avoid disturbing any of these

Friends taking in the view on the way down Mount Abraham

endangered plants or the surrounding soils. Walk only on the marked trail, and sit only on the bare rock.

Beyond the summit, enter the woods and continue along the ridge until you reach the summit of Little Abe and then the 3,975-foot summit of Lincoln Peak—with a viewing platform just east of the LT—at 1.6 miles.

After you have enjoyed the summit of Lincoln Peak, follow the left edge of the ski clearing. Approximately 50 yards after you enter the clearing, the trail reenters the woods through a small gap. Look for the sign and white blazes marking the trail. For the entire day, it is important to remember that all ski trails between Lincoln Gap and

Appalachian Gap go to the right (or east), whereas the LT is always the leftmost trail. The ridge between Lincoln Peak and General Stark Mountain is excellent moose habitat. You should look for their large prints in the muddy sections of the trail.

Continue your hike over the rocky trail on easy grades until you ascend Nancy Hanks Peak (named after a member of a prominent local family) at 2.2 miles. The trail then descends to the Castlerock chairlift. Bear left, and follow the ski trail 100 yards to Holt Hollow, where the trail enters the woods at 3.0 miles. A small spring is located 200 feet west of the trail along a short spur that starts where the LT leaves the ski slope.

Central Vermont

Ascend the ridgeline over rolling terrain to the summit of Cutts Peak at 4.1 miles. Shortly after Cutts Peak, climb to the wooded 4,083-foot summit of Mount Ellen. Just past the summit is a ski trail clearing with excellent views. The trail out of the ski area is small and frequently unsigned. The LT descends steeply to the left, just before a large board fence. Reenter the woods to the left, and descend the steep western face of the mountain until you reach the northern boundary of the Green Mountain National Forest at 4.9 miles.

At 6.3 miles, you reach the junction with the Jerusalem Trail, which leads 2.4 miles west to Jim Dwire Road in Jerusalem. Continue on the LT to the junction with the Barton Trail that leads 0.3 mile east to Glen Ellen Lodge. The lodge was built in 1933 by the GMC's Long Trail Patrol. The lodge has a reliable source of water, except during droughts, and is worth the side trip to fill water bottles, sit in the sunshine, or step inside on a rainy day to make some hot coffee or soup.

From Glen Ellen Lodge, return to the LT and begin your last major ascent up General Stark Mountain. After reaching the 3,662-foot summit, the LT continues along the ridge and follows a ski trail to the top of Mad River Glen's historic single chairlift at 7.9 miles. The trail passes Stark's Nest on the uphill side, briefly descends a ski trail, and then bears left into the woods. You briefly reenter the ski trail before returning to the woods. The trail between General Stark Mountain and VT 17 overlaps several small Mad River Glen ski trails. Remember that all ski trails descend to the east (right), whereas the LT bears left and maintains the ridge.

After a ladder that helps you over a particularly difficult spot, you will come to Theron Dean Shelter at 8.6 miles. Theron Dean was a close friend of Will Monroe and an active member of the GMC during the club's early years. The shelter is actually on a short spur to the left of the LT. The trail passes to the right of the shelter clearing. There is no water source at Theron Dean Shelter. After resting at the shelter, it is worthwhile to explore Dean Cave, a short underground passage that leads back to the main trail 150 feet from the upper junction.

After Theron Dean Shelter, you come to one last chairlift. The LT bears left into the woods across a perennially muddy patch and ascends a small rock face. Follow the trail on long switchbacks through a scenic birch forest. Then climb over one final knob before descending to VT 17 at Appalachian Gap at 10.4 miles and the end of your hike.

31

Hires and Sensory Trails

Total distance: 1.2-mile loop (1.9 km)
(total for the two hikes described)

Hiking time: ¾ hour

Vertical rise: 200 feet (61 meters)

Rating: Easy

Maps: USGS 7.5' Hinesburg; 7.5'
Huntington

Trailhead GPS Coordinates: N44°
20.81', W72° 59.8'

Both of these easy trails are located at the Green Mountain Audubon Center, a 250-acre nature center owned and operated by Audubon Vermont, a local chapter of the National Audubon Society. The grounds are open every day from dawn to dusk. The visitors center is usually open weekdays and weekend afternoons, depending on staff availability, and offers a summer Ecology Day Camp, seasonal programs, workshops, classes, and more. We recommend that you pick up a brochure and map of the trails at the visitors center. Donations to maintain the center are welcome, and you can also purchase a variety of books and other items.

The Hires Trail goes to a lookout with an exceptional view of both Mount Mansfield and Camel's Hump. The Sensory Trail is a hiking trail designed with interpretive stations to help hikers enjoy and experience the area through all five senses. In addition to these two trails, there are several other trails open for walking, which are shown on the map available at the nature center. Please remember to stay on the trails, and do not remove any natural objects from the area. Dogs are not allowed on the Hires and Sensory trails; dogs on a leash are permitted on some of the trails across the road from the visitors center.

Just 0.5 mile past the visitors center on Sherman Hollow Road is the Birds of Vermont Museum, which displays hundreds of woodcarvings of birds by founder Bob Spear, Jr., as well as paintings and photographs of birds and a bird-feeding station frequented by wild birds. The museum is

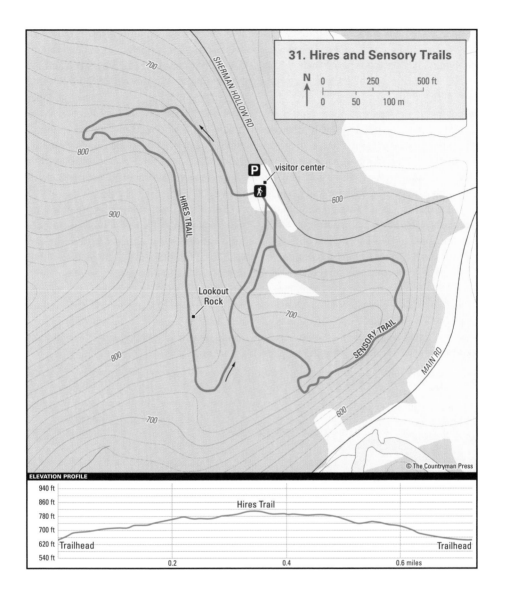

31. Hires and Sensory Trails

N 0   250   500 ft
   0   50   100 m

SHERMAN HOLLOW RD

visitor center

HIRES TRAIL

Lookout Rock

SENSORY TRAIL

MAIN RD

© The Countryman Press

ELEVATION PROFILE

940 ft
860 ft
780 ft   Hires Trail
700 ft
620 ft Trailhead   Trailhead
540 ft
        0.2   0.4   0.6 miles

open daily from May 1 to October 31 from 10 AM to 4 PM. Admission is seven dollars for adults.

HOW TO GET THERE

To reach the Green Mountain Audubon Center, take exit 11 off I-89, and take U.S. 2 east toward Richmond. At the traffic light, turn right (south) onto Bridge Street toward Huntington. At 0.3 mile, cross the Winooski River. The road bears right (now Huntington Road) and winds uphill before leveling again. Stay left (on the main road) through two junctions. At 5.1 miles, you reach a AUDUBON NATURE CENTER 300 sign and turn right onto Sherman Hollow Road. The center is the first building on the left. Parking for 8 to 10 cars is available, and a trail signboard shows the location of the numerous hiking trails.

THE TRAILS

Hires Trail: This trail was named for Christine Hires, who donated the land for the center. The trail starts to the right, behind the signboard in the parking lot. Hike up a short bank and bear right. Notice that you are hiking parallel to Sherman Hollow Road as you walk up the hillside through mixed forest on moderate grades. You soon bear left at the junction with the Brook Trail and climb through birch and then small softwoods.

Continue uphill to a spur trail on your right that leads to Lichen Rock, a large, moss-covered boulder. Return to the main trail and quickly reach a junction. Follow the unblazed main trail uphill along several rock outcrops through a hemlock forest. Pass the junction with the Bob Spear's Founder's Trail, and reach a rock shelf called Lookout Rock at 0.4 mile. Enjoy the nice views of Camel's Hump and a unique view of Mount Mansfield to your left. From the overlook, gradually descend through mixed forest until you are below the overlook. Begin a moderate descent to a junction with the Sensory Trail on your right. Leave the woods, enter an overgrown field, cross a mowed lawn, and reach the visitors center at 0.7 mile.

Sensory Trail: This unique 0.5-mile-loop trail begins on the porch of the visitors center, crosses fields, and winds through the woods. What makes the trail unique is that it is designed to help hikers experience the landscape with all five senses. This trail will help you more fully appreciate the sounds and smells around you. Any description would be woefully inadequate—this trail must be experienced!

Heading for the top of Jay Peak (hike 42)

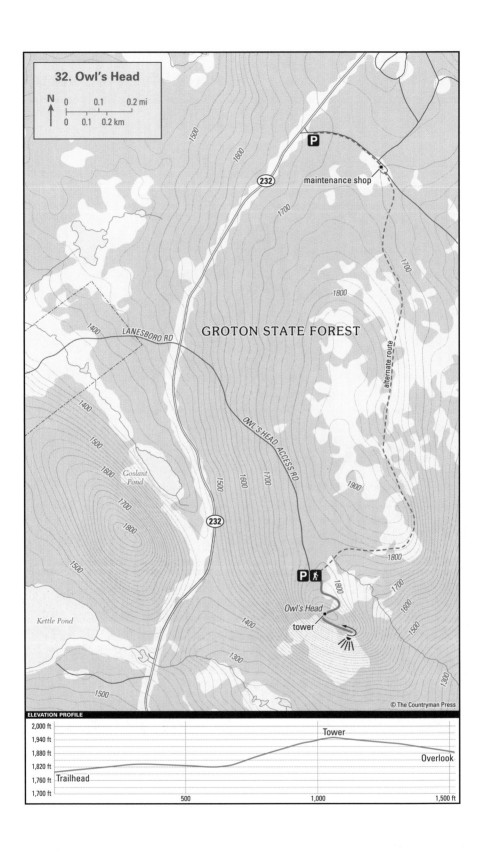

32. Owl's Head

N

| 0 | 0.1 | 0.2 mi |
| 0 | 0.1 | 0.2 km |

1500

1600

P

232

maintenance shop

1700

1700

1800

GROTON STATE FOREST

1400

LANESBORO RD

alternate route

1400

1500

1600

Goslant Pond

1700

OWL'S HEAD ACCESS RD

1500

1600

1700

1900

1800

232

1800

1700

1800

P 🚶

1600

Kettle Pond

Owl's Head tower

1500

1400

1300

1300

1500

© The Countryman Press

ELEVATION PROFILE

			Tower	
2,000 ft				
1,940 ft				
1,880 ft				Overlook
1,820 ft				
1,760 ft	Trailhead			
1,700 ft		500	1,000	1,500 ft

32

Owl's Head

Total distance: 0.5 mile (0.8 km)
Hiking time: ½ hour
Vertical rise: 160 feet (49 meters)
Rating: Easy
Map: USGS 7.5' Marshfield
Trailhead GPS Coordinates: N44° 17.9', W72° 17.69'

This relatively short hike takes you to the summit of Owl's Head in Groton State Forest. The Civilian Conservation Corps (CCC) constructed the summit's stone fire tower, trail, and picnic shelter at the trailhead in the 1930s. Because of its accessibility, this is an excellent outing for families with young children. There is even a small rock tunnel for kids to explore on the trail to the summit.

During the off-season, the 0.9-mile road to the picnic shelter is gated. The hike from VT 232 up the closed road makes a good snowshoe trip during winter and a firm-footed hike during spring's mud season.

Since acquiring the first tract of land in 1919, the state of Vermont now owns

Boulder cave on Owl's Head

approximately 26,000 acres in Groton State Forest. The Vermont Department of Forests, Parks, and Recreation manages the forest for summer and winter recreation, forestry, and as wildlife habitat.

HOW TO GET THERE

Drive east on US 2 from Marshfield to the junction of VT 232 at 1.0 mile. Turn right onto VT 232 and drive past the New Discovery State Park Campground entrance (5.4 miles). Continue beyond this entrance, pass the road to the park's maintenance shop on the left (5.9 miles), and reach a left turn marked by an OWL'S HEAD sign (6.6 miles) opposite signs for Lanesboro Road and Ethan Allen Corners (during off-season the OWL'S HEAD sign is down, and the road is blocked by a gate). Turn left and follow the gravel road to the parking lot and picnic pavilion (7.5 miles). From the south via US 302, the Owl's Head road is 8.0 miles north on VT 232.

THE TRAIL

Before or after your hike, take a moment to enjoy a view of Kettle Pond from the picnic shelter overlook, from a wide path that leaves the right side of the parking lot.

From the parking lot, enter the trail at a sign for the Owl's Head scenic view and begin a very gradual hike through mixed hardwoods up the first set of CCC-constructed steps. You soon reach another set of steps as the trail bears left and then right. Be sure to notice the extensive CCC rock work.

At 0.25 mile you reach the top of Owl's Head and the octagonal stone fire tower built by the CCC in 1935. A rock outcrop beyond the tower provides fine views to the south

Kettle Pond from Owl's Head

Stone hut on the summit of Owl's Head

and west. Visible to the west is Kettle Pond, framed by Hardwood Mountain to the left of the pond and Kettle Mountain to the right. In the far distance on a clear day is Camel's Hump. Looking further to the left you will see Spruce Mountain, with its fire tower sticking up from the trees at the summit. To the far left is Lake Groton. A better view of the lake is available by taking a short spur trail through the woods to another rock outcrop.

For those seeking more of a workout, there is a 3.0 mile round-trip hike to Owl's Head that begins at the entrance to the maintenance shop on VT 232. Park off to the side of the gravel road to the maintenance shop, being careful not to block either the road or the gate, which is closed on weekends and at 3:30 PM during the week. Walk around the gate and up the road, past the large brown automotive shop building on the right. Continue straight, passing the blacksmith shed on the right, and enter the woods. About 100 feet past the blacksmith shed, turn right at a sign for the Owl's Head Trail.

The blue-blazed trail is level for the first 0.2 mile, until it reaches an intersection with an old woods road, marked with a sign pointing to Lake Groton. Continue straight and begin a gradual climb. As you hike, you'll notice the trail is strewn with a number of rocks and boulders, left behind by the glacial action that formed all the lakes and ponds in the Groton State Forest more than 13,000 years ago.

At about 1.0 mile the trail dips down into a sag, crosses a set of puncheon, and then emerges at the Owl's Head parking area. Make note of the sign on your left reading NEW DISCOVERY 1.5 MI., as this is the entry point for the walk back to your vehicle. From the parking lot, follow the directions above to the summit and the view.

33

Prospect Rock (Johnson)

Total distance: 2.0 miles (3.2 km)
Hiking time: 1 hour
Vertical rise: 540 feet (165 meters)
Rating: Easy
Map: USGS 7.5' Johnson
Trailhead GPS Coordinates: N44° 39.13', W72° 43.73'

This short hike offers superb views, including Whiteface Mountain and the Lamoille River as it meanders through the valley below on its way to Lake Champlain.

Before or after your hike, be sure to check out the Green Mountain Club's 100-foot suspension bridge across the Lamoille, on the other side of the road from the trailhead.

HOW TO GET THERE

From Johnson, drive 1.5 miles west on VT 15 to the highway bridge over the Lamoille River. Just before the bridge, turn right onto Hog Back Road, and continue another 1.2 miles to a pullout on the right side of the

Lamoille River from Prospect Rock

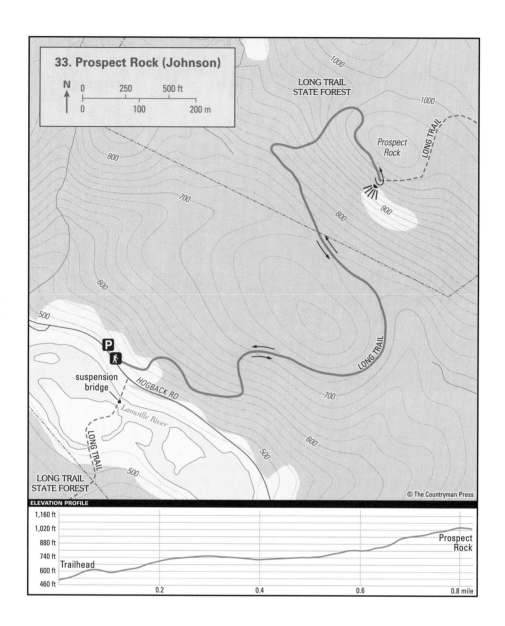

33. Prospect Rock (Johnson)

LONG TRAIL
STATE FOREST

Prospect Rock

LONG TRAIL

suspension
bridge

HOGBACK RD

Lamoille River

LONG TRAIL

LONG TRAIL
STATE FOREST

© The Countryman Press

ELEVATION PROFILE

1,160 ft
1,020 ft
880 ft
740 ft
600 ft
460 ft

Trailhead

Prospect
Rock

0.2   0.4   0.6   0.8 mile

road, just past the Ithiel Falls Camp. There is additional parking 200 feet ahead on the left.

THE TRAIL

Entering the woods at a hiker crossing highway sign, the white-blazed Long Trail (LT) climbs southeast through a hemlock stand on a bank high above the road and the Lamoille River. Sounds of cars and water begin to fade away as the trail levels off, reaches a group of white birch, and swings north.

Four large boulders line the trail, most likely having tumbled down long ago from the cliffs above. Just past the boulders, the

View of Whiteface Mountain from Prospect Rock

trail begins to climb more steeply. As the trail skirts the base of Prospect Rock, from this angle trees rooted in a thin layer of soil appear to be shooting up directly from the ledges.

The LT suddenly changes direction (as indicated by the double white blaze on a tree) and begins a short, steep climb up the back of the rock outcrop. The trail soon levels off and the Sterling Range becomes visible through the trees. Breaking out of the woods, the trail opens to a 180-degree view, with Whiteface Mountain ahead to the south, and the Lamoille River winding through the valley to the west. Return via the same route.

34

Mount Philo

Total distance: 2.0 miles (3.2 km)	
Hiking time: 1½ hours	
Vertical rise: 600 feet (198 meters)	
Rating: Moderate	
Map: USGS 7.5' Mount Philo	
Trailhead GPS Coordinates: N44° 16.67', W73° 13.33'	

Mount Philo State Park in Charlotte was Vermont's first state park, donated in 1924 by Mrs. Frances Humphreys of Brookline, Massachusetts. Mrs. Humphreys and her husband, James, were frequent summer guests at the Mount Philo Inn, located south of the state park entrance on Mount Philo Road, and they purchased 27 acres around Mount Philo in 1901, deeding it to Frank Lewis, owner of the inn. In the spring of 1903, workmen built the first carriage road to the summit, cleared paths, installed benches, and built a three-story observation tower on top. Lewis deeded the land back to Mrs. Humphreys in 1914 after her husband's death and she subsequently donated it to the state in 1924 for recreational use. The present entrance was built in 1929 and the road in 1930.

The Mohawk Indians called the mountain *Tyontkathotha,* or "lookout place." The Abenaki word for it was *Mataguesaden* or "rabbit place." Legend has it that the current Philo was the name of a locally famous hunter and Indian fighter who camped along its hillsides and used the mountain as a lookout for hostile marauders. Another theory has the mountain named during a burst of enthusiasm for classical names, hence *philo* from the Greek for friend or dear. Whatever the name, this small mountain has many big features: crumbly rock ledges, precarious drop-offs, and spectacular views.

In the 1930s, the Civilian Conservation Corps planted Scots pine, red pine, Norway spruce, and other nonnative tree species on the side of the mountain, which was denuded from years of livestock grazing. An ice storm in January 1998 devastated the trees and the park was closed that year while mechanical harvesting equipment cleared blowdowns and removed dangerously overhanging limbs. The road also was rebuilt. Although most of the trees suffered ice damage, the native species, such as sugar maple, fared better than the nonnative. It is a credit to the work crews that the storm damage and subsequent cleanup are practically unnoticeable.

In late April and early May, the hillsides and roadside are covered with white trillium, trout lily, bloodroot, bellwort, coltsfoot, rose-twisted stalk, white and purple violet, mullein, Dutchman's britches, and the ubiquitous dandelion. From the summit ledge, birders can observe the annual autumn migrations.

HOW TO GET THERE
State Park Road is located off US 7, 1.2 miles north of North Ferrisburgh or 2.5 miles south of the stoplight near Charlotte. Turn

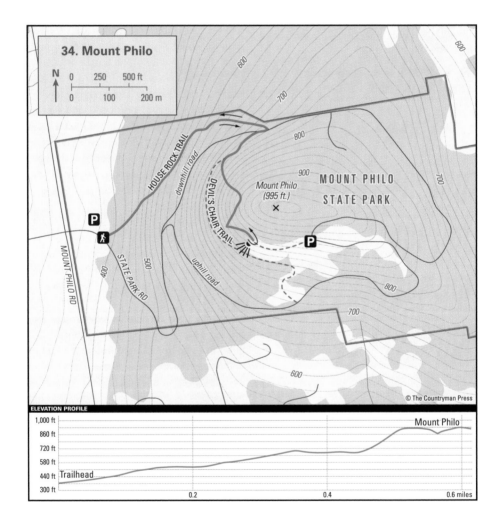

Lake Champlain with the Adirondacks beyond, from Mount Philo

east at the blinking yellow light onto State Park Road, and continue 0.5 mile to the park gate, immediately after crossing Mount Philo Road. Parking is in the large parking area at the base of the mountain. From Memorial Day through October, the state park charges a day-use fee. A brochure with a map is available at the entrance booth. Although the park is officially closed in winter, it sees as much or more use as a favorite destination for walkers and sledders. The paved summit road makes an excellent mud-season alternative when the trails at higher elevations are too soft for hiking.

THE TRAIL

The blue-blazed trail, cut in 1996 by the Vermont Youth Conservation Corps, begins just beyond the gate and a signboard with a map of the park. It climbs steeply for about 100 yards, then gently ascends to an overhanging boulder known as House Rock. Climbing moderately over recently improved tread way, the trail turns sharply right onto a switchback before crossing the "downhill" road at 0.4 mile. The trail follows the road downhill to the right a short distance before reentering the woods on the left. It climbs steeply for 50 yards to a junction with the trail to Devil's Chair, a challenging 0.5-mile walk along a narrow path through a rock maze and under overhanging ledges complete with caves. The Devil's Chair is a rock bench ideally suited for quiet contemplation of the forest or an afternoon with Emily Dickinson. This side trail then descends steeply to the "uphill" park road.

Beyond the junction with the Devil's Chair Trail, the main trail bears left, passing a marked trail to the campground, as it climbs steeply to the top of a ledge and the first of many west-facing lookouts. From here, the grade steepens, then moderates as the trail passes a spur to another viewpoint: an open rock on the right 20 feet from the trail. Below toward the Adirondacks, Thompson's Point juts into Lake Champlain—with Garden, Cedar, and tiny Picket islands just to its north. The trail turns sharply left and continues gently uphill a short distance to the summit (0.75 mile).

From the highest lookout point behind a metal railing, Split Rock Mountain can be seen across the lake in New York. To the southwest, Snake, Buck, and Shellhouse mountains undulate from right to left. Below and to the south, the rooftops of the former Mount Philo Inn are visible when the trees are leafless.

There are several options for the return route. From the top of the summit ledge, a path continues southwest to a gravel parking area where both the "downhill" and "uphill" roads lead back to the park entrance. A trail on the left descends to the campground and the "downhill" road.

35

Black Creek and Maquam Creek Trails

Total distance: 2.3 miles (3.7 km)

Hiking time: 1 1/4 hours

Vertical rise: Minimal

Rating: Easy

Map: USGS 7.5' East Alburgh

Trailhead GPS Coordinates: N44° 56.66', W73° 9.08'

These self-guided nature trails are in the 6,729-acre Missisquoi National Wildlife Refuge, which occupies much of the Missisquoi River delta and consists of marsh, open water, and wooded swamp. The name *Missisquoi* comes from the language of the native Abenaki people and is said to mean "place of the flint." The refuge was established in 1943 and provides feeding, nesting, and resting areas for 20,000-plus ducks and other migrating waterfowl. The largest concentrations of waterfowl occur during April, September, and October. A variety of

Black Creek and Maquam Creek trails

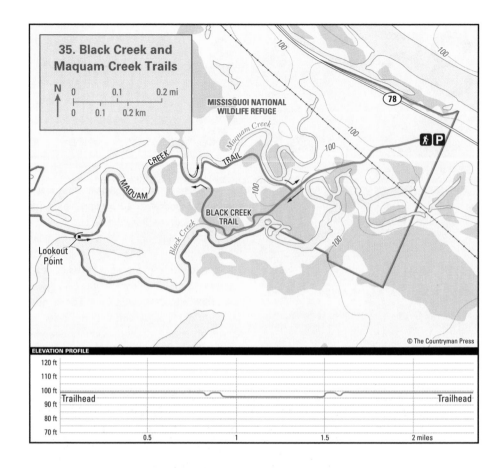

35. Black Creek and Maquam Creek Trails

N

0   0.1   0.2 mi

0   0.1   0.2 km

MISSISQUOI NATIONAL
WILDLIFE REFUGE

78

Maquam Creek

CREEK   TRAIL

MAQUAM

BLACK CREEK
TRAIL

Black Creek

Lookout
Point

© The Countryman Press

ELEVATION PROFILE

120 ft
110 ft
100 ft
90 ft — Trailhead
80 ft
70 ft

Trailhead

0.5   1   1.5   2 miles

other birds are present during spring, summer, and fall, including great horned owls, barred owls, ospreys, and bald eagles. The refuge also is home to Vermont's largest great blue heron nesting colony.

Remember to bring binoculars, and walk slowly and quietly so you don't disturb the birds and wildlife. Time needed to hike this loop will vary depending on how long you stop to observe your surroundings.

HOW TO GET THERE

From the north end of the town green in Swanton, drive 2.4 miles west on VT 78 to the wildlife refuge's large gravel parking area

on the left side of the road. A picnic table and outhouse are just off the parking area.

THE TRAIL

Start at the large information board with a map of the refuge at the back of the parking area. A box at the board includes a pamphlet and map, *Black Creek and Maquam Creek Nature Trails*. It notes that the paths here total about 1.5 miles; the walk is farther because some segments are out-and-back.

The trail starts at the information board and crosses a large meadow and active railroad tracks into a wooded area. You may immediately begin to hear birds as you follow the trail along the wide, mowed path and across the tracks. Through the brush on your left, look for a meandering creek and possibly some beaver activity. Also, watch for game trails, which crisscross this section of the trail. On your right, you will soon see an area that was clear-cut and has begun to regrow. This area was established in 1992 to provide habitat for woodcock. A sign explains that woodcock are among many species requiring forest habitat that is periodically disturbed to make way for new vegetation.

At 0.3 mile, another gravel roadway, the Maquam Creek Trail, enters from your right. You will return by this trail. Continue straight ahead to the end of the roadway and the beginning of the Black Creek Trail, which follows the bank of the Black Creek. Dark and slow moving, the creek lives up to its name. If you wish, sit on the bench and take time to observe the reflections of the trees and the swirls of brilliant green duckweed that pattern the water surface in summer. Enjoy your time, but be prepared for a few (maybe many!) mosquitoes and blackflies during bug season.

In motion again, traverse the first of many sections of elevated boardwalk that carry visitors over wet areas. At 0.7 mile, you reach a trail junction, where a sign points to the end of the Maquam Creek Trail. Turn left and

Boardwalk on the Black Creek and Maquam Creek trails

Water flower

walk parallel to Maquam Creek. Look for lots of ducks along the creek as well as nesting boxes on poles. The trail may be wet or even flooded on occasion, although extensive boardwalk—much of it built by the Vermont Youth Conservation Corps in 2010—keeps walkers above many trouble spots.

At 1.2 miles, you reach the end of the trail at Lookout Point, with a view of the creek and marsh. Return to the junction at 1.7 miles and bear left along the Maquam Creek Trail, which soon enters an area with a more open understory, carpeted with ferns. At 2.0 miles, reach the junction with the road on which you entered. Turn left and hike back to refuge headquarters at 2.3 miles.

36

Little River History Loop

Total distance: 3.5 miles (5.6 km)	
Hiking time: 2½ hours	
Vertical rise: 880 feet (268 meters)	
Rating: Easy to moderate	
Map: USGS 7.5' Bolton Mountain	
Trailhead GPS Coordinates: N44° 23.6', W72° 45.99'	

Established in 1962, Little River State Park occupies 1,100 acres within the 37,000-acre Mount Mansfield State Forest. The park's principal feature, Waterbury Dam, was built after two serious floods of the Little River, first in 1927 and again in 1934. The U.S. Army Corps of Engineers and the Civilian Conservation Corps completed the original structure in 1938. Reconstruction of the current dam was completed in 2005.

This hike offers a pleasant view into the past as it winds past abandoned settlements with stone walls, cemeteries, overgrown roads, foundations, orchards, and more.

A thriving community once lived and worked here. And, in the right place and time, it seems they still do. Early on a quiet summer's morning, with birdsong and cicadas chattering from the forest, the imagination can easily picture a sweat-soaked farmer cutting a field of sweet grass with a scythe. A teacher's voice drifts on the still air from the community's one-room schoolhouse. Smells of bread baking and apple pies cooling combine with the aromas from newly cut fields and blooming orchards.

This community lives on, if only in the imagination. Treat it with respect during your visit. Please take photographs of the area and any artifacts you find, but do not remove any items from the park.

HOW TO GET THERE

From the junction of US 2 and VT 100 in Waterbury, drive west on US 2, paralleling I-89. At 1.4 miles, turn right (north) onto the road to the Little River State Park, and cross under I-89. Continue to the Waterbury Dam at 4.2 miles. The road bears left, ascends the bank of the dam, and at 4.5 miles reaches the park entrance. The park charges a day-use fee and offers several maps and guides, and has a pamphlet available that provides a history of the area. Pass to the right of the entry station, and bear left behind the ranger's residence. Continue on this road past the gated Stevenson Brook Trail on the left (the end point of your hike), and go across a bridge at 5.0 miles. Go past the nature trail parking area at the bridge, and park in the small history hike lot (space for ten vehicles) on the right, across from a gated road.

THE TRAIL

Leave the parking area, and cross the main road to the gated Dalley Road. A kiosk here displays a map and some local hike information. Climb gradually uphill along the roadway through birch, hemlock, maple, and hobblebush, as the sound of Stevenson Brook rushes to the left. Shortly, turn right off Dalley Road and follow the blue-blazed Dalley Loop Trail. At 0.3 mile, cross a culvert and begin a short but steep climb. Wild violets often grow near the stream, as do hemlock and ferns. A large, flat rock at the top of the slope in a pine forest provides a sheltered spot to read the history pamphlet. A settlement of subsistence farmers lived and worked here in the 19th century, before they abandoned their pastures and the forest reclaimed the land. Today, only a sunken road bordered by rock walls marks the old pastures. Arrive at the Gideon Ricker Farm (site 16) with an old road and foundation on the left (0.5 mile) and farm implements and relics scattered around the site.

Continue on the main trail as it narrows slightly, following the foundation between two stone walls. Wind through white birch until you reach Ricker Cemetery (site 15).

Today native birch and spruce crowd out the nonnative white cedar (also known as "arbor vitae" or "tree of life") planted by the settlers to symbolically give life to the dead.

Beyond the cemetery the Dalley Loop Trail leads to the former Tom Herbert farm (site 14), first settled in 1856. This site includes a stand of roses, two cellar holes, and an old well. The well, approximately 50 feet to the southeast of the cellar holes, is 27 feet deep.

Just before a clearing, cross the stone wall near the William Randall farm (site 13). At 1.0 mile, you reach the William Clossey farm (site 12). Just beyond the farm, the Patterson Loop Trail enters, leading to Cotton Brook and the town of Moscow. Beyond the junction, on the right, lies the Ricker Mountain School (site 11), one of five in the area. A lack of pupils forced the school's closing in the late 1800s. It reopened in 1908, but the school permanently closed in the early 1920s.

Continuing on the main road, the Kelty (Patterson) Loop Trail leaves again at 1.3 miles. The James Carney farm (site 10) sits to the right, and the Upper Cemetery (site 9) lies uphill in the woods. Beyond the cemetery, the trail begins a long descent, past the Montgomery Trail junction, until it reaches a major signed junction at 1.5 miles. Many of these multiuse trails include snowmobile routes and other postings.

Go past the sign that notes the sawmill to the right. Turn left at the signpost to continue on Dalley Loop Trail, following the main road. Before hiking on the Sawmill Loop junction to your right (1.7 miles), follow the main road downhill 0.2 mile to visit the last remaining structure in the park. The Almeron Goodell Place represents the only surviving farmhouse in the Little River area. Almeron Goodell bought the land around 1864 and built the house of hewn timbers

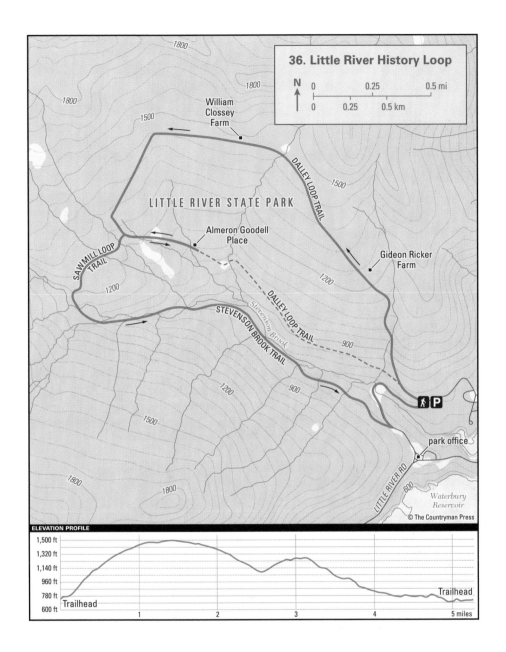

36. Little River History Loop

N
| 0 | 0.25 | 0.5 mi |
| 0 | 0.25 0.5 km | |

William Clossey Farm

DALLEY LOOP TRAIL

LITTLE RIVER STATE PARK

SAWMILL LOOP TRAIL

Almeron Goodell Place

Gideon Ricker Farm

STEVENSON BROOK TRAIL

Stevenson Brook

DALLEY LOOP TRAIL

park office

LITTLE RIVER RD

Waterbury Reservoir

© The Countryman Press

ELEVATION PROFILE

1,500 ft
1,320 ft
1,140 ft
960 ft
780 ft
600 ft
Trailhead
Trailhead

1   2   3   4   5 miles

and hand-split shingles. One story of the time describes this disabled Civil War veteran as an escaped slave befriended by an area Goodell family.

After exploring the site, retrace your steps and walk uphill to the Sawmill Loop Junction at 2.1 miles. In spring you might hear local birds, such as the brown creeper, black-throated blue warbler, and ovenbird in the forest.

Old stone foundation

Turn left, and enter a beech/birch forest, following old stone walls and hiking across a gully. Where the trail levels, cross another small stream on a footbridge. Again notice the old road and farm implements. Descend to a switchback, follow and then cross a brook on stepping-stones, ascend a steep bank on a small rock stair, and reach the junction of the Stevenson Brook Trail at 2.4 miles. A short spur to the right leads to the remains of the Waterbury Last Block Company Sawmill. Constructed in 1917, and in operation until 1922, two steam-powered 150-horsepower boilers ran this band sawmill. It employed 35 men, 44 horse teams, and one truck. Workers turned timber into ammunition cases and gun stocks and hauled the finer wood to Waterbury for cobblers' lasts (shoe molds). Today, only a large boiler, truck chassis, and various band saws remain.

Return to the junction, making sure to avoid the snowmobile trail beyond the sawmill. Return along the Stevenson Brook Trail, past a few large ash trees, a grove with significant undergrowth, and trilliums, aster, and other wildflowers visible in season. Nettles also intrude on this overgrown roadway. The old road widens as you descend along Stevenson Brook and reach the abutments of old road bridges. A new footbridge crosses the sometimes swift-running brook. The historical map describes the old fords as "difficult crossings."

Some evidence of former settlements appears next to the brook. Beech and birch trees predominate in the woods. You soon enter a hemlock grove and reach a junction where the Link Trail crosses Stevenson Brook to join Dalley Loop Trail. Continue descending along the right bank of the brook on the old road. Soon you bear upward to the right and leave the brook. Pass through the gated entry at 3.3 miles to reach the paved park road; then turn left and follow the road to your car (3.5 miles).

37

Stowe Pinnacle

Total distance: 2.8 miles (4.5 km)

Hiking time: 2½ hours

Vertical rise: 1,520 feet (463 meters)

Rating: Moderate

Map: USGS 7.5' Stowe

Trailhead GPS Coordinates: N44° 26.32', W72° 40.04'

This short, occasionally steep hike to a rocky knob provides extensive views of the entire Worcester Range, the Green Mountains, the Waterbury Reservoir, and the surrounding area. It offers visitors a comfortable hike, picture-book views, and an impressive vantage point overlooking local farms, forests, and the quaint resort village of Stowe.

HOW TO GET THERE

Take VT 100 to the village of Stowe and turn east on School Street (directly opposite the Stowe Community Church). At 0.3 mile afterward, bear right at the fork on the Stowe Hollow Road. At the next intersection (1.8 miles), go straight and follow the Upper Hollow Road. The road then crosses a brook. Continue uphill, and bear right. At 2.3 miles pass Pinnacle Road on the left, and at 2.4 miles reach a parking lot on the left (east) side of the road. If the parking lot is full, there is additional parking at the upper lot at the Pinnacle Meadows trailhead. (Take Pinnacle Road and go left at 0.1 mile, turn right onto Upper Pinnacle Road [0.3 mile], go straight at 0.9 mile onto Pinnacle Heights Road, and follow it to the gate at the end of the road. To the left of the gate there is a parking lot with space for about a dozen cars.)

THE TRAIL

There are two approaches to Stowe Pinnacle. One begins at the lower parking lot and climbs moderately for about 1 mile before intersecting with the trail from the upper parking lot, which takes a more level route that

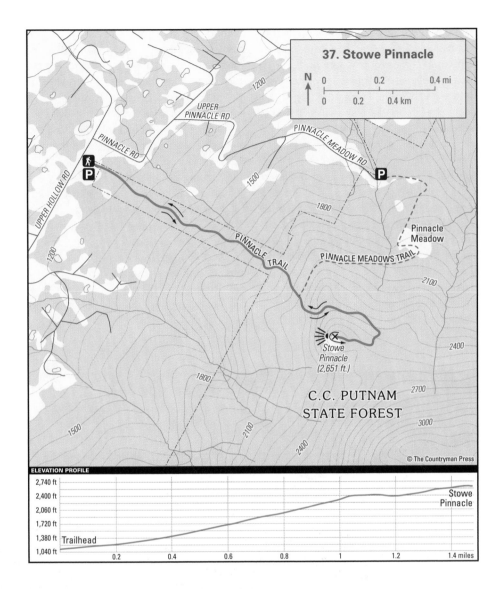

Stowe Pinnacle (2,651 ft.)

C.C. PUTNAM STATE FOREST

© The Countryman Press

ELEVATION PROFILE

passes through a high-elevation meadow with a spectacular view.

The blue-blazed trail from the lower parking lot begins by crossing a field and overgrown pasture on puncheon (wooden beams that provide a raised, dry path over muddy spots). Volunteers from the Green Mountain Club and the Long Trail Patrol installed this puncheon—as well as water bars and rock steps you cross later in the hike—to minimize trail erosion and provide an improved footpath.

The Worcester Range and the Stowe Pinnacle appear directly in front of you; Mount Mansfield rises behind you. Soon you will pass a large boulder, an erratic probably dropped as the glaciers retreated. The trail becomes quite rocky and begins to ascend. At 0.4 mile, cross a gully, turn right, cross another gully, and begin to climb through mature hardwoods. Look carefully at the smooth beech bark for claw marks. In the fall and early winter, bears climb these trees and feed on beechnuts, leaving the impression of their claws in the bark of these "bear trees." You may also hear the staccato *tap-tap-tap* of woodpeckers as they search out insects in the trees. The insects invade the tree, woodpeckers weaken it with their pecking, and a strong wind knocks it down, where the tree decays on the forest floor and nourishes new growth.

A series of switchbacks help moderate the ascent before a sharp right turn leads onto a plateau. The trail swings left and you ascend over an impressive series of rock steps installed by the Long Trail Patrol. As you reach the top of the rock stairs, a short spur on the left leads to a limited view of Mount Mansfield through the trees and a better view of Camel's Hump to the left.

The trail levels out and circles behind the pinnacle, descending slightly and then resuming its climb. As you gain elevation, the trail becomes rockier; you'll encounter short fir trees indicating your approach to the summit. A trail enters from the left, leading to the Skyline Trail, which traverses the Worcester Range to Mount Hunger.

The Pinnacle Trail bears right and begins its final ascent to the summit, mostly over rocks. A couple of wood ladders have been anchored into the rock to assist you over the trickier spots. Breaking out of the

View from Stowe Pinnacle with Camel's Hump to the far right

Mount Mansfield from Stowe Pinnacle

woods, follow the blue blazes painted on the rocks to the viewpoint. Directly ahead is Mount Mansfield, with Camel's Hump rising in the distance to the south. Elmore Mountain stands alone to the north, while the Worcester Range is behind you. The body of water in the foreground is the Waterbury Reservoir.

The other approach, the Pinnacle Meadows Trail, begins at the upper parking lot. The trailhead is marked by a sign that indicates you are passing through the C. C. Putnam State Forest. Go around the metal gate and begin a gentle climb on a wide woods road. As the road swings around to the left, you'll soon come to Pinnacle Meadow, an open field with a semicircular rock bench—a great place to remove your pack for a few minutes and admire the sweeping vista of Mount Mansfield and the Stowe area. Pinnacle Meadow was conserved by the Stowe Land Trust in 2002, and the rock bench features a plaque with the names of donors who are "champions of land conservation."

The trail enters the woods to the right just beyond the rock bench and continues on easy grades until intersecting with the trail from the lower parking lot.

38

Bluff Mountain

Total distance: 3.6 miles (5.8 km)	
Hiking time: 2½ hours	
Vertical rise: 1,080 feet (329 meters)	
Rating: Moderate	
Map: USGS 7.5' Island Pond	
Trailhead GPS Coordinates: N44° 49.52', W71° 52.57'	

Bluff Mountain is one of those deceptively modest climbs that fools people into thinking they'll be up and down in no time at all. Although its starting point is very close to downtown Island Pond, a hike to the lookout near this peak's lower, south summit (2,380 feet) makes the rest of the world seem much further away. NorthWoods Stewardship Center in East Charleston maintains the expanding network of trails on this mountain.

Located just north of the village of Island Pond, Bluff Mountain gets less attention from the hiking community than more prominent peaks, but it still offers a good workout and an impressive view. Hikers have been climbing to its south-facing lookout for decades, but the route they've taken has evolved over time. A recent relocation on the middle portion of this trail offers a more direct approach to the summit. It can also be hiked in combination with the much steeper Lookout Trail.

HOW TO GET THERE

From its junction with VT 114 in the village of Island Pond, follow VT 105 east across the railroad tracks, and then turn immediately left onto South Street. After a short distance, turn right onto Mountain Street (0.3 mile), opposite the covered footbridge. Follow Mountain Street to a small parking area on the left (1.0 mile), which should accommodate four to six vehicles. Larger groups should plan on carpooling or walking to this trailhead from the village.

THE TRAIL

From the parking lot, follow the blue blazes

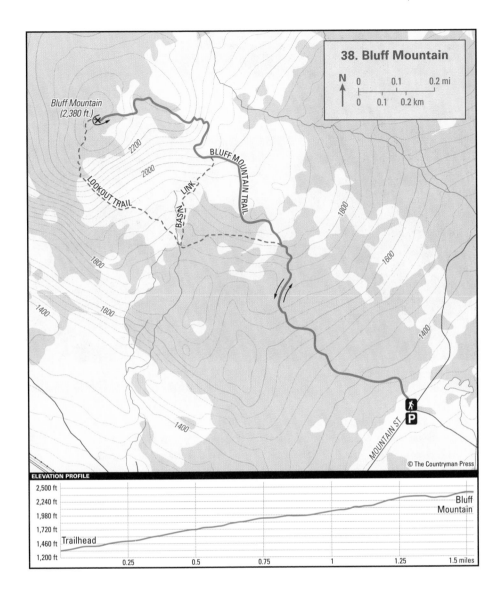

38. Bluff Mountain

N   0   0.1   0.2 mi

0   0.1   0.2 km

Bluff Mountain
(2,380 ft.)

2200

2000

LOOKOUT TRAIL

BLUFF MOUNTAIN TRAIL

BASIN LINK

1800

1800

1600

1400

1600

1600

1400

1400

MOUNTAIN ST

© The Countryman Press

ELEVATION PROFILE

2,500 ft					
2,240 ft					Bluff
1,980 ft					Mountain
1,720 ft					
1,460 ft	Trailhead				
1,200 ft	0.25	0.5	0.75	1	1.25 1.5 miles

carefully on the lower segment of this trail, which rises through a red pine plantation that is so orderly it can be disorienting. The trail soon passes a register box at the upper end of this area (0.1 mile). (Signing in will document trail usage, which is helpful when local trail crews seek funding for continued maintenance of this route.) The forest quickly gives way to a more natural mix of hardwoods. After crossing an overgrown skidder path (0.4 mile), the trail begins a steadier climb to the northwest. Following a sharp turn to the left, which is marked by an arrow (0.6 mile), the main pathway soon reaches a junction with the Lookout Trail on the left (0.7 mile). This yellow-blazed trail

Bluff Mountain

189

Brighton Pond from Bluff Mountain

forms a loop with the Bluff Mountain Trail, but it involves a very steep rock climb that is unsuitable for young children or dogs.

Continuing from the junction with the Lookout Trail, where the blue blazes lead to the right, this newest section of the Bluff Mountain Trail offers an easier, more direct approach to the summit. After a short descent on an impressive stone staircase (0.8 mile), the trail gradually climbs to the Ridge Junction (1.1 miles), where it is met by the Basin Link. By providing another connection with the Lookout Trail, the Basin Link might come in handy for those who have abandoned their attempt to ascend that steeper route.

Bearing right at the Ridge Junction, the Bluff Mountain Trail continues its ascent on some increasingly steeper terrain, which includes another relocation. After rejoining the older route again, it soon crosses a boggy depression on a series of puncheons (1.4 miles). Climbing more gradually, the trail reaches a final junction near the south summit (1.6 miles), which is located at the end of a 50-foot spur path on the right. From this junction, the yellow-blazed Lookout Trail makes an easy descent to a fine vista (1.8 miles) of Island Pond and the village that shares its name. Among the surrounding hilltops, East Mountain is the easiest one to identify. The large building, which is clearly visible on its summit, is part of an abandoned radar base that dates back to the Cold War era.

While the Lookout Trail provides an alternate way back to the trailhead, its steep terrain is better suited for an ascent. Returning along the same route is likely the best option, especially if these trails are wet.

39

Spruce Mountain

Total distance: 4.4 miles (7.1 km)
Hiking time: 3 hours
Vertical rise: 1,180 feet (360 meters)
Rating: Moderate
Maps: USGS 7.5' Barre East; 7.5' Knox Mountain
Trailhead GPS Coordinates: N44° 14.09', W72° 22.67'

This trail leads to an abandoned fire tower as well as several lookouts with excellent views of northern and central Vermont and western New Hampshire. Children especially enjoy exploring a very large split rock 1.6 miles up the trail.

Most of the trail up Spruce Mountain is located in the L. R. Jones State Forest, a 642-acre parcel of land located in the town of Plainfield. This forest—the first parcel purchased by the state of Vermont on November 23, 1909—was formerly called the Plainfield State Forest. The name was changed to honor Professor L. R. Jones, a University of Vermont professor of botany, for his efforts to establish the state tree nursery and create the position of state forester. The summit of Spruce Mountain is located in Groton State Forest.

HOW TO GET THERE

Take US 2 to Plainfield. Turn south at the flashing yellow light, cross a bridge, and immediately bear left onto Main Street. At 0.4 mile, turn right onto East Hill Road, which quickly turns to gravel. At 2.0 miles, Spruce Mountain is visible ahead. Ignoring various roads on the left and right as you go downhill, turn left at 4.3 miles onto Spruce Mountain Road. At 4.7 miles, bear left at a wooden sign that indicates the trailhead is another 0.5 mile away. Continue uphill on the twisting and rough road past a pullout at the site of the old gate and parking area. Continue to the end of the road at a sign reading L. R. Jones State Forest, where there is a gate and trailhead parking for as many as 15 cars. Please park in this upper lot, which is located on state rather than private land.

THE TRAIL

The Spruce Mountain Trail follows a path well-worn by fire wardens on their way to the tower. The first half of the route follows an old logging road, and the second half follows an obvious foot trail. The route is unsigned but is sporadically marked with blue blazes.

Begin your hike along the roadway past the gate. During this 1-mile woods-road walk, notice the frequent views of Spruce Mountain, the fragrant spruce-scented air, and (in the fall) a few beautiful full-color maple trees along the way. Also, look for ruffed grouse in the woods—you may startle one into sudden flight. Although numerous old logging roads intersect the roadway, be sure to stay on the main road. Don't be concerned that you appear to be walking away from Spruce Mountain.

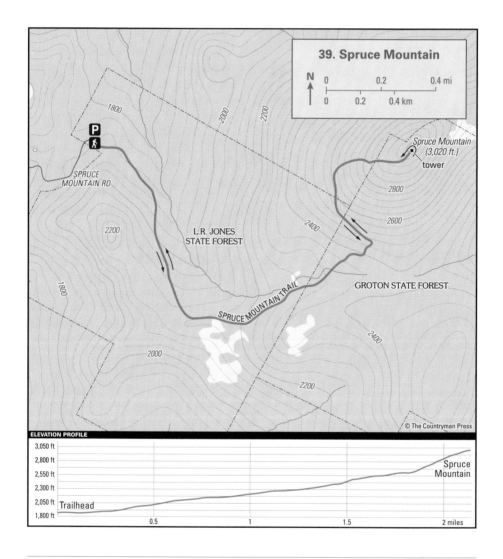

© The Countryman Press

Trail up Spruce Mountain

The wide road ends at an old log landing. Continue straight ahead, ignoring woods roads to the right and left, to pick up the old foot trail. You soon cross an unusual area of small, round rocks—or as one hiker describes it, "a baby boulder field." The relatively level, rocky trail continues past a large boulder engulfed by the roots of a birch tree. You soon cross a brook and, at 1.5 miles, you turn right and climb a switchback to avoid an old, eroded part of the trail. The trail finally levels somewhat, and you reach a large rock outcrop split by the freezing and thawing of water. This is a good place to take a break and explore the rock.

The trail continues past the rock and ascends along a hillside by the bottom edge of a sloping, exposed rock slab. Follow the slab to 1.9 miles, where you swing right for a steeper ascent. The trail returns to a mix of hardwoods and softwoods and enters a small open area of ferns before returning to the woods. Climb a short distance farther to reach an overlook to the south.

Immediately past the overlook is the summit, with an old fire tower and the old foundation of a fire warden's cabin at 2.2 miles. The summit trail, cabin, and original tower were built in 1919. In 1931, the original tower was replaced, and in 1943–44, the current steel lookout tower was transferred to Spruce Mountain from Bellevue Hill in St. Albans Town. Although not used as a fire lookout since around 1974, it was repaired in 1987 and placed on the National Historic Lookout Register in 1994. The state trail crew has been making small repairs to the stairs in recent field seasons.

A series of paths near the old cellar hole lead to various points on a rock outcrop that provides nice views of Groton State Forest, including Pigeon and Noyes ponds. From the tower, enjoy extensive views of central Vermont and the Green Mountain range to

Spruce Mountain fire tower

the west. To the east, Mount Moosilauke, the Franconia Ridge, and the Presidential Range in western New Hampshire are all visible.

After enjoying the views, hike back down the same trail to your car.

40

Elmore Mountain Loop

Total distance: 4.2 mile-loop (6.8 km)	
Hiking time: 3 hours	
Vertical rise: 1,470 feet (448 meters)	
Rating: Moderate	
Map: USGS 7.5' Morrisville	
Trailhead GPS Coordinates: N44° 32.39', W72° 32.16'	

Good views, a refurbished fire tower, old stone foundations, a glacial boulder, and a beautiful lake at the foot of the mountain make this hike a wonderful choice for a day of outdoor activities in Elmore State Park.

The park, which charges a day-use fee, was established in 1933 when the town of Elmore deeded approximately 30 acres of land, including the beach on Lake Elmore, to the state. During the early 1940s, the Civilian Conservation Corps (CCC) constructed the bathhouse, a picnic area, and a summit fire tower and caretaker's cabin. This 706-acre park offers access to camping, a picnic area, hiking trails, swimming, boating, fishing, hunting, snowmobiling, cross-country skiing, and a winter weekend of dogsled racing. Lake Elmore is 204 acres in size and averages 8 feet deep, with a maximum depth of 15 feet. The lake is classified as a fair to good warm-water fishing area. The most sought-after fish in Lake Elmore is northern pike; an abundant perch population has limited the numbers of other species. Little Elmore Pond is upstream and has better fishing as it is stocked annually with brown trout. Most of the park is forested, and the steep terrain limits the availability of commercial timber.

HOW TO GET THERE

Elmore State Park is located on VT 12 in Elmore, just north of the center of town. In-season (Memorial Day to Columbus Day) parking is available in the park. From the park entrance, drive past the contact station and straight into the woods, ignoring roads on

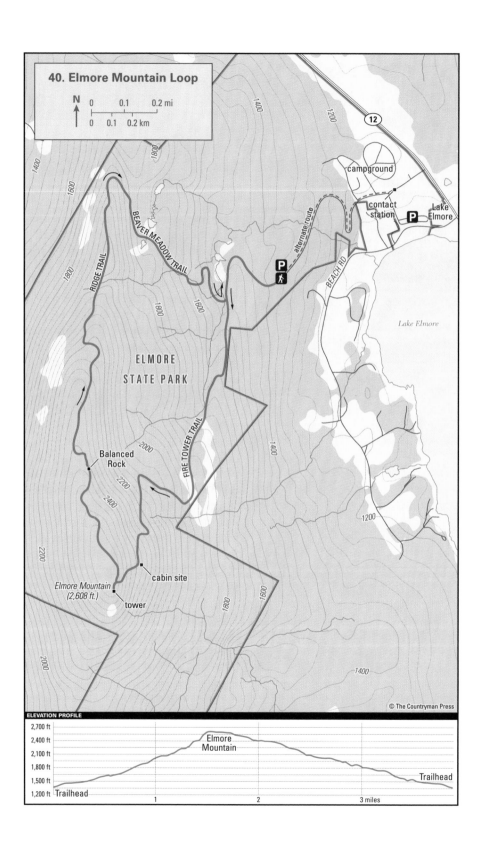

40. Elmore Mountain Loop

N
0   0.1   0.2 mi
0   0.1   0.2 km

12

1400
1200
campground
contact
station
Lake
Elmore
P

1400
1600
1800

BEAVER MEADOW TRAIL

RIDGE TRAIL

alternate route

BEACH RD

1800

1600

1800

P

Lake Elmore

1600

ELMORE
STATE PARK

1400

FIRE TOWER TRAIL

2000

Balanced
Rock

2200

2400

1200

2200

*Elmore Mountain
(2,608 ft.)*

cabin site

tower

1800

1600

2000

1400

© The Countryman Press

ELEVATION PROFILE

2,700 ft
2,400 ft   Elmore
2,100 ft   Mountain
1,800 ft
1,500 ft   Trailhead
1,200 ft Trailhead
                    1   2   3 miles

the left (to the beach) and right (to the camp-ground). Follow the winding gravel road up-hill to a turnaround and parking area at the end of the road by the gate. Alternatively, to add an additional 0.5 mile to the hike, simply park near the park entrance. During the off-season when the main gate is locked, use the park's Lower Lot—accessible by Beach Road, just south of the main entrance.

THE TRAIL

The hike follows blue-blazed trails for its entire distance. The trail starts at the gate and continues up the gravel road.

At the top of the first grade, the Beaver Meadow Trail (our return route) branches right. Continue on the road past a rock cut and uphill to a junction at 0.5 mile where the Catamount Trail, a cross-country ski trail, continues ahead on the road. At this point the trail makes a sharp right turn, climbs the road bank on steps, and enters the woods. Follow a gully uphill with a small brook on your right as the trail ascends with occasional views of the lake on your left. Be sure to stay on the blue-blazed trail and avoid the many side trails in this section.

At 0.9 mile, you switch back to the right and immediately make two steady ascents. At the top of the second ascent, pass through a rock cut, and continue over more level terrain. Next, cross a small brook, swing left, and ascend again. As you follow this gully upward, the trail terrain ahead looks very steep. Don't worry—the trail bears to the left and begins a series of sweeping uphill switchbacks.

As you ascend the last long climb, white birch appear ahead. At 1.4 miles, a spur leads left 100 feet to a clearing, the former site of the fire warden's cabin, which burned in 1982. All that remains is the foundation and chimney, yet the flowers planted by the warden near the foundation continue to

Busy day on the Elmore fire tower

bloom each spring and summer. From the clearing you have a good view down to the lake, of Spruce Peak in the foreground to the east, and of the White Mountains in the distance to the east.

The trail continues behind the cabin site and begins a final climb to the summit. The short summit has been much improved in the past decade with the placement of rock stairs, and in one stretch with footholds drilled into the steep schist bedrock.

Once atop the ridge, at 1.7 miles you reach a junction with the Balanced Rock Trail. Bear left onto the main trail, and continue a short distance to the 60-foot steel tower which is in excellent condition. It ceased to be used as a fire tower in the fall of 1974 but was repainted and repaired in

1987 by the state of Vermont. The tower is used by birdwatchers every spring and fall during hawk migrations.

The spectacular views from the tower include the Worcester Range to the south as well as the entire Green Mountain Range north from Camel's Hump, including Mount Mansfield. To the north are Laraway Mountain, Belvidere Mountain (with its asbestos mine "scar"), and Jay Peak. To the northeast are the Lowell Mountains (with wind turbines) and the Pilot Range in the northern White Mountains beyond. To the east is the White Mountain chain from Mount Moosilauke to Mount Washington.

After resting and enjoying the views, return to the Balanced Rock Trail junction, and follow this side trail along Elmore's ridge to a series of rock outcrops with beautiful views. The trail swings up and away from an eastern outcrop, climbs a shelf, and continues northwest over the ridge to a western outcrop. Continue along the ridge to the north behind the outcrop, descend slightly, and reach another outcrop with deep cracks created when weathered rock plates slid off the mountain. Be sure to enjoy the impressive views through these cracks. At 2.25 miles, you reach Balanced Rock, a boulder perched high on the ridge, left by a glacier that receded during the last Ice Age.

About 30 feet above (before) the boulder,

Rest time on the ladder

Trying to push over Balancing Rock

our route continues along the north spur, alternately meandering along the spruce-dense ridgetop and dipping to the fern-lush eastern slope where deciduous species dominate. Where the trail takes a left-right turn at 3.1 miles, the ledge just to the west offers limited views west and south of Mount Mansfield, Stowe Pinnacle, and Nebraska Notch.

Finally the trail drops more steeply at 3.3 miles, soon leveling and turning briefly southward to the crossing of Beaver Meadow. Formerly an active area of beaver ponds, these wet meadows host a variety of wetland species. The last 0.5 mile here sometimes crosses wet areas on puncheon (narrow boardwalk of planks or logs) before returning to the road where we began.

Elmore Mountain Loop

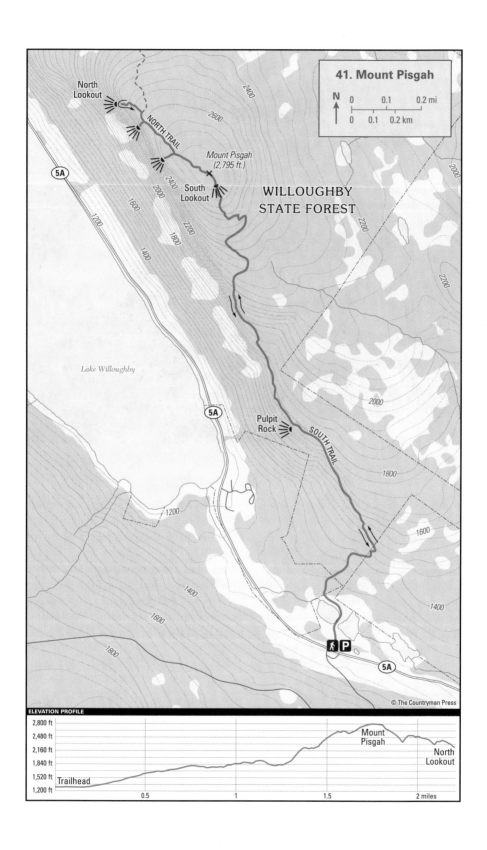

41. Mount Pisgah

N

| 0 | 0.1 | 0.2 mi |
| 0 | 0.1 0.2 km |

North Lookout

NORTH TRAIL

Mount Pisgah
(2,795 ft.)

South Lookout

WILLOUGHBY
STATE FOREST

5A

Lake Willoughby

5A

Pulpit Rock

SOUTH TRAIL

2400

2600

2400

2000

2200

1800

1600

1400

1200

1600

1800

1400

2000

2200

2200

2000

1800

1600

1400

1200

5A

© The Countryman Press

ELEVATION PROFILE

2,800 ft					
2,480 ft				Mount Pisgah	
2,160 ft					
1,840 ft					North Lookout
1,520 ft	Trailhead				
1,200 ft					
	0.5	1	1.5		2 miles

41

Mount Pisgah

Total distance: 3.8–4.8 miles (6.1–7.7 km)	
Hiking time: 3 hours	
Vertical rise: 1,590 feet (485 meters)	
Rating: Moderate	
Map: USGS 7.5' Sutton Provisional	
Trailhead GPS Coordinates: N44° 42.65', W72° 1.43'	

Willoughby Gap is an iconic geological feature in the Northeast Kingdom of Vermont. It consists of three parts: Mount Hor to the west, Lake Willoughby in the center, and Mount Pisgah (this hike's destination) to the east. Sculpted by glaciers, the adjacent sides of Pisgah and Hor drop dramatically to the lake, then continue underwater to form the deepest lake that is entirely within the state of Vermont (over 300 feet in places).

The area surrounding this lake is a four-season destination for outdoor enthusiasts. Residents and visitors enjoy a wide variety of activities. They include hiking, snowshoeing, cross-country skiing, biking (mountain and road), paddling, sailing, snowmobiling, hunting, and ice fishing. Despite its popularity, the 8,000-acre Willoughby State Forest remains a quiet and peaceful place, with hermit thrushes and ovenbirds easily drowning out road sounds.

HOW TO GET THERE

A large parking area for the South Trail to Mount Pisgah is situated about 0.6 mile south of Lake Willoughby on the east side of VT 5A. Additional parking can be found immediately across the road. This popular trailhead is located 5.6 miles north of the junction of US 5 and VT 5A in the village of West Burke and an equidistant 5.6 miles south of where VT 16 and VT 5A intersect at the north end of Lake Willoughby.

THE TRAIL

Starting at the south end of the parking lot on the east side of VT 5A, this trail soon

Autumn snow in the Northeast Kingdom

crosses over an old beaver pond on two footbridges. After reaching a register box (0.2 mile), the trail turns right. For the next 300 yards it passes through a beautiful glade strewn with glacial erratics. These boulders were torn from the nearby mountainsides by a south-flowing glacier.

A sharp turn to the left signals the beginning of a much steeper section of this trail (0.4 mile). Rock staircases, water bars, and switchbacks are used extensively in this area to help minimize soil erosion. This part of the trail tends to color its overall reputation as a steep climb, but it doesn't last too long. Eventually the trail continues on easier grades until it reaches a short spur path to Pulpit Rock (1.0 mile), where you'll find a dramatic view of Lake Willoughby. As with most of the vistas on Mount Pisgah, Pulpit Rock can be intimidating. Anyone hiking with children or dogs should exercise caution when using these side trails, which can end abruptly at a sheer cliff.

Beyond Pulpit Rock, the main trail begins to ascend again, but after another steep climb, it levels off once more. As the trail veers away from the cliffs on some switchbacks, it soon passes through an ecotone where the forest of mostly maple and birch gives way to one dominated by balsam fir and red spruce. With patches of bedrock becoming more commonplace, this trail finally reaches a short-but-steep pitch that leads directly to the South Lookout (1.9 miles). It's worth stopping to appreciate this excellent view of Burke Mountain with the White Mountains of New Hampshire in the background, since the nearby summit is heavily wooded. The South Trail reenters the woods at the top of this ledge and travels another 200 feet before it reaches a junction with the North Trail and a short spur path on the left, which leads 25 feet to the unmarked summit. At this point you can say you've climbed Mount Pisgah, but the best views on this mountain are located further down the North Trail. The total round-trip distance from the summit to all of these west-facing lookouts is just under 1 mile.

After some minor ups and downs near the summit, the North Trail descends to a junction with the first of three lookout spurs on the left (2.0 miles). The side trail to this upper lookout descends steeply for 200 feet to a small ledge similar to Pulpit Rock. It offers the best perspective on the cliffs of Mount Hor. Continuing downhill to the next junction (2.2 miles), a 90-foot spur path makes a nearly level approach to what is arguably the finest overall view of the lake and its surrounding terrain. The third and final side trail is just 150 feet below the second and begins with a gentle turn to the left at a point where the North Trail turns sharply right. It then descends for a distance of almost 500 feet to the broadest and least intimidating of these lookouts. This particular vantage point has a slightly better view to the far north.

When returning to your car, follow the same route back.

42

Jay Peak

Total distance: 3.4 miles (5.5 km)

Hiking time: 3 hours

Vertical rise: 1,638 feet (499 meters)

Rating: Moderate

Map: USGS 7.5' Jay Peak

Trailhead GPS Coordinates: N44° 54.76', W72° 30.26'

Jay Peak, the northernmost high peak in the Green Mountain chain, was named in honor of John Jay, the first chief justice of the United States who was instrumental in settling a controversy between the state of Vermont and the state of New York. The summits of Little Jay, Big Jay, and Jay Peak; 3 miles of the Long Trail (LT); and the Jay Peak Resort are all included in Jay State Forest, which is managed primarily for recreation, wildlife, and watershed protection. An enclosed aerial tramway at the Jay Peak

Jay Peak

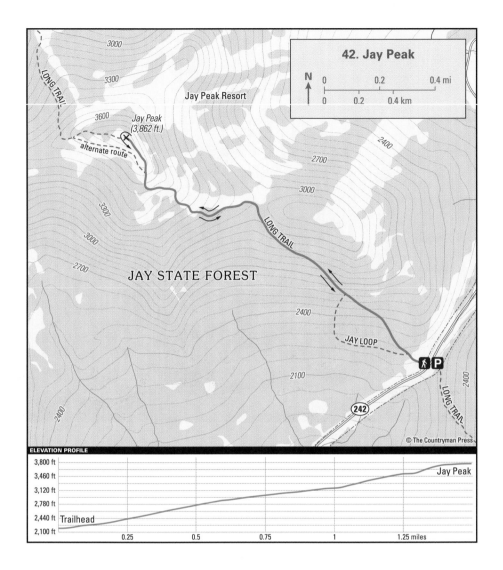

ELEVATION PROFILE

3,800 ft					
3,460 ft					Jay Peak
3,120 ft					
2,780 ft					
2,440 ft	Trailhead				
2,100 ft					
	0.25	0.5	0.75	1	1.25 miles

Resort allows year-round visits to the summit, so hikers should expect a few other visitors. Lying to the west of Jay Peak, the 3,674-acre Black Falls tract was added to Jay State Forest in 2001, bringing the total holding to more than 5,000 acres.

HOW TO GET THERE

The trailhead parking area for 15 cars is located at the height-of-land on the south side of VT 242, approximately 1.4 miles west of the Jay Peak Resort access road and 6.6 miles east of VT 118 in Montgomery Center.

THE TRAIL

The entire hike from the VT 242 parking lot to the summit of Jay Peak follows the white-blazed LT. Begin by following the path north,

Northern Vermont from Jay Peak

up the bank opposite the parking lot. At the very beginning of the trail is the Atlas Valley Shelter, a small lean-to not designed for overnight use. Made from plywood and plywood cores donated by the Atlas Valley Company, the shelter was prefabricated at the company's Morrisville plant and assembled on-site by Green Mountain Club (GMC) volunteers in 1967.

Almost immediately, the LT reaches the trail junction for the south end of the blue-blazed Jay Camp Loop Trail. This trail leads a short distance to Jay Camp, a frame cabin constructed in 1958 and renovated in 2009. The camp is maintained by the Northern Frontier Section of the GMC for the use of long-distance hikers. Continue straight through the junction on the LT—climbing gradually, then more steeply, through a hardwood forest—and continue past the signed north end of the Jay Camp Loop Trail.

The trail turns to the west and climbs on moderate grades for some distance, eventually leaving the hardwood forest, first for a stand of white birch and ultimately for the aromatic spruce-fir zone. There are limited views to the south and west in areas where storms have knocked over large trees, creating holes in the canopy. The LT turns left at 1.0 mile to avoid a ski trail, and then scrambles over some steep ledges and rougher terrain. The trail turns left again at 1.2 miles and begins a steeper climb over jumbled rocks until it emerges through a wooden fence onto a ski trail. There are good views here to the east and south, and on a sunny summer day the ski trail looks like a grassy alpine meadow. The LT continues directly across the ski trail (look for the white blazes on the rocks) and climbs steeply, at times scrambling up ledges, to reach the summit at 1.7 miles. As you climb into the scrub near tree line here, be careful to get your bearings on the final climb to the summit so you can descend in the right direction.

On the summit is the upper tram station of the Jay Peak Resort; please respect their buildings and property. On a clear day, there are views of Canada to the north, the Adirondack Mountains to the west, the White Mountains to the east, and most of northern Vermont. The large lake to the northeast is Lake Memphremagog, near Newport, Vermont. The summit of Jay Peak is exposed and can be a dangerous place in inclement weather. Limited shelter is available under the tram building.

From the summit, you may simply descend the way you came; however, there are two opportunities to vary the route of your return. First, you can use the alpine ski trails to leave the summit to the *north* and loop back to the point where the LT crossed the ski trail on the ascent. To do this, from the tram station on the summit, follow the white-blazed LT north along an alpine ski trail, making a steep descent to a ski trail junction. Here the LT passes through a fence and enters the woods. Do *not* follow it! Rather, turn left at the junction, and follow the alpine ski trail to the southeast, passing a ways below the tram station. This is the ski trail you crossed on your ascent—so keep a sharp lookout on the right for the white blazes and a small Long Trail sign just after the ski trail begins its descent. Note that the ski trails are not blazed like the LT.

Second, you may vary your descent route near the bottom of the mountain by following the blue-blazed Jay Loop Trail at its signed upper junction, where it departs steeply to the right from the LT. The Jay Loop Trail passes Jay Camp and returns to the LT a short distance above the parking lot on VT 242.

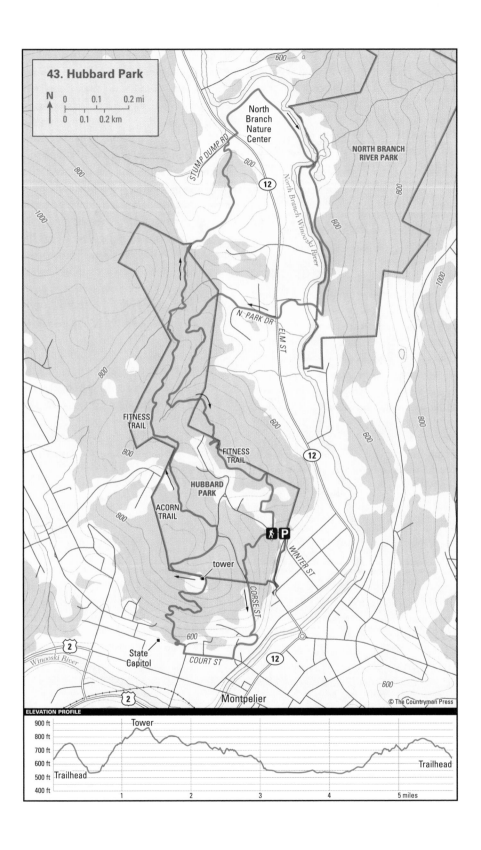

43

Hubbard Park

Total distance: 5.8 miles (9.3 km)	
Hiking time: 3½ hours	
Vertical rise: 374 feet (114 meters)	
Rating: Moderate	
Map: USGS 7.5' Montpelier	
Trailhead GPS Coordinates: N44° 16.04', W72° 34.42'	

Hubbard Park is a quiet—even wild—place in the heart of Montpelier, Vermont's capital city. The high point of the park is Capitol Hill, whose evergreen forest forms the backdrop for the golden dome of the state capitol building. The Hubbard family settled in Montpelier in 1799 and used the park land for various enterprises through the 19th century before donating it to the city in 1899. The city parks commission has made a few additions to the park over the years, most notably the construction of an impressive observation tower on the summit of Capitol Hill, but the majority of the park has been left in its natural state. The park is mostly a second-growth forest with a mixture of hardwoods and softwoods. It has a variety of habitats including steep ground with dry soil and plants unusual for the area; hardwood forest with moist soil; a high diversity of spring wildflowers; several marshy areas; and elevated, rocky cliffs.

In recent years, the Montpelier Parks Department has done excellent work connecting the trail systems of the parks and natural areas in the city limits. This has made possible a substantial new day-hike loop that connects historic neighborhoods, great mountain views, quiet forest glades, and wild natural areas, as well as grassy playing fields and picnic spots.

Hubbard Park is a great place to hike with your dog. Expect to meet many four-legged friends along the way!

HOW TO GET THERE

The trail begins at the Winter Street gate of Hubbard Park in Montpelier. From the corner

Bridge at the North Branch Nature Center

of State Street and Main Street in the center of the city, go one block west on State Street (toward the capitol building), and turn right onto Elm Street at the court house. Follow Elm Street 0.3 mile and turn left onto Winter Street. Follow Winter Street up a hill to the park gates. There is parking for about eight cars.

THE TRAIL

From the park gates at Winter Road, walk past the "Frog Pond" and over a small wooden bridge. Climb through the woods on a narrow path. Come to a four-way intersection of paths and turn left. The path ends at a road. Turn left and follow the road through the park gates. Continue downhill on Corse Street, a narrow, winding city

street lined with old wooden houses. To the left is a view of downtown Montpelier: roofs and steeples nestled in a green valley formed by the Winooski River and the North Branch of the Winooski. Downtown Montpelier is on the National Register of Historic Places as a well-preserved example of a typical 19th-century New England town. Turn left onto Cliff Street, and then left again onto Hillside Avenue. Hillside soon ends at Court Street, which is a slightly larger street with a sidewalk. Turn right onto Court Street, follow it a few blocks until it ends, and turn right onto Greenwood Terrace. The golden dome of Vermont's state capitol building rises to your left. Continue straight up Greenwood Terrace, and enter the woods on a set of wide stone stairs. There is a sign that reads

TOWER. The trail winds up a steep hill for just more than 0.5 mile. Near the top of the climb a number of smaller trails fan out to the sides; stay on the main trail to reach the observation tower at the top of the hill.

From the observation tower there are panoramic views of the mountains and valleys of central Vermont. It is said that on a clear day, one can see seven mountain ranges. The tower was built over a period of 30 years using stone salvaged from old walls in the surrounding woods. It is made to have a "ruined castle" look, but is well maintained and it is safe to climb the staircase inside.

In front of the tower is a gravel road. Facing the road, with your back to the tower, turn left onto the road and continue past a dozen large boulders lining the road. Pass a stone obelisk on the left side of the road. Come to a grassy area with a picnic table and turn right off the road onto a narrow path in the woods. The trail descends into a ravine with sheer rock outcroppings rising on both sides. Below the ravine, the trail intersects with a dirt road. Turn left and follow the dirt road for approximately 100 feet to where a footpath crosses the road. Turn left onto this path, marked the Acorn Trail, and reenter the woods. Several smaller paths branch off from the main footpath, but stay on the most obvious path that goes generally straight. After a while, the trail makes a sharp right turn and travels through a small bog on a narrow ridge of solid ground. Cross a dirt road, and continue on the footpath down a hill; a house may be visible through the trees to the left. At the bottom of the hill, join Hubbard Park's fitness trail, a series of exercise stations scattered through the park. Follow the posted instructions to test your strength and endurance against the likes of the ladder walk and the vault bar. Turn left and cross a small wooden bridge. After a short way, the trail crosses a dirt road. Turn left onto the dirt road and leave the fitness trail behind for now.

The dirt road ends in a cul-de-sac. There is an outhouse, grassy picnic area, and several stone fireplaces. Walk straight through the grassy area, and follow the footpath on the far side. Come to a four-way intersection of paths, and continue straight through. The path quickly forks; go left, entering a deeryard. Dogs should be kept on a short leash here in the winter. The trail comes to a T intersection near a brook; turn right. The trail forks again. Go left, following the sign to the nature center. After the sign, the trail goes over a small rise, and then crosses a wooden bridge. The path diverges from the brook, climbing uphill past a sign for the nature center (don't follow the faint path that parallels the brook). The path leaves the woods and

Stone tower in Hubbard Park

enters a meadow. Enjoy views of forested hills to the north. The glimpse of a graveled area in the foreground is the Montpelier City Dump. The trail follows the crest of a long, level hill with more good views to the east, and then descends through the woods to Stump Dump Road.

Turn right on the road, and carefully cross VT 12 to the North Branch Nature Center, a 28-acre reserve along the North Branch of the Winooski River. A small white house to the right is a nature center open to the public Monday through Friday, 9:00 AM to 4:00 PM. Turn left at the entrance to the parking lot, and follow the road around the edge of the large field. Pass a community garden and tree nursery, then follow along the edge of the North Branch. Turn left across the river on a large steel bridge, and enter the city of Montpelier's North Branch River Park. There is a "blind" on the left just past the bridge. Stand patiently in the blind to catch a glimpse of wildlife in the wetlands along the riverside. The trail follows a wide path through meadows and woods along the edge of the river. (Several other paths on the left ascend the forested hill. Please note that these paths do not all connect back to the main trail.) After about 0.25 mile, take a hard right into a grassy recreation field with picnic tables and a volleyball net. Cross back over the river on a large wooden bridge, and enter a parking lot. Pass between the pool and the tennis courts. Continue around behind the white pool house, and climb up to VT 12 on the paved path.

Again, cross the road at the marked crosswalk, and continue up North Park Drive for 200 feet or so. The road bends left, and the hiking trail takes off to the right, descending through a field to a boardwalk, then climbing back into the woods and reentering the boundaries of Hubbard Park. Take a left trail fork, then another left trail fork. At this second fork, the trail leaves behind the Hubbard Park deeryard (where dogs should be leashed in the winter). The trail winds through quiet woods along the edge of the park. At a four-way trail intersection, turn left. Reach a dirt road, and turn left. Follow the road 100 feet, and when the road bends right, follow the footpath that takes off to the left. Come to a T-intersection with another trail, and turn left again. Begin passing fitness trail exercise stations again. Enter a grassy area with a road and parking area to the right. This is a popular area for dogs to play and run free. Continue straight across the grass, and reenter the woods on the footpath. When the trail forks, go left. The trail goes through rolling woodland, climbing and descending on wooden stairs. Smaller trails take off to each side, but stay on the most obvious trail. The trail skirts the edge of a meadow with a picnic pavilion visible to the right. The meadow opens up to the left. Go down the hill through the meadow to the road. A mown path leads to the Winter Street park gate and your car in the parking area next to Frog Pond.

44

Mount Hunger

Total distance: 4.4 miles (7.1 km)
Hiking time: 3 hours
Vertical rise: 2,285 feet (696 meters)
Rating: Moderately strenuous
Map: USGS 7.5' Stowe
Trailhead GPS Coordinates: N44° 24.15', W72° 40.52'

This hike goes to the open south summit of Mount Hunger which, at 3,539 feet, provides excellent views of the Green Mountains to the west and the White Mountains of New Hampshire to the east. Mount Hunger is part of the Worcester Range, which begins near the Winooski River to the south and ends at Elmore Mountain to the north.

HOW TO GET THERE

From US 2 in Waterbury, take VT 100 north toward Waterbury Center and turn east onto Howard Avenue. This turn is south of the Cold Hollow Cider Mill at a dip in the road opposite the Waterbury Reservoir Road. Drive straight for 0.3 mile, and turn left (north) onto Maple Street. Just past the fire station, at 0.5 mile, turn right onto Loomis Hill Road, which turns to dirt at 2.4 miles. Bear left at Sweet Farm Road, and continue on Sweet Farm Road until you reach a parking area on your right at 3.9 miles. A sign at the parking area identifies the WATERBURY TRAIL TO HUNGER MOUNTAIN trailhead, which is also the site where stones were crushed during construction of the interstate highway.

THE TRAIL

Your pathway begins behind the parking area and passes through the remains of the crusher site. There are no blazes at this point, but the trail is obvious. Blue blazes appear at the trail register and begin a series of switchbacks through huge, moss-covered boulders. Cross a small gully and begin your climb along a side slope with numerous rock outcrops. At 0.6 mile the trail levels, crosses a small brook, and resumes climbing along a moderate slope through a beautiful northern hardwood forest filled with large sugar maple, yellow birch, and beech trees.

Arrive at a brook at 1.0 mile with a series of cascades and pools that provide cool, welcome relief on a hot summer day. For those with kids or looking for a shorter hike, this could be an enjoyable destination unto itself. Continue uphill through birches until you reach a sharp left bend in the trail. Climb through rocks and roots, crossing several small streams, until you reach a lovely field

of ferns at 1.6 miles. The trail now enters a hemlock stand and becomes steeper as you pass over large rocks. At 1.8 miles, you reach the junction of the Bob Kemp Trail, which branches to your right and leads to the summit of White Rock.

From the junction, continue on the main trail, which steeply ascends a short distance to a view of White Rock. As you near the summit, scramble over rocks to the south summit of Mount Hunger. Stay on the rocks to avoid trampling the fragile alpine vegetation.

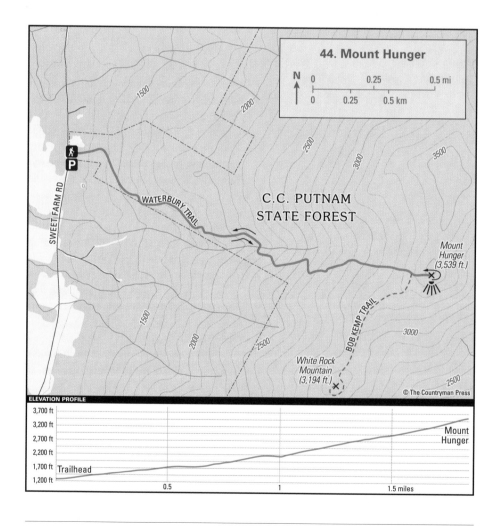

Early morning on Mount Hunger

The south summit at 1.9 miles offers spectacular views of Waterbury Reservoir, Camel's Hump, White Rock, Mount Mansfield, the White Mountains, the Worcester Range, and area valleys. Enjoy the patterns created by the roads, fields, forests, ponds, and rivers below you.

As you prepare to return, be sure to avoid the blue-blazed Middlesex Trail, which descends to the other (east) side of Hunger Mountain. Another trail, the Skyline Trail, heads to the northern end of the Worcester Range.

On the way back to your car, take time to admire the many stone steps and water bars built by the Vermont Youth Conservation Corps to protect the trail bed. Like many Vermont mountain trails, this trail is subject to wear by hikers' boots and erosion by water.

45

Mount Monadnock

Total distance: 4.8 miles (7.7 km)

Hiking time: 4 hours

Vertical rise: 2,108 feet (664 meters)

Rating: Moderately strenuous

Map: USGS 7.5' Monadnock Mountain, VT–NH

Trailhead GPS Coordinates: N44° 54.08', W71° 30.52'

Mount Monadnock in tiny Lemington, Vermont, should not be confused with its famous cousin of the same name in southern New Hampshire. New Hampshire's Mount Monadnock lends its name to a general class of isolated mountains that are composed of harder rocks that have resisted erosion more effectively than the surrounding terrain. Vermont's Monadnock is a member of this class and takes its name from it.

Overlooking the northern reaches of the Connecticut River, Mount Monadnock is less than ten miles from the Canadian border and is the easternmost mountain in Vermont. The fire tower on the summit offers a commanding view of southern Quebec, New Hampshire's massive Coos County, and Vermont's remote Northeast Kingdom.

HOW TO GET THERE

Parking for the trail is available along the southern edge of a gravel pit on VT 102 at 0.1 mile north of where it meets VT 26 at the bridge to Colebrook, New Hampshire. Entering through the gate, notice the sign that says PARKING FOR TRAILHEAD ONLY. Bear left until you come to a sign that says NO VEHICLES BEYOND THIS POINT. THANK YOU. Please help hiker-landowner relations by parking well to the left and out of the way. The parking area is 7.6 miles south of the junction of VT 114 and VT 102 in Canaan, Vermont, and 13.1 miles north of the junction of VT 105 and VT 102 in Bloomfield, Vermont.

THE TRAIL

After following the lightly used gravel road

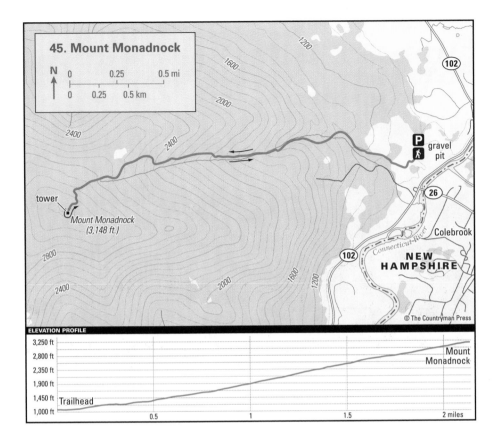

45. Mount Monadnock

N 0   0.25   0.5 mi
  0   0.25   0.5 km

tower

Mount Monadnock
(3,148 ft.)

gravel
pit

Colebrook

NEW
HAMPSHIRE

Connecticut River

© The Countryman Press

ELEVATION PROFILE

3,250 ft
2,800 ft
2,350 ft
1,900 ft
1,450 ft   Trailhead
1,000 ft

Mount
Monadnock

0.5   1   1.5   2 miles

100 yards past the No Vehicles sign, you will notice a trail register to your left. At this point you should also note a 4-foot-tall wooden stake whose top has been painted yellow. This is the first of several markers that will lead you through the confusing preamble to the trail. For the next 250 yards the trail follows these markers along a gently worn footpath that meanders through a field that is in the process of returning to forest. It is worth mentioning at this point that the trail up Mount Monadnock receives less traffic than most of the hikes in this book. In order to enjoy the positive benefits of this, hikers need to maintain a heightened awareness of the trail. To an attentive hiker, the trail is well maintained and obvious; however, it is narrower and blazed less frequently than major routes to popular destinations.

At 0.2 mile the trail enters the forest and ascends through a mix of pine and fir. A short while later the trail meets up with a small mountain stream that will be audible, and frequently visible, for most of the hike. Bearing to the right, in order to keep the stream on your left, you pass under an impressively broken outcrop of bedrock at 0.5 mile. At 0.6 mile, the trail crosses the stream on stepping-stones and later turns right onto a forest road at 0.7 mile. This turn is marked by a rock cairn that should be noted and remembered when you are descending the trail.

For the next 0.3 mile, the trail ascends the

Mount Monadnock

road, which becomes steeper, rockier, and narrower as you go. The trail does not leave the road; instead, the road gradually narrows back down to the width of a hiking trail. At 1.0 mile the trail recrosses the stream on a wooden bridge that is just above a small but beautiful waterfall. From here, the trail continues to climb over rocky terrain. At 1.7 miles the trail swings to the right, moves away from the stream, and begins to traverse longer stretches of exposed bedrock. At last the trail swings left into a dry spruce forest and the fire tower comes into view. One last climb brings you to the top of Mount Monadnock at 2.4 miles.

The solid stairs and decking attest to the fact that the aging tower is still being maintained in climbable condition. A short trail at its base leads to a stone chimney and foundation that marks the site of the former ranger cabin. The view from the top offers a unique perspective on the north country of Vermont, New Hampshire, and southern Quebec. The Connecticut River winding past the foot of the mountain is not much more than a mountain stream this far north. Jay Peak can be seen off to the west. Looking southward, the White Mountain's Presidential Range is partially obscured by a jumble of smaller mountains standing just across the river from Monadnock. The highest peaks in this range top out around 3,700 feet and include Mount Blue, Sugarloaf Mountain (another peak that shares a name with more famous mountains), and the Percy Peaks. When it is time to head down, return to your car along the same trail you just hiked.

46

Sterling Pond and Elephant's Head

Total distance: 7.7-mile loop (12.4 km)	
Hiking time: 5 hours	
Vertical rise: 1,650 feet (503 meters)	
Rating: Strenuous	
Map: USGS 7.5' Mount Mansfield	
Trailhead GPS Coordinates: N44° 31.99', W72° 47.2'	

This trail begins at the lower portion of Smugglers' Notch, a beautiful passageway between Mount Mansfield and the Sterling Range and a once-favorite route for smuggling goods into and out of Canada. In 1807, northern Vermonters faced a serious hardship when President Jefferson passed an embargo act, which forbade American trade with Great Britain and Canada. With Montreal such a close and lucrative market, however, many Vermonters continued illegal trade with Canada by herding cattle and transporting other goods through the notch. In the mid-1800s, fugitive slaves used the notch as an escape route to Canada. In the 1920s and 1930s, the notch was once again used to smuggle liquor from Canada during Prohibition.

Geologists date the rocks of the notch from about 400 million years ago. Today's rocks—originally the bottom of a shallow sea—contain clay particles, sand, and animal shells deposited on the seafloor. Over time, pressure from the ocean above pressed these particles into shale-type rocks. About 100 million years later, an uplift pushed up the seafloor and created the Green Mountains. When subjected to tremendous pressure and high temperatures associated with the uplift, these sedimentary rocks rearranged the minerals into the banded patterns seen today. This "metamorphosed" rock, called schist, primarily contains the minerals mica, albite, and quartz and occasionally garnet, magnetite, and chlorite.

Although uncertain about the formation of the notch, most geologists believe that

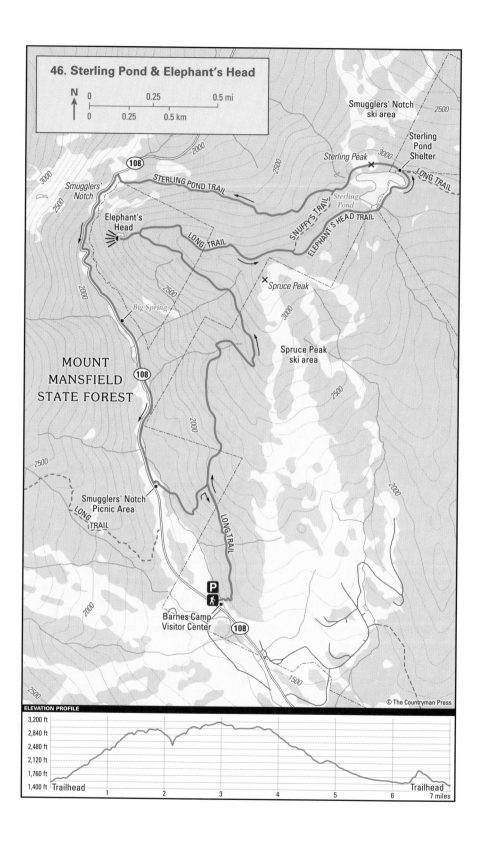

46. Sterling Pond & Elephant's Head

N

| 0 | | 0.25 | | 0.5 mi |
| 0 | 0.25 | | 0.5 km | |

Smugglers' Notch ski area

Sterling Pond Shelter

Sterling Peak

2500

3000

LONG TRAIL

108

2000

STERLING POND TRAIL

2500

3000

Smugglers' Notch

2500

Elephant's Head

LONG TRAIL

SNUFFY'S TRAIL

Sterling Pond

ELEPHANT'S HEAD TRAIL

2000

Spruce Peak

2500

Big Spring

3000

MOUNT MANSFIELD STATE FOREST

Spruce Peak ski area

108

2500

2000

2500

2000

2000

Smugglers' Notch Picnic Area

LONG TRAIL

LONG TRAIL

2500

P

Barnes Camp Visitor Center

108

1500

2500

© The Countryman Press

ELEVATION PROFILE

| 3,200 ft |
| 2,840 ft |
| 2,480 ft |
| 2,120 ft |
| 1,760 ft |
| 1,400 ft |

Trailhead 1 2 3 4 5 6 Trailhead

7 miles

a southward-flowing river carved it. They speculate that as the first glacier retreated twelve thousand years ago, ice on the eastern (warmer) side of the Green Mountains probably melted first. On the western (colder) side, the glacier continued to block any westward-flowing meltwater. Over time, a river of melted ice rushed through the path of least resistance—the notch—and down into the valley where Stowe is located today.

This geologic activity carved the magnificent cliffs of the notch into shapes resembling people or animals. Our forebears named them the Smuggler's Face, Singing Bird, Elephant's Head, and Hunter and His Dog. The cliffs also contain some of the rarest and most endangered plants in Vermont. Water, constantly dripping in the cliff's cracks, breaks down the rock minerals and nourishes the few plants that manage to grow on the outcroppings. Other factors—such as a steep face where few plants can survive, a cold microclimate, and a constant supply of mineral-rich water—combine to form an unusual plant environment, called a "cold calcareous cliff community." Please take extreme care neither to disturb nor pick any plants in the notch.

This hike follows the Long Trail (LT) north to the Spruce Peak Ski Area. Note that while the LT is blazed in white, there are some remnant blue blazes along this 3-mile section. The route leaves the LT as it continues northeast on the Elephant's Head Trail (blue blazes), circling the beautiful Sterling Pond before rejoining the LT at the Sterling Pond Shelter. It then turns south on the LT, crossing the top of the Smugglers' Notch Sterling ski lift that affords some nice open views. A short descent back to the pond is followed by a short climb to the intersection with the Sterling Pond Trail (blue blazes), which descends to the notch.

The ascent from the road provides views of the ski slopes and summit of Mount Mansfield as well as Taft Lodge, the largest of the LT shelters. A spur leads to the top of the Elephant's Head buttress and offers views into the top of the notch, and the hike concludes with a road walk through the base of the notch. This road walk can be eliminated if you have a second car to spot at the top of the notch, 1.5 miles north of Barnes Camp.

This strenuous hike—particularly the LT section up to Elephant's Head from VT 108—requires crossing often-slippery exposed bedrock, scrambling over rock/landslides, steep sections, and sometimes traversing the hillside using handholds provided by exposed rocks and roots. This rugged trail offers a great deal of satisfaction and unique views of the notch and surrounding cliffs. Although definitely not a technical climb, it requires some physical effort and demands proper equipment and preparation. Think carefully about starting this hike late in the day or if poor weather threatens.

HOW TO GET THERE

To reach the trail, take VT 108 (the Mountain Road) from VT 100 at the three-way stop in the center of Stowe (for 7.7 miles) or from VT 15 in Jeffersonville (for 10.0 miles) to the Barnes Camp Visitors Center on the east side of the road where there is parking for several cars. If the Barnes Camp Visitors Center lot is full, and for overnight parking, use the large ski-area parking lot across the road and to the left.

THE TRAIL

Begin hiking on the northbound white-blazed LT at the Barnes Camp Visitors Center and ascend a long grade through a beech and birch forest, with intermixed fir trees and hobblebush.

Continuing along the trail, it ascends in a series of switchbacks, with rock steps in the

Sterling Pond, with a friend

path. The trail levels out slightly before reaching a series of often-slippery bedrock sections, with seasonal flows of water crossing the path. Continue uphill on moderate grades through a mixed forest of birch and maple. At 1.6 miles, cross the lower portion of a 1985 rock-and-mud slide. Ascend some steep sections and slowly enter a boreal forest dominated by coniferous trees (spruce, fir, and pine) with intermixed birch trees. The trail climbs steadily, parallel to the slide. It crosses a second bigger slide path at 1.8 miles. This area of loose scree rock with a very large boulder makes a good rest stop, with the ski slopes of Mount Mansfield, Adam's Apple, and the Chin visible across the notch.

The trail levels out slightly (2.1 miles), crosses a small stream, and reaches a flat spot above the second slide with views across the notch. Continue on the now-narrower tread way, across gulches filled with fallen trees and boggy areas. This portion is essentially a long traverse with rolling terrain. In time you will reach the "Mayan Steps" built by the Long Trail Patrol in 2005.

After admiring this excellent Green Mountain Club trail work, continue along toward the optional spur tail (2.4 miles) that takes you to the top of the iconic Elephant's Head buttress. This cliff has a long history and has been a Vermont test piece among rock climbers. The cliff area is now home to nesting peregrine falcons thanks to the work of Vermont Institute of Natural Science (VINS). The falcons were successfully reintroduced by VINS in the early 1980s and have been returning annually ever since, using thermals and wind currents to soar to the top of nearby peaks. In early spring, state naturalists evaluate the trails and locate any nesting sites, which sometimes requires closure of the Elephant's Head spur in order to protect these beautiful birds from disturbance. Please obey any trail signs during nesting season (February through mid-July; the introduction contains additional information about falcons).

Turn left onto the spur and descend steeply left (0.2 mile round-trip) to the top of the cliffs overlooking Smugglers' Notch. The views here are breathtaking and dramatic; just be safe, and stay back from the edge! Looking 700 feet straight down into the notch, the road forms a horseshoe turn. When you reach the road walk near the end of your hike, use this turn as a marker to locate the cliffs. Across the road are the sheer walls of Mount Mansfield and the scar left by a 1983 landslide.

Return via the spur to the main trail, and resume hiking north on the LT. The trail crosses several boggy areas using puncheon and ascends to a saddle just below Spruce Mountain. The trail continues to level and climb until it reaches Snuffy's Trail (3.3 miles), a rough road (ski trail) that connects the Spruce Peak Ski Area and Smugglers' Notch Ski Area at Sterling Pond.

At this point, the LT turns northward (left) toward the Sterling Pond Trail, offering you another hiking option. To shorten the hike (by 0.8 mile) and return to VT 108, follow the LT as it descends along Snuffy's Trail and reaches a junction with the Sterling Pond Trail (on the left) in 0.3 mile. You may descend farther (0.1 mile) along the LT and reach the outlook of Sterling Pond or take the Sterling Pond Trail south 1.1 miles to the highway.

To continue the loop hike, cross Snuffy's Trail and follow the blue-blazed Elephant's Head Trail. This portion of the route crosses a knoll through the forest, passing through some wet areas, rock outcroppings, and a cavelike opening going counterclockwise around Sterling Pond.

The shallow, spring-fed Sterling Pond contains stocked trout; beavers frequently construct dams near the outlet. The pond formed after the last glacier cut a depression in a large talc deposit. Talc, a fine-grained mineral used in talcum powder and as a paper coating, feels soft and soapy, and makes *certain stones extremely slippery along the tread way*. Use caution when circling the pond. Only the remoteness of the pond saved it from development as a talc mine.

Begin the Elephant's Head Trail on easy rolling terrain, which soon comes to a steep, short climb. The terrain continues rolling with moderate ups and downs through the beautiful high-elevation spruce-fir forest, ledge, and wet areas. While crossing the knoll, some distant northerly views are seen through openings in the trees on the left. Later, at a view out to the east of the Sterling Range, the trail begins to descend in earnest toward a saddle where it reaches the shore of the pond. Here the hiking trail crosses a faint ski trail (exiting right) that connects to Spruce Peak ski trails. During ski season skiers shuffle across the pond ice to reach this connector and ski the trails at Stowe.

Following along the edge of the pond, the terrain is rough and rolling as it comes and goes from shoreline. Each reconnection with shore yields another beautiful view angle to be enjoyed. Continue on as you climb up, over, around, and through huge jagged boulders—eventually reaching a cavelike feature. Remember to keep an eye out for the slippery talc, which is lighter in color. If one is lucky with birds you might even encounter a ruby-crowned kinglet! Meandering along the small coves, you eventully pass the site of the old Watson Camp above the trail on your right. This historic shelter was removed in 2011 due to environmental concerns. At the next intersection (4.0 miles) bear left and climb up to the Sterling Pond Shelter (going right leads back to the old Watson shelter site). At the shelter the Elephant's Head Trail ends (4.1 miles including the spur) and it is back to the white blazes of the LT heading south.

This next short stretch of the hike runs along a ridge on the northern side of the pond. The trail traverses openings at the top of the Smugglers' Notch Ski Area. The route crosses under the Sterling lift line, back into the woods, and then over a ski trail and into the woods again. Continue following the white blazes to a steep descent down a set of wooden steps that lead to the pond shoreline once again. This is the outlet of the pond and it affords beautiful views across the water, including the summit of Madonna Mountain to the east. After taking in the views cross the pond outlet on a small bridge, bear right, and ascend the steep rocky ski trail (LT south) for a short distance to the intersection with the Sterling Pond Trail (4.4 miles).

Leave the LT and turn right onto the Sterling Pond Trail following the blue blazes to begin the hike down to VT 108 in Smugglers' Notch. This descent follows a series of plateaus—crossing a number of streams, rivulets, and steep grades. At times streams and the trail are one! This is one of the heaviest-used trails in Vermont and has had significant work done by the Long Trail Patrol. The Green Mountain Club's extensive work has created many rock stairs and water bars to help minimize erosion and protect the tread way. As you approach the lower portion of the trail, there are views into the western part of the notch. You begin to hear traffic noise, and then you reach long sections of stairs—finally reaching a nice plateau traverse and the crossing of a drainage gully.

Continue down the last run of steep rock stairs to complete this section of the hike (5.4 miles) at the trail register and the road (VT 108). Turn left on VT 108 for the next section, which is the road walk back to Barnes Camp Visitors Center.

Follow the road a short distance up and over the height-of-land, being careful of the often heavy traffic. The road is very narrow so walk tight to the edge, facing traffic for safety, as you pass through a series of large boulders (including King Rock, a large boulder that fell in 1910) and blind hairpin curves.

Walk down the hill to the big horseshoe bend. You might want to cross the road and look up for a view of the Elephant's Head cliffs, where you viewed this road from the terminus of the spur trail several hours previously. Pass Big Spring (6.0 miles), the original location of a mountain hotel and a popular water source. Despite its scenic location, treat all water found in the woods before drinking. See the introduction for more information about waterborne diseases.

Continue descending on VT 108 until you reach the Smugglers' Notch Picnic Area (6.8 miles) on your left. Proceed through the picnic area to the blue-blazed connector trail at the southeast corner of the picnic area. The trail crosses a small brook via rock steps, turns left immediately before a closed log structure, and descends to a ford of the Notch Brook. During the spring or at other times of high water, you may need to detour upstream to find a suitable crossing.

After crossing another smaller drainage, bear right along a traverse. Look for the beginning of a large wetland complex on your right and reach the LT (7.2 miles). Turn right (south) on the LT and return to the Barnes Camp Visitors Center (7.7 miles).

Note: The section of this hike between the Smugglers' Notch Picnic Area and the Barnes Camp Visitors Center is scheduled to be relocated in 2015. This is part of the restoration of historic Barnes Camp and a multiyear relocation of the LT in this area.

47

Mount Mansfield

Total distance: 6.7 miles (10.8 km)
Hiking time: 5 hours
Vertical rise: 3,200 feet (975 meters)
Rating: Strenuous
Maps: USGS 7.5' Mansfield
Trailhead GPS Coordinates: N44° 31.99', W72° 47.2'

With an elevation of 4,393 feet, Mount Mansfield is the highest peak in Vermont. The Abenaki called the mountain *Moze-o-de-be-Wadso* or "mountain-with-the-head-of-a-moose." Europeans probably named the mountain for the town of Mansfield, a sparsely populated mountain community that was dissolved in the mid-1800s. Today, the southern parts of the mountain are part of Underhill and Stowe, while the northern portion lies in Cambridge.

This National Natural Landmark resembles the profile of an elongated human head with the body lying flat and looking up at the sky. From the east (Stowe) side and traveling south to north on the ridge, observers can see the Forehead, Nose, Upper Lip, Lower Lip, Chin, and Adam's Apple. In the route described here, hikers climb from the east—reaching the ridgeline at the Chin and then following the ridge south to just below the Nose.

The summit ridge supports a rare and beautiful arctic-alpine plant community, notably sedges and heaths usually found 1,000 miles north in the Canadian tundra. These fragile plants may resemble common grass and appear undistinguished, but their existence depends on hikers staying on the trails and rock outcrops.

Owned by the University of Vermont, the ridge attracts more than forty thousand hikers each year and is included in the Vermont Fragile Areas Registry. Through the cooperation of the University of Vermont; the Mount Mansfield Company; the Vermont Department of Forests, Parks, and Recreation; and

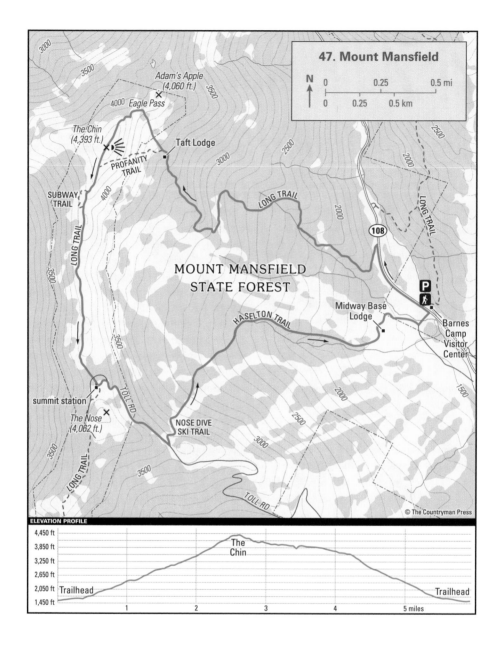

47. Mount Mansfield

Adam's Apple
(4,060 ft.)
Eagle Pass
The Chin
(4,393 ft.)
Taft Lodge
PROFANITY
TRAIL
SUBWAY
TRAIL
LONG TRAIL
LONG TRAIL
LONG TRAIL
108
MOUNT MANSFIELD
STATE FOREST
HASELTON TRAIL
Midway Base
Lodge
Barnes
Camp
Visitor
Center
summit station
TOLL RD
The Nose
(4,062 ft.)
NOSE DIVE
SKI TRAIL
LONG TRAIL
TOLL RD

© The Countryman Press

ELEVATION PROFILE

The
Chin

Trailhead
Trailhead

the Green Mountain Club (GMC) summit caretakers provide detailed information about the alpine zone and its inhabitants during the hiking season. (See "Arctic-Alpine Vegetation" in the introduction.)

Visitors to the summit arrive by many routes, including the direct, less demanding drive up the auto toll road; a ride on the ski area gondola followed by a short, rugged hike (not recommended in wet weather);

and strenuous ascents on the Long Trail (LT) or one of the many side trails. Hikers can choose from 9 approach trails to the summit ridge, more than 15 other trails along the ridge, and 31 trails in the Mount Mansfield area.

This hike begins at the Barnes Camp Visitors Center on VT 108 at the bottom of Smugglers' Notch and follows the LT south past Taft Lodge and to the Chin. It continues on the LT to the summit station, where it descends via the auto toll road, Nose Dive Ski Trail, and Haselton Trail. In addition, several other route options lead to points of interest, such as the Adam's Apple, the Subway, and the Forehead. Note that certain trails at the summit remain closed for ecological or safety reasons, including the trail to Lake of the Clouds and to the Nose. Anyone hiking into the alpine zone is wise to bring warm clothing, rain gear, water, and a first-aid kit. The weather at the summit changes frequently and may not resemble the weather at the trailhead.

HOW TO GET THERE

To reach the trail, take VT 108 (the Mountain Road) north 7.7 miles from the three-way stop in the center of Stowe to the Barnes Camp Visitors Center on the east side of the road, where there is parking for several cars. If the Barnes Camp Visitors Center lot is full or being used for overnight parking, use the large ski area parking lot across the road and to the left.

THE TRAIL

From the Barnes Camp Visitors Center, follow the white-blazed LT south.

Note: At the time of publication, the LT south from the Barnes Camp Visitors Center follows VT 108 for 0.4 mile before turning left off the highway. When walking along VT 108, be sure to stay on the left *side of the road, facing traffic. A relocation to the east side of VT 108, through wetlands on a boardwalk, is scheduled for development in 2015.*

Cross VT 108 and bear right on easier grades through a beech and yellow birch forest. The GMC has built steps and water bars over the years to slow the impact of heavy trail use.

Following a brook, then zigzagging uphill, the LT bears right up a set of stairs and crosses a small brook twice. Elephant's Head, a great cliff across the way on the east side of the notch, may be glimpsed through the trees.

A series of switchbacks ends at a rocky ledge (1.6 miles), with views of the Nose and summit towers. Bearing right and ascending sometimes steeply, the trail transitions into boreal forest with the Spruce Peak Ski Area and Madonna Mountain coming into view across the notch. The LT passes the Hell Brook Cutoff on the right before reaching a spur trail to Taft Lodge at 2.2 miles. Directly ahead, the LT continues south to the Chin. A short trail to the right leads to a privy. Taft Lodge, the largest and oldest shelter on the LT, dates from 1920. The GMC and other volunteers, under the direction of Fred Gilbert, rebuilt the lodge in 1996. It contains bunk space for 24 people, with a small fee charged for overnight use. A resident GMC caretaker stays at the lodge during the hiking season to assist hikers, maintain the trails, and compost sewage to protect water quality. Because of the area's fragile nature, tent camping is not permitted, and there are special policies for waste disposal. Hikers are asked to follow instructions while at the lodge.

Above Taft Lodge, the LT continues south past the junction with the Profanity Trail. This 0.5 mile trail, which connects Taft Lodge with the LT south of the Chin, offers a sheltered—but steep—alternate route to the ridge, especially in poor weather. With the Long Trail, it provides the option for a loop to the summit and back.

The LT continues up the mountain through a field of ferns to a trail junction at Eagle Pass (2.5 miles) where the LT, Adam's Apple Trail, and Hell Brook Trail meet. The open summit of the Adam's Apple is a short 0.1 mile from the junction and much less popular than the sometimes crowded Chin. The aptly named Hell Brook Trail descends steeply 1.5 miles to VT 108 in Smugglers' Notch.

Individuals with vertigo—and some pets— may find the route to the summit from Eagle Pass difficult. It also can become slippery when wet. The more sheltered Profanity Trail may be a more suitable route to the summit ridge, although it too is appropriately named.

From Eagle Pass, the LT continues south, ascending the steep face of the Chin to the summit at 2.8 miles. Staying on the marked trails and rock outcrops avoids disturbing the fragile alpine vegetation and thin mountain soils. Many of these protected plants look like ordinary grass and are easily damaged by stray footsteps.

On a clear day the Chin, the highest point on the ridge at 4,393 feet, offers panoramic views with the Sterling Range, Laraway Mountain, Cold Hollow Mountain, Belvidere Mountain, Big Jay, Jay Peak, and Mount Pinnacle (in Canada) to the northeast. To the east lies the Worcester Range and beyond it the Granite Hills and peaks of the Northeast Kingdom. Mount Washington in New Hampshire and the White Mountains south of the Connecticut Lakes can be seen in the southeast. The southerly view follows the spine of the Green Mountains to Killington Peak. The Adirondack Mountains in New York, including Whiteface Mountain and Mount Marcy, loom up across Lake Champlain in the west.

And on an especially clear day, it is possible to make out the skyscrapers of Montreal to the northwest.

From the summit, the LT continues south on the ridge for 1.4 miles, passing the Profanity and Sunset Ridge trails. At 3.2 miles, the Subway comes in from the right. This fun and exciting trail is extremely difficult, especially if attempted with a full pack. It steeply descends the west side of the mountain through rock fall, demanding maneuvering around caves, crevices, and boulders—making for a long, slow 0.3 mile.

From the junction, the LT continues along the ridgeline past a large rock cairn, Frenchman's Pile, where lightning struck and killed a hiker many years ago. Hikers caught on the mountain during a thunderstorm should leave the ridge and seek the shelter of grouped trees, avoiding tall, solitary trees, and rock outcrops. Caves and shallow overhangs are dangerous because ground currents can jump through these gaps after a strike.

The stunted spruce and fir trees on the exposed ridge attest to the severity of the winter weather. Snow covers them during the winter, and wind and ice prevent normal growth. Although small, some of these trees may have survived one hundred years. At this elevation, the distinctive musical call of the white-throated sparrow or the raucous cackling of ravens may be heard; an occasional peregrine falcon may be seen soaring on the thermals.

Stones on both sides of the footpath mark the trail and are placed to prevent people from walking on the fragile vegetation. In addition, the GMC has installed puncheon over some boggy areas.

At the summit station and visitors center (4.2 miles), this route departs the LT and bears left to begin descending via the auto toll road. The LT continues south over the Forehead. In summer, the summit station is

Hiking south from the chin, along the Mount Mansfield summit

staffed by GMC caretakers who can answer questions about the mountain.

The Mount Mansfield Summit House, one of New England's most successful summit hotels until 1958, once occupied the land now devoted to the auto toll road parking lot. Writing about the Summit House on a visit in 1862, the poet and essayist Ralph Waldo Emerson wrote that "a man went through the house ringing a large bell and shouting 'Sunrise,'" every morning. Vigorous guests rolled out of bed and climbed the Nose for a prebreakfast view of the emerging dawn. Because of the various communications towers now occupying the Nose, the trails to its summit are closed.

From the summit station, this part of the loop descends via the auto toll road to the Nose Dive ski trail, a former ski racecourse. A trail sign for the Haselton Trail marks the point at which the trail leaves the road. A piped spring to the right of the road allows hikers to replenish their water supplies. Local people informally refer to this as the "runny nose." Water from this source requires treatment before drinking. Descending the ski trail (zig, zag, and zig), the route enters the woods on the left at a sign for the Haselton Trail. This trail, one of the oldest on the mountain and the original route of the LT between the summit house and the Stowe Valley, is named for Judge Seneca Haselton, the first vice president of the GMC.

The Haselton Trail follows a brook downhill, leaving the woods at a ski area service road immediately above the Midway Base Lodge parking lot. Passing under the gondola and in front of the Midway Lodge (6.3 miles), it crosses another gravel service road and reaches the upper parking lot of the Stowe Mountain Resort and the Gondola Base Station. From the parking lot, the paved access road leads to VT 108 at the Barnes Camp Visitors Center (6.7 miles).

48

Camel's Hump

Total distance: 7.4 miles (11.9 km)

Hiking time: 6 hours

Vertical rise: 2,645 feet (806 meters)

Rating: Strenuous

Maps: USGS 7.5' Waterbury; 7.5' Huntington

Trailhead GPS Coordinates: N44° 18.98', W72° 50.98'

This challenging hike to the 4,083-foot summit of Camel's Hump begins in low-elevation forest dominated by birch, beech, and maple—then ascends through boreal (spruce-fir) forest to an alpine plant community at the summit. The route crosses streams, passes beaver ponds, and gives tantalizing glimpses of the stark open rock leading to the summit cone.

The Waubawakee Indians called Camel's Hump *Tawabodi-e-wadso*, which means "the saddle mountain." Legend says that Samuel de Champlain's explorers thought the mountain looked like a resting lion and so called it *le lion couchant*, or "the couching lion." In 1798, Ira Allen referred to the mountain as Camel's Rump on a historical map. From that name, Zadock Thompson in 1830 called the mountain Camel's Hump.

During the Civil War, Camel's Hump served as a well-known resort with horse and carriage trails leading to guest houses at the base and near the summit. Its popularity waned, however, with competition from the Mount Mansfield resort complex. In the early 1900s, area businessmen restored the trails and the summit house. Later, Professor Will S. Monroe of the Couching Lion Farm (the trailhead for this hike) continued these efforts by developing a section of the Long Trail (LT) called the Monroe Skyline.

In 1911, Colonel Joseph Battell gave 1,000 acres, including Camel's Hump, to the state of Vermont for one dollar, specifying that the entire forest be "preserved in a primeval state." The summit and surrounding land became a Natural Area in 1965 and the

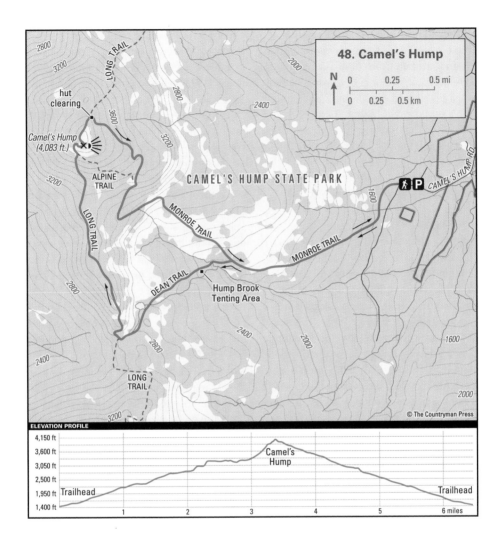

48. Camel's Hump

CAMEL'S HUMP STATE PARK

ELEVATION PROFILE

National Park Service designated Camel's Hump a registered National Natural Landmark in 1968. The Camel's Hump State Forest was established by the Vermont legislature in 1969. It is bordered by VT 17 to the south, the Huntington River to the west, the Winooski River to the north, and the Mad River to the east.

As one of the highest backcountry use areas in Vermont, Camel's Hump averages ten to fifteen thousand visitors a year, primarily day hikers. The volume of traffic widens the pathway and demands extensive and difficult trail maintenance.

Protecting the summit's fragile arctic-alpine vegetation remains a high priority. Those "fields of grass" on the summit are actually rare and endangered tundra species limited to an area of approximately 10 acres (Mount Mansfield supports the largest tundra in Vermont, about 250 acres on the ridgeline). Excessive trampling of plants and soil leads to the loss of rare vegetation and precious soil necessary for regeneration. Green Mountain Club (GMC) summit caretakers, on duty during the hiking season, assist hikers and explain the fragile nature of this environment. Visitors can help by following their instructions and walking only on trails and durable rock surfaces. The introduction contains additional information about this unique plant community in the "Arctic-Alpine Vegetation" section.

HOW TO GET THERE

From the junction of US 2 and VT 100 off I-89 exit 10 in Waterbury, follow VT 100 south under a railroad trestle and past playing fields on the right. At 0.1 mile, turn right on Winooski Street, cross a bridge over the Winooski River, and turn right on River Road (0.4 mile). At 5.0 miles, turn left (south) on Camel's Hump Road. Several side roads branch off this road, but stay on the main road. At 6.4 miles, bear left at the fork and cross the bridge. Continue across another bridge and past a sign that reads WELCOME TO CAMEL'S HUMP STATE PARK. A side road to the left leads to parking for the Camel's Hump View Trail and also serves as the winter parking lot and overflow summer lot. Continue up the rough, steep, narrow road to the summer parking lots. On the right at 8.5 miles, opposite a gated road, is a large parking area with space for 20 to 25 cars. The road ends at 8.7 miles in the Couching Lion Farm parking area with space for an additional 20 to 25 cars.

Emergency vehicles, residents, and others require access to the trailhead, so please avoid blocking the gated road and do not park along the roadside.

THE TRAIL

The blue-blazed Monroe Trail enters the woods at the western end of the upper parking area. Immediately on the left is a memorial to American service personnel killed in a 1944 crash of a B-24 bomber near the summit. Within a few yards, the trail passes a composting privy on the right and a trail registration box and information board. A map shows the trails followed for this loop hike and the bulletin board contains displays about the natural history of the area. Trail users should sign in at the registration box.

At this elevation, the forest is made up of mixed spruce and fir, with beech, birch, oak, and maple trees common. Ferns, moss, and lichen grow in the wetter areas along the trail. Early morning is a good time to hear thrushes and song sparrows. Beyond the registration box, the trail crosses the first of three footbridges, crossing the third bridge at 0.8 mile on a moderate climb to a junction at 1.3 miles. This loop follows the left fork—the Dean Trail, a narrow, less-traveled footpath. The right fork, the Monroe Trail, is the return route. At 1.6 miles, the Dean Trail passes a spur to the Hump Brook Tenting Area, a popular primitive campsite. The trail continues its moderate climb to another spur leading right to a beaver pond and view of the rocky summit of Camel's Hump.

The trail climbs steadily past several glacial erratics—large boulders deposited by glaciers—and through a notch to the LT at Wind Gap. The Allis Trail, on the left, was the original route of the LT. Straight ahead, the LT leads 0.2 mile to Montclair Glen Lodge, a log-and-frame cabin originally built in 1948 by the Long Trail Patrol. A GMC caretaker lives here during the hiking season, with a fee charged for overnight use.

Turning right, the route follows the white-blazed LT north over steep ledges to a rock face overlooking the beaver pond. From the top are views of the pond and valley below, and Mount Ethan Allen to the south. The trail climbs along another rock outcrop, enters a

Camel's Hump

cleft at 2.6 miles, and reaches an overlook. Ascending another knob, it opens to a view of Camel's Hump summit.

As the trail descends the west side of the ridge, the forest becomes denser with spruce and fir trees and the temperature cools as it passes through boggy areas. Dropping into a col, and then ascending again at 3.4 miles, the trail traverses the southwest face of the mountain, providing several views of the summit. At 3.8 miles it reaches a junction with the yellow-blazed Alpine Trail, which circles the summit to the east and provides a bad weather bypass of the exposed Camel's Hump summit. Continuing north over exposed rock, the LT reaches the alpine summit at 4.0 miles. Besides the fragile ecosystem, Camel's Hump is home to the call of the white-throated

sparrow and sightings of ravens, juncos, and peregrine falcons.

To the north, the profile of Mount Mansfield is easily recognizable and far beyond it the white scar of the asbestos mine on Belvidere Mountain. To the south, the ridge of the Monroe Skyline continues over Mount Ethan Allen and Mount Ira Allen. Ribboning ski trails identify Mad River Glen and on a clear day, it's possible to see all the way to Pico Peak and Killington Peak. To the east lie the Worcester Range, Barre's Granite Hills, and the rugged peaks of New Hampshire's White Mountains. To the west lie the expanse of the Champlain Valley and New York's Adirondack Mountains, most notably Whiteface Mountain standing alone as the northernmost of the high peaks.

From the summit, the LT descends

Winter day on Camel's Hump

steeply to the Camel's Hump Hut Clearing (4.3 miles), the site of a summit house built in the mid-1800s and three tin-roofed shelters in use from 1912 to the 1950s. A caretaker stayed in one hut while the others provided separate lodging for women and men.

Three trails diverge at the hut clearing: The Burrows Trail descends west 2.1 miles to Huntington Center. The LT continues north to the Winooski River via Bamforth Ridge. The Monroe Trail leads 3.1 miles east back to the parking area at Couching Lion Farm.

Turning right, the route follows the blue-blazed Monroe Trail. It descends steadily to meet the yellow-blazed Alpine Trail at 4.9 miles. Continuing downhill through mixed hardwoods and softwoods, it crosses Camel's Hump Brook at 5.2 miles, and then passes the base of a large rock face, reaching the Monroe/Dean Trail junction at 6.1 miles, thereby completing the loop. The parking area is 1.3 miles straight ahead (7.4 miles total).

Note: Older maps and guidebooks may list the Monroe Trail as the Forestry Trail. The name change in 1997 to the Monroe Trail honors Will S. Monroe, a legendary LT pioneer and trail builder.

49

Belvidere Mountain

Total distance: 7.9-mile loop (12.7 km)	
Hiking time: 5½ hours	
Vertical rise: 1,980 feet (603 meters)	
Rating: Strenuous	
Map: USGS 7.5' Hazens Notch	
Trailhead GPS Coordinates: N44° 47.45', W72° 31.17'	

Belvidere Mountain is a gorgeous but challenging hike. The fire tower at the summit affords a dramatic 360-degree view. This loop hike from the east begins and ends at the trailhead located at the end of Tillotson Road in the town of Lowell. From the trailhead, it is possible to hike to the summit and make a 7.9-mile loop, ascending via the Forester's Trail and returning by following the Long Trail (LT) north from Belvidere Saddle to Tillotson Camp and then descending on the Frank Post Trail. Optionally, you can hike to the summit on the Forester's Trail and return the same way for a hike of 5.8 miles. The description that follows describes the 7.9-mile loop hike.

HOW TO GET THERE

From VT 100 in Eden Mills, follow North Road (which becomes Mines Road at the county line) 5.2 miles north. Turn left on Tillotson Road, a gravel public road. Follow Tillotson Road to the trailhead parking area (5.8 miles). Tillotson Road is also 3.1 miles south of VT 58 in Lowell via Mines Road.

Note: The Green Mountain Club (GMC) conducts ongoing sustainable timber harvesting in an area of hardwoods above the parking area. If there is timber staged in the parking area or evidence of logging activity, please park in a manner which does not block access.

THE TRAIL

From the parking area enter the woods on the blue-blazed Frank Post Trail, named for a former Boy Scout leader and GMC

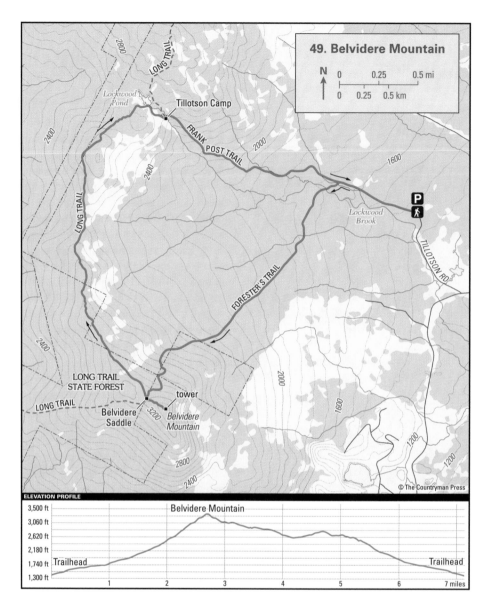

49. Belvidere Mountain

N
0   0.25   0.5 mi
0   0.25   0.5 km

ELEVATION PROFILE

3,500 ft	Belvidere Mountain
3,060 ft	
2,620 ft	
2,180 ft	
1,740 ft	Trailhead ... Trailhead
1,300 ft	1 2 3 4 5 6 7 miles

© The Countryman Press

Burlington Section member. Reach a junction with the Forester's Trail (0.6 mile). Turn left on the Forester's Trail, also marked with blue blazes. Ascend, gradually at first, crossing a small brook and then the larger Lockwood Brook, which can be quite high during spring melt. Cross several more small brooks and old woods roads, and then climb some switchbacks to the LT at Belvidere Saddle (2.7 miles). Turn left and continue uphill to the summit of Belvidere Mountain (2.9 miles).

The summit of Belvidere Mountain features a fire tower maintained by the GMC.

From the tower, the Green Mountains are visible south to Camel's Hump; Big Jay and Jay Peak are prominent to the north and to their right Owl's Head and other Canadian mountains in Quebec near Lake Memphremagog and Gore Mountain and Middle Mountain in the Northeast Kingdom. On a clear day the White Mountains are visible to the east. An inactive asbestos mine, once a mainstay of northern Vermont's economy, lies at the eastern base of the mountain, with another inactive mine on the south slope.

Return to Belvidere Saddle (3.1 miles). (From here, you can turn right on the Forester's Trail and return to the trailhead on the same trail you ascended for a hike of 5.8 miles.) From Belvidere Saddle, follow the white-blazed LT north. The trail here has rough footing and passes through spruce-fir forest devastated by Hurricane Floyd in 1999. After some ups and downs on the west side of the ridge, it steeply descends into a sag at Lockwood Pond. Bear right to skirt the south shore of the pond and reach the blue-blazed Frank Post Trail (5.9 miles).

Turn right on the Frank Post Trail and in 50 feet reach Tillotson Camp. This camp was built in 1939 and renovated by the GMC's Long Trail Patrol in 2007. From the front of the camp, there is a view east to the Lowell Mountain range with its 21 wind turbines.

From the camp, descend steeply on the Frank Post Trail. The trail then follows an old woods road (sometimes wet) for 6.5 miles, descending more moderately. Cross a brook and reach a junction with the Forester's Trail (7.3 miles) on the right. Stay left on the Frank Post Trail and reach the trailhead and parking area at Tillotson Road (7.9 miles).

Foggy day on Belvidere Mountain

50

Gile Mountain

Total distance: 1.4 miles (2.25 km)	
Hiking time: 1 hour	
Vertical rise: 413 feet (126 meters)	
Rating: Easy	
Map: USGS 7.5' South Strafford	
Trailhead GPS Coordinates: N43° 47.37', W72° 20.57'	

A trip to the top of Gile Mountain is an easy hike with a grand payoff. The summit's fire tower offers commanding views of the Connecticut River valley; Mount Ascutney and Mount Cardigan; and more distant views to Killington Peak, Camel's Hump, and New Hampshire's White Mountains. It's a popular local destination for families with kids and dogs. This trail is maintained by the Norwich Conservation Commission Trails Committee. The parking lot at its trailhead is plowed in winter.

HOW TO GET THERE
From the junction of VT 10A and US 5 (near exit 13 on I-91) in Norwich, head north on US 5 (Main Street). After passing the town green on the right, stay straight on Main Street (do not follow US 5 where it turns right) and continue past Dan & Whit's general store on the left (0.4 mile). Turn left onto Turnpike Road (1.0 mile), which eventually changes to gravel (3.6 miles). This road gets narrower and starts to climb before it reaches the entrance to a small parking area on the left (6.2 miles).

THE TRAIL
Shortly after leaving its trailhead parking lot, the blue-blazed Gile Mountain Trail bears left onto an old woods road. It soon diverges from this roadbed and crosses a small bridge (0.2 mile) before making an easy ascent to the cleared right-of-way for a transmission line that carries electricity from the Wilder Dam.

Once it crosses this power line clearing

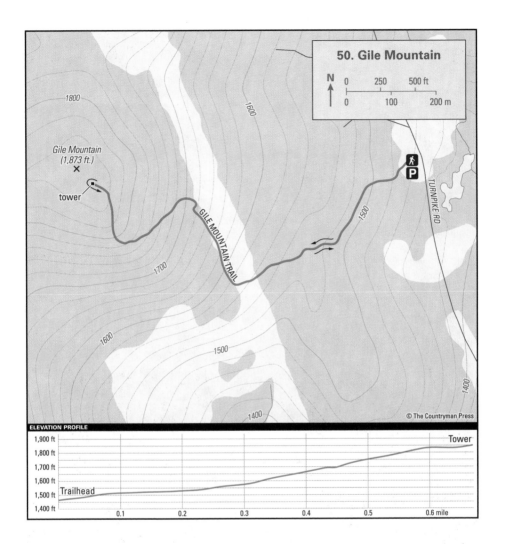

50. Gile Mountain

Gile Mountain (1,873 ft.)

tower

GILE MOUNTAIN TRAIL

TURNPIKE RD

© The Countryman Press

ELEVATION PROFILE

Tower

Trailhead

(0.3 mile), the trail resumes a gradual climb on some wide switchbacks. Significant improvements have been made in recent years to help prevent further soil erosion on the upper section of this heavily used hiking trail. Eventually, it reaches a junction near an old shelter (the former ranger's cabin). Skirting to the left of this building, the trail leads to the nearby summit (1,873 feet) and fire tower (0.7 mile). Several safety upgrades were added to this lookout tower during an extensive renovation project back in 2001. These improvements have made it much safer for children to climb to the top of this structure, which measures nearly 68 feet from its base to the cab floor, making it the tallest fire tower in Vermont.

Please take note: At several points along this ascent, a second trail crosses the main hiking trail. This alternate route was laid out by Thetford, Vermont, ski trail designer John Morton. It takes a less direct approach to the

Nice, easy trail

tower using longer switchbacks that are intended for mountain biking and cross-country skiing. Hikers should also make sure they do not follow the new Ridge Trail when leaving the summit, since it doesn't reconnect with the main trail or Turnpike Road.